Rita Louise, PhD

Copyright © 2004 Rita Louise, Ph.D.

All rights reserved.

Editing by Ian Rule
Copy Editing by Arlene Prunkl
Illustrations by Roberto Sabas
Interior Book Design by Fiona Raven
Book Cover Design by Book Cover Express

No part of this book may be reproduced or transmitted in any form or by any means, electronic or mechanical, including photocopying, recording, or by information storage and retrieval systems without permission in writing from the copyright owner.

ISBN 0-9758649-0-4
Library of Congress Control Number: 2004094542

First Printing September 2004
Printed in the USA

Published by SoulHealer Press
Dallas, Texas

SoulHealer Press
www.soulhealer.com
rita@soulhealer.com
tel 972-475-3393

~ *For Kiko* ~

To Veronica
Keep on keepin On!

Acknowledgments

I would like to thank all the people who helped make this book possible. Special thanks to Marilynn Macky, Charles Lightwalker, Susan Zajone and Earl Hall for their unique insights and guidance. To Ian Rule, for his outstanding job of editing this manuscript and his persistence in correcting the multitude of spelling errors. Many thanks to Tana Holderman for her inspired guidance and loving support.

I would also like to thank my husband, Jim Baker, who supported my efforts, encouraging me and my work. I am especially grateful for all of the times he held up the light at the end of the tunnel for me to see and walk toward. For this, I will be forever thankful.

We whispered,
"God, speak to us"
And a meadowlark sang.
But we did not hear.

So we yelled
"God, speak to us!"
And the thunder rolled across the sky.
But we did not listen.

We looked around and said,
"God, let us see you."
And a star shone brightly.
But we did not notice.

And we shouted,
"God show us a miracle."
And a life was born.
But we did not know.

So, we cried out in despair,
"Touch us God, and let us know you are here."
Whereupon, God reached down and touched us.
But we brushed the butterfly away and walked on…

— Unknown

Table of Contents

Foreword ix
Introduction xi

Section 1 – Our Energetic Nature

The Nature of Wholeness   3
The Energy of Life   9
In Search of Subtle Energy – A Historical Perspective   21
The Physical Body and Beyond   29
The Chakras – An Introduction   36
Energy Flow and the Subtle Body   45
The Qabalah   56

Section 2 – From Spirit to Self: The Nature of the Subtle Bodies

The Causal Body   67
The Mental Body   71
The Emotional Body   81
The Etheric Body   92
The Meridians   95
The Physical Body   98

Section 3 – Experiencing the Power of the Chakras

Before We Get Started… 115
The First Chakra 117
The Second Chakra 132
The Third Chakra 150
The Fourth Chakra 161
The Fifth Chakra 176
The Sixth Chakra 191
The Seventh Chakra 207

Section 4 – Avoiding the Cosmic 2 x 4

Finding Wholeness 217
How to Avoid the Cosmic 2 x 4 223
Experiencing Wholeness 231

Appendix

Guidance on Your Path to Wholeness 239
About the Author 258

FIGURES

Figure 1 – Wavelength and Frequency 13
Figure 2 – The Subtle Body 31
Figure 3 – The Seven Major Chakras 37
Figure 4 – The Chakras and Their Associated Nadis 47
Figure 5 – Movement of Subtle Energy Through the Bodies 49
Figure 6 – Qabalistic View of Subtle Energy Flow 52
Figure 7 – Black Holes and White Holes 53
Figure 8 – The Tree of Life 58
Figure 9 – The Lightning Path 62
Figure 10 – Nodal Points in the Psychosomatic Network 104
Figure 11 – Illustration of Balanced Energy 167
Figure 12 – Illustration of Imbalanced Energy 170

Foreword

I was delighted one day to receive an e-mail with the greeting "Hello from Rita Louise." It had been several years since I had heard from her, several years since she had completed her training with me in Transpersonal Hypnotherapy/NLP. I often wondered over the years what had become of this sensitive, funny, very open-minded and warm-hearted student. Where had she gone? Was she using the perspectives and techniques she had learned in my training? Had she continued with her work as a psychic? Had she integrated hypnotherapy with her psychic work?

My questions were finally answered when Rita contacted me. I was surprised and delighted to discover she had become a Naturopathic Physician (N.D.), had completed her Ph.D., and was practicing as a medical intuitive.

It was obvious that Rita had not only integrated her

psychic ability with hypnotherapy, but also with natural medicine, and with teachings about subtle energetic levels of our being from several ancient traditions.

What I found in *Avoiding the Cosmic 2 × 4* is Rita's clear explanation of the different energetic levels of our being and how they manifest health or disease when they are balanced or imbalanced. You will learn from her examples with clients how she reads the deep energetic roots of presenting symptoms and provides solutions based on her understanding of how these subtle energies affect our physical bodies. Rita also includes wonderful exercises that you can use immediately to uplift your mood and energize your being.

Even after sixteen years of using energetic visualizations in my hypnotherapy work with clients and students, I found renewed inspiration in Rita's presentations of the *chakras*, the subtle bodies, and the Qabalah's teachings about energy flow in our being. I immediately began to use visualizations inspired by Rita's for myself and with my clients with great results.

You are about to treat yourself to some soulful nourishment and very likely to an expansion of your notions of who and what you are and what it is possible for you to achieve in the areas of health and healing. This book offers a doorway to a whole new way of living.

Peace,

Jack Elias, CHT

Author of
Finding True Magic: Transpersonal Hypnotherapy/NLP©
www.findingtruemagic.com

Introduction

About ten years ago, I met a woman who challenged my view of health and wellness. Because of our encounter, my eyes were opened to an entirely different, much deeper realm than I had been aware of in the past. At the time, I was living just north of Seattle, WA, where I ran a monthly psychic fair – The North End Psychic Fair. In addition to hosting this event, I also provided medical intuition evaluations and clairvoyant readings to its patrons.

It was at one of these regularly scheduled events that I met Mary. Seeming about sixty-five years young, she sat down at my table for a fifteen-minute session. As I do with all of my clients, I asked her to repeat her full name three times, so that I could tune into her energetic vibration. With my eyes closed while she repeated her name, I felt the dynamics of her energy quickly come into focus.

Opening my eyes as I collected my thoughts, I reported to Mary the first thing I noticed in her aura: the subtle energy field around the body. What I observed was an area of dark black energy that was situated in the center of her chest. This dark energy appeared old and seemed almost dried up and crusty. It was as if it had been sitting there for many years. Probing deeper, I was given the impression that the tar-like mass that covered her heart chakra was somehow related to some unresolved issues she had with her mother.

Without a breath, Mary responded, informing me that she couldn't have any unresolved issues with her mother, for she had been adopted at birth and had never known her birth mother. I smiled and nodded at her reply. Instead of probing further, as I normally would do, I let this issue go and we continued on with our session without a hitch.

When I think back upon our interchange, I can still relate to her response regarding her mother, that is, when I think about it on an intellectual level. But energetically, it was very clear to me, then and now as well, that the unexpressed or the denied emotions she had concerning her birth mother were actually being expressed in her body and appeared in her aura in the form of a dark mass.

It was sometime later that afternoon when one of the vendors at the show asked me how my session with Mary had gone. Apparently the vendor had referred Mary to me. She believed that I could help Mary or at least provide her with some insights into her health concerns. It was then that my friend revealed to me that Mary was recovering from quadruple bypass surgery.

Later that evening, all of the pieces came together for me. The unacknowledged and unresolved emotions Mary had about her birth mother, the feelings of abandonment, the feelings of "who am I?" and "why am I here?" had not only manifested in her aura as a crystallized accumulation of energy, but had solidified even further where it manifested in her physical body as heart disease.

Prior to that time, based on my understanding and experience, I had viewed disease as manifesting in the physical body in one of three ways: from environmental causes such as bacteria, viruses, toxins or pollutants, from genetic causes, and from accidents and injuries to the body. After my experience with Mary, my perspective on disease and the disease process was no longer the same.

It was made abundantly clear to me that the blockages she experienced in the arteries that led to her heart were caused by the lack of subtle energy flowing into and out of her fourth chakra. This happened because her unconscious mind worked overtime in its efforts to suppress the pain, anger and/or frustration her conscious mind was unable to bear. The more she suppressed these unacknowledged feelings, the more the flow of energy into her body slowed, which, in the end, manifested in the physical body as heart disease.

Over the years, my view of health and wellness continued to broaden. As I worked with my clients, I became more aware of the underlying thoughts and emotions they had that impacted their well-being. It became evident to me that negative or limiting beliefs and unresolved emotional traumas play an overwhelming role in our ability to experience health. In fact, what I came to know from the depths of my being was that the mental and emotional conflicts we experience in life, while often thought of as a symptom of a yet-to-be-manifested physical issue, is in fact the disease itself but in an uncrystallized form.

I also came to recognize that we are a whole, integrated unit, made up of body, mind, spirit and emotions; that there must be a consistency or congruency between our inner and outer selves that is reflected in our thoughts, ideas, beliefs, opinions, feelings, intentions and actions. I found that from this place of wholeness our life force energy, our *chi'*, can flow through us unhindered. I also realized that an imbalance of any one of our parts hinders the unfettered flow of this life force energy through us. This interferes with our ability to be whole.

My definition of disease had changed. While bacteria, viruses, genetics, accidents and injury play a role in our ability to maintain health, my own observations suggested that the number of individuals that manifested health concerns brought about by unresolved mental and emotional issues was staggering. I finally understood why many people refer to disease as "dis-ease." The definition I had always heard was dis-ease means "lack of ease." From this viewpoint, the concept of dis-ease can include not only our physical bodies, but also any pain or discomfort we may experience in our interpersonal relationships and within ourselves. With my increased awareness, I was now able to expand upon this notion, because I understood both how and why disease occurs.

Because of the revelation I experienced in my encounter with Mary, the focus of my work shifted. I found myself compelled to look at and identify the mental and emotional imbalances my clients were experiencing. I was driven to help them restore health, harmony and wholeness in their lives. I felt that it was essential for me to go back to school and get a degree in Naturopathy. This stirring sensation didn't let up once I was done with that degree, and I found myself again back in school working on a Ph.D. in Natural Health Counseling.

Deep down inside, I had an inner conviction that it was critical for me to follow this path and that somewhere down this road I would experience wholeness in my own life. What I didn't realize was that this work, while extremely important on some levels, was only the outer shell that housed a vast transformation that was occurring inside.

Sometimes it is not until you get to the end of the road that you recognize its beginning.

It was the beginning of March, 2003 when I sat down to write the last chapter of this book, the chapter on the seventh chakra. It was not that this was the subject matter of the book's final chapter, but it was the last chapter that I actually sat down to write. If the truth were told, I had written the chapters on the other chakras months before. For some reason, unbeknownst to me, I was unable to put pen to pad and write.

As time went on, I would constantly remind myself that I needed to write this missing section, but never felt inspired nor compelled to work on it. In retrospect, it is interesting because a part of me felt as if I were procrastinating or somehow afraid to write these final words. At the time I wondered why I was experiencing such resistance. I wasn't having difficulty working on the other chapters, so why was I having so much trouble with this one? No matter how much I thought about it, I just couldn't figure it out.

I remember sitting down at my computer, determined to write it. I started typing, outlining the basics of the seventh chakra. As I sat trying to organize my thoughts, to bring in, own and surrender to the feeling that is our seventh chakra, my dog had a seizure.

At almost seventeen, Kiko, my miniature poodle was like a child to me. Old, deaf and having difficulty seeing, her health over the past few weeks had been deteriorating quickly. By the time she had the seizure, she had barely eaten or drunk anything for almost a week. From the time she was fifteen, as she went through a number of health issues, Kiko had shown me very distinct images of how she wanted to pass. She didn't want to go to the vet and be put down. Instead, she would show me pictures of me holding her in my arms as I had thousands of times before. This is how she wanted to take her last breath.

As I held her in my arms, her body shaking violently, I prayed and asked that she be taken quickly. I knew that she was ready and the end was near. When the seizure passed and I got her comfortable in her bed that sat behind my desk, not knowing what else to do in that moment, I turned my attention back to my writing. I found the words flowing through me. As I worked, I finally realized why I had been unable to write about the seventh chakra until then.

The seventh chakra represents the point of initiation, the seed from which all life springs forth, the place upon which the outflowing breath brings life and the indrawn breath the end of life, but death. I was unable to write about the seventh chakra because I was meant to experience and comprehend its meaning to the depths of my being. It was not that I was procrastinating, or was afraid to put the words to paper, but instead because I was not destined to write those words until that moment in time.

With this recognition, and through my tears, I put my ego to the side and allowed the words to come to me. I knew that all was right; all was perfect and happening as it was supposed to, even though it wasn't fun. In fact, it was an experience I would just as well have avoided.

I decided to share this story with you because I feel it reflects the intent and purpose of this book. If I were to encapsulate how wholeness is achieved, it would be in one word – surrender. The dictionary defines surrender as the following: to give up, give back or abandon; to give over or resign to something, as to an emotion.

When we repress or suppress who we really are, we create distortions in the flow of our life force energy. It is only when we are our authentic self that we can experience health and well-being. We are whole. When we are authentic, the flow of life-giving energy moves freely in and out of our bodies. Being authentic allows us to follow our inner guidance going wherever it takes us, even if it is not fun.

Avoiding the Cosmic 2 × 4 is all about dis-ease and the dis-ease process. It talks about the nature of our subtle self and how our life force energy flows through it. It also delves into the aspects of our makeup that can impact the flow of energy through our systems. By understanding ourselves and our subtle nature, we can take the first step in becoming our authentic selves and finding health, happiness and wholeness in our lives.

Throughout this book, I will be making reference to a number of specific terms to describe our energetic nature. For ease of reading, I have simplified the different concepts and systems, choosing one word or system to represent a number of different words that can be used interchangeably.

For example, all the way through the text, the Yogic system of the bodies, chakras and *nadis* is used to explore the working of subtle energy. It is not because it is the only system available, but because many people are already familiar with the basic ideas and concepts this system provides. Much of the information provided is a synthesis of the Yogic system with that of Jewish Mysticism, the Qabalah. Unless specifically noted, these two systems are in agreement with one another.

In addition, throughout the book, I will refer to the guiding, prompting presence that is part of us by using the words "God" and "soul." When I make reference to God, it is not from a religious sense, such as the notion of a white-haired man sitting on a throne and telling us what to do. Instead, I use it to simplify a multitude of concepts that denote this originating energy, whether the term you are accustomed to using is Allah, Jehovah, Supreme Being, Cosmic Conscious, Divine Spark, The Universe, The Source, etc.

The same holds true for the usage of the word "soul." Separate from the notion of God, the concept of the soul can be thought of or termed our higher self or inner self. For the sake of clarity, I have decided to use these terms, but feel free to substitute whatever name feels appropriate for you.

It is my hope that, as you read this book, you will be able to find wholeness in your own life and learn to avoid the cosmic 2 × 4.

Section 1

Our Energetic Nature

The Nature of Wholeness

> *The universe is no longer seen as a machine, made up of a multitude of objects, but has to be pictured as one indivisible dynamic whole whose parts are essentially interrelated and can be understood only as patterns of a cosmic process.*
>
> — FRITJOF CAPRA

Mist covers the floor of a thickly forested woodland. The sun, inching its way up the sky, is reflected in the dew that rests on the leaves and branches of the tall trees, appearing as thousands of miniature rainbows as they glisten in the first light of the early morning. The dimness of the morning sky gives rise to the fullness of a summer's day. Hour by hour, the moisture that cloaked the deep green foliage of the woodland slowly evaporates, filling the air with subtle amounts of humidity.

Around the world, this same process occurs, in the forests and on the plains and over the oceans, on the tallest of mountains and in the deepest of valleys. In time, the evaporated moisture, collected from plant and animals alike, accumulates and condenses, filling the sky with soft billowy clouds.

As the noonday sun rises high in the sky, clouds form, gathering into darkened masses. Rain begins to fall from the now murky sky, saturating the earth and nourishing the trees, plants and grasses, each drop seeding the earth with water so that another cycle can begin.

Simple as this example may be, everything on the earth is interconnected through a variety of cycles and feedback systems and is held together in a delicate web of interdependencies and a precise balance or homeostasis. Homeostasis is defined as the tendency toward a relatively stable equilibrium between interdependent elements. It is the tendency of an organism to compensate for internal and external changes and disturbances in order to maintain stability. This means that each part that makes up the system must remain in balance with the other parts or the system will ultimately fail. This is achieved through a series of checks, balances and feedback loops.

When a system is stable and balanced, it can be said that the system is working as a whole. In the natural world there is an inherent longing for wholeness. But what is wholeness? According to the Merriam-Webster dictionary, wholeness is a state of internal integrity that exists at the core of any organization or system. When we think of something that is whole, we think of a solid unified entity; of something undivided, and always working for a unified cause or objective.

The concept of wholeness used here implies that: 1) the whole is made up of a number of component parts or elements, 2) the whole and its various parts are aspects of one another and are continually influenced and modified by one another, and 3) the whole and all of its parts are pliant and moldable. It is this flexibility and adjustability between each of the parts that permits balance and harmony to exist throughout the system. When something is whole, there is a place for all its parts, with the positive, negative, good or bad perceived as just aspects of the whole.

The question is, what happens when the delicate balance needed to keep this system operating correctly is threatened? What happens when its checks, balances and feedback loops falter?

If we look again at the natural world, we can see that balance is essential to its healthy functioning. Over the last few years concern has been raised regarding climatic changes (global warming) on the earth. Scientists believe that the earth's temperature is progressively rising due to the number of greenhouse gases that are being released into the atmosphere. These gases come primarily from the burning of fossil fuels, which release carbon dioxide (CO_2) into the atmosphere. In July 1997, former President Bill Clinton stated, "The overwhelming balance of evidence and scientific opinion is that it is no longer a theory but now a fact that global warming is real."

Projections based on computer models show that the average daily temperature will rise approximately 3° Celsius by the end of the twenty-first century. Put into context, the increase in global temperatures responsible for bringing us out of the Ice Age was only 4 – 5° Celsius. This increase, however, occurred over thousands of years, thus allowing the earth's systems to adjust gradually. Even with this gradual change in global temperatures, a large number plants and animals still fell prey to worldwide extinction. In the scenario proposed by scientists today, it is believed that such rapid change in temperature will cause major ecosystem failures. They will fail because their internal systems will be unable to adapt to the temperature changes in such a short period of time.

There is an ancient saying that states, "As above, so below." This philosophical principle is often used to describe the correspondence between the heavens above reflected on the earth below: our inner world reflected by our physical reality or the divine reflected in the mundane. It suggests that the universe is reflected in the essence of man, man is reflected in the essence of each of our cells, the cells are reflected in the essence of the atom, the atom is reflected ... and so on, ad infinitum.

As in nature, the principle that necessitates balance and harmony, or homeostasis, also holds true for us. It ensures the healthy functioning of our bodies and is critical to our survival. The concept of homeostasis is well established in biology. In the human body, for example, we maintain a core temperature of 98.6° Fahrenheit despite variations in the temperature around us. The pupils of our eyes change in relation to the intensity of light. Our bodies are constantly adjusting and readjusting to both internal and external stimuli and stressors in an effort to maintain balance.

When the balance and harmony of these systems are disrupted or somehow impaired, we experience disease. Disease is routinely defined as an unhealthy condition of the body or mind. It is identified as any harmful change that hinders or impairs the normal function, structure or appearance of the physical body or any of its parts. It can be the result of trauma to the body, an inherited abnormal gene, exposure to an infectious bacteria or virus or of internal chemical imbalances.

Doctors and scientists are taught to think of the human body as a sophisticated biological machine where the origin of disease can only be found under a microscope. This outlook towards health and wellness is based upon a Newtonian view of the world, which sees life as a series of intricate mechanisms and us as being made up of a complex series of biochemical processes. This view of health, healing and medicine has been around for hundreds of years.

According to this model, disease is seen as a function of our physical being, where it is observed as afflicting one part of the body or another. Migraines, ulcers and high blood pressure are viewed as being separate and unrelated to one another. Doctors diagnose the visible pathology and consider it to be the cause of the illness or the illness itself and seek to treat it by chemical means. It is sad to say, but many physicians, in the diagnosis and treatment process, tend to overlook some of the simple laws of health that include good food, fresh air and exercise. Scientists have long understood that in nature an imbalance in one aspect of a system can disrupt the functioning of the entire unit, causing it to break down and ultimately fail. If we are a reflection of the world around us, then we too should be impacted by imbalances in our systems and subsystems and, according to many modern researchers, we are.

The Energy of Life

> *Misdirected life force is the activity in the disease process. Disease has no energy save what it borrows from the life of the organism. It is by adjusting the life force that healing must be brought about.*
>
> — THE QABALAH

In Western medicine, researchers have only recently begun to appreciate the impact our thoughts and emotions have on our health, and have started to investigate the link between the mind and the manifestation of disease in the body. Their work has led them to identify a number of reasons why people get sick. For some, illness and disease is a way in which individuals express unresolved distress and trauma. For others, getting sick may actually provide the person some kind of benefit, even if the benefit is based on an unhealthy belief.

There are other reasons people get sick. Illness may provide them with an excuse to not live up to high expectations; it may provide them with a way of expressing inner mental or emotional conflicts; it may help them, in a roundabout way, to solve a problem. Disease may also be used to punish ourselves, receive attention from others or find incentive to manifest internal changes or modify unwanted habits.

There are a growing number of skilled observers who believe that issues such as diabetes, cancer or heart disease only represent a symptom of a larger pattern of disorder and disharmony within the body. Renée Weber, Ph.D., expressed the cause of disease in this way: "The primary cause of disease is the disconnectedness from the flow and rhythm of the whole, both within the single organism and also among groups of organisms."

Disease can be seen as the manifestation of some undesirable condition within us that has been brought into physical form so it can be dealt with and eliminated. It can be thought of as a reflection of the conflict between our inner state and outer existence or as our soul trying to get our attention. It works to let us know that our true self is being thwarted or that we are being pulled in two directions at once. It is brought about by our habitual or limiting thoughts and our negative feelings and emotions.

According to Edward Bach, M.D., the father of flower essence therapy, to understand the true nature of disease, certain fundamental truths have to be acknowledged:

1. Man has a soul, which is his real self and the body is but a reflection of it.
2. Our personalities are here for the purpose of gaining knowledge and experience through our earthly existence so we can bring into balance the parts of us that are lacking.
3. Our bodies are but temporary instruments through which the soul works. While our life here on earth is but a moment in the course of our evolution, our soul is immortal.
4. When the soul and the personality are in harmony, all is joy and peace, happiness and health. It is when our personalities are led astray from the path laid down by the soul that conflict arises. This conflict is the root cause of disease and unhappiness. As long as we are working in alignment with the soul, all is well. Regardless of our job or occupation, we will always be provided with the lessons and experiences necessary for our personal development.
5. There is a unity to all things. While we may seem separate and individualized, we are part of a collective whole. Thus, any action we take against ourselves or another affects the whole because an imperfection in a part is always reflected in the whole.

Researchers now believe that the body is not only made up of a series of organs, glands and biological processes, but of a complex network of interdependent and interconnected energies which interact with one another in a web of mutually conditioned relationships. If one looks at the concept of disease from the perspective of all living things being part of this interconnected network, disease can be seen as a lack of harmony, an imbalance, a disturbance or lack of wholeness somewhere within our being.

The idea that we are made up of a network of interconnecting energies is often referred to as the "Einsteinian paradigm," which recognizes that there are invisible forces that operate in and around all of nature including us as human beings. These forces, or subtle energies, although not readily discernible to the naked eye, are believed to have a direct impact upon the state of our health on physical and even cellular levels and on mental and emotional levels as well.

We have learned from Einstein's theories that matter and energy are one and the same. If we take matter down to its simplest subatomic components, we find that it is energy in motion. Thus the atoms and molecules that make up the physical body are actually a form of vibrating energy, vibrating within a specific frequency range.

Physicists believe that all systems in nature have their own particular way of vibrating. Everything in the universe, every thought, feeling, event, word, and all life, has its own rate of vibration or resonance. This is what makes each type and form of energy distinctive and unique. From the swing of a pendulum to the waves in the ocean to the light that brightens the sky each day, each of these oscillates at its own particular rate or frequency. The same holds true for sound, heat, light and magnetism. They are each made of waves of vibrating energy, differing from each other only by their frequency and the way they move through time and space.

Things such as rocks and minerals vibrate very slowly at a rate that is imperceptible to us. Living beings such as plants and animals vibrate faster and appear to be alive. Based on current technology, electromagnetic radiation vibrates at the highest frequency we know of in the universe.

Visible light, such as the light that is emitted by the sun or even a light bulb, is a kind of electromagnetic radiation. Microwaves, infrared radiation, ultraviolet rays, X-rays and gamma rays are also forms of this kind of energy. Combined, they make up the electromagnetic spectrum. All electromagnetic energy radiates at the speed of light, 186,000 miles per second. The difference between each of these forms of energy is their wavelength – the shorter the wavelength, the higher the frequency.

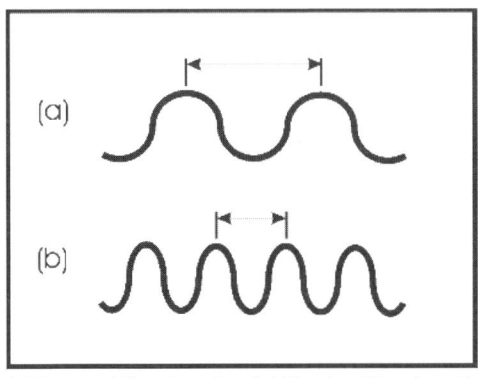

(a) Longer Wavelength; (b) Shorter Wavelength

Figure 1
Wavelength and Frequency

Radio waves, for example, are used to transmit radio and television signals. Each wavelength can be as little as one centimeter to tens or even hundreds of meters in length. The wavelengths of microwaves, like those used to cook food, can range from one millimeter to about twelve inches in length. Visible light, i.e., the section of the electromagnetic spectrum we can see, comprises wavelengths ranging from 400 to 700 billionths of a meter in length. Ultraviolet light, the kind of energy that tans the skin in lower doses or causes cancer or cataracts in higher amounts, has a wavelength of 400 billionths of a meter to ten billionths of a meter. X-rays possess a wavelength of ten billionths of a meter to about ten trillionths of a meter, while gamma rays have a wavelength of less than ten trillionths of a meter.

It is theorized that the subtle energy that makes up our being vibrates at a frequency faster than electromagnetic radiation. According to Don Paris, author of *Regaining Wholeness Through the Subtle Dimensions,* everything in the universe – every living thing as well as every nonliving object – emits subtle energy so, in a sense, everything is alive. This unseen yet undeniable part of who we are is something that many of us take for granted, yet it is always with us, every minute of every day. It fills us from the tops of our heads down to the tips of our toes, ever moving and flowing in and around us. Subtle energy provides an organizing principle to nature – if it weren't for this predisposition, we would only be a collection of cells or disordered pile of chemicals.

Western scientists have traditionally ignored the energetic implications of our being, primarily because they have been unable to document them. Scientists who have investigated the movement of subtle energy in the body assumed that they would find it on physiological levels where it would work like our nervous or circulatory systems. When they were unable to find "it," they concluded that it didn't exist or was the stuff of myth. They never considered the notion that the tools they were using might be insufficient or that their assumptions might be wrong. Yet, throughout time, the greatest advancements and breakthroughs in science have occurred because of the discovery of a new scientific instrument or groundbreaking technology. Recent findings in quantum physics are now validating the existence of subtle energy and subtle energetic systems.

If you think about it, only in the last century have scientists been able to measure, validate, harness and utilize electromagnetic radiation in the form of medical x-rays, indoor lighting and microwave ovens. For example, it is common knowledge that if you go outside on a sunny day, you run the risk of getting burnt, but only recently has this effect been attributed to ultraviolet radiation. So while we have all experienced ultraviolet radiation on a qualitative level, this is based purely on its effect. Even today, while scientists understand the laws and principles upon which electromagnetic radiation is based, they still don't know exactly how or why it works.

The concept of a person being made up of subtle energy has actually been around for millennia. Described by ancient schools of healing in both the East and the West, this mysterious life force energy is the basis of all life. Its life-giving properties are referred to in almost every spiritual tradition and culture worldwide. According to a National Institutes of Health study, there are well over 50 different and distinct terms used to describe this subtle life force energy including chi', prana, holy spirit, manna, ether, orgone, biomagnetism and zeropoint.

Doctrines that incorporate the concept that we are made up of energy can be found in ancient philosophical traditions, particularly those of India and China. It also is part of the teaching of the Qabalah, the basis of Jewish mystical traditions. Each of these schools of thought agrees upon a number of points regarding subtle energy, especially the concept that our life force energy is the basis of all life and the source of all movement, not only in the human body but in the universe as well. Dion Fortune, in his book *The Mystical Qabalah* states, "And when we find three of the great metaphysical systems of the world in complete agreement, we may conclude that we are dealing with established principles and should accept them as such."

Each of these philosophical traditions holds a piece of the puzzle as we seek to understand subtle energy and how it interacts with the world around us. In China, Taoists view all life as being whole and undifferentiated as it moves and flows, ever-changing and dependent upon the viewpoint of the observer. Here the concept of subtle energy is called chi'. Taoists believe that we are all filled with chi' that runs through the bodies in a series of energetic veinlike structures called meridians. It is thought that the meridians are lines of communication that carry the necessary information to guide the growth of a fetus and play a pivotal role in the repair and healing of the body proper.

According to Taoist beliefs, the whole of life is dualistic in nature with the two parts, the yin and the yang, being aspects of and composing the whole. The movement of chi' is likewise expressed in the form of the yin/yang. The yin/yang speaks purely of energy and the energy dynamics found in the universe. The universe and all things within it are seen as positive or negative, light or dark, male or female.

In the Yogic tradition, an ancient philosophical doctrine from India, the nature of subtle energy is described in a more structured manner. According to this system, we are more than just a physical body. In fact we are made up of five separate but equal bodies, each vibrating at different frequencies, which include the physical body, the etheric body, the emotional body, the mental body and the causal body. Each is seen as controlling an aspect of our physical form as well as regulating our action/reaction to stimuli from the world around us.

We are also made up of a number of unique energetic components including the aura or electromagnetic field around the body, the chakras or energy centers within the body, and the nadis or energetic channels that run through the body. In this tradition, our life force energy is called "prana."

In the Qabalah, the concept of our energy-based self takes on an even more pragmatic appearance. The movement of subtle energy is expressed in a linear format, where its creative, formative and limiting nature is identified. It explores the dynamics of energy and energy flow, thus providing a detailed and comprehensive explanation of its workings.

These concepts are represented by the Tree of Life, which is made up of ten sephiroth or centers of energy on seven separate yet distinct levels. The sephiroth are arranged on three pillars, one positive, one negative, and the last one neutral. According to Qabalistic traditions, consciousness manifests itself in four different worlds: Azilut, Beriah, Yezirah and Asiyyah.

In a healthy system, energy and information should flow smoothly and freely through each layer of the subtle body and then back out again. (We will go into greater detail regarding the nature and function of each of the subtle bodies later in the book.) The flow of energy through our subtle body, however, is capable of either preserving or diminishing our inner resources. When energy is active and moving without obstruction through the bodies, we experience health. When the flow is inhibited or distorted, disease ensues.

Imagine your life force energy as a fast-moving mountain stream. It is flowing strong and unyielding through you, filling you with unfettered life force energy. Now consider what it would feel like if a large stone were placed in the center of your stream. Your life force energy would be forced to yield and deviate around the stone blocking its path. The flow of your stream has become imbalanced.

If, for example, the first time you feel invalidated a large stone was placed in your stream, its effect on the flow of your energy may not be great. If you are invalidated again and another stone is added to your stream, the blockage becomes bigger. Your life force energy must yield and deviate even more to get around the even larger blockage. These blockages can grow instance by instance, cycle by cycle, stone after stone, lifetime after lifetime, until the body starts to manifest these issues as disease.

Another way of looking at the flow of energy through our subtle body is in electrical terms, where our negative thoughts, ideas, feelings and emotions can be thought of as resistors that resist the flow of energy through the body. Resistance is a measure of how hard it is for a charge to move through a circuit. A resistor in turn is a component that resists the flow of current. Resistors can limit or protect a current, reduce its voltage or provide large amounts of heat or light. When our energetic channels are open and our energy is flowing, it indicates that our resistance is low, whereas if our energetic channels are closed, it signifies that our resistance has increased, and that consequently the flow of energy through our system has decreased.

Imbalances in the flow of energy through the mental body can manifest as narrow-mindedness, disrespect for life and nature, or materialism. Imbalances of the emotional body manifest as anger, rage, phobias, depression and hate. Imbalances of the etheric body are expressed through the physical body as illness and disease, manifesting in the form of a cold, back pain, arthritis or cancer. If not addressed, imbalances to our life force energy will continue to grow, creating more pressure on an already stressed system. If not addressed and the pressure released, even greater issues can manifest in our bodies.

Everything is in the universe is dependent on the life-giving power this neutral energy provides, including ourselves. Even though it is unseen, we experience it through its actions. It is generally agreed upon that, if we were deprived of this life-giving animating energy, we would cease to exist.

When we are healthy, energy and information flow easily and effortlessly through the bodies. However, based on our life experiences, the flow of energy through our system can become inhibited. If our response to a particular stimulus is in congruence with our inner self, the flow of energy through our energetic system is enhanced. If our response is repressed or suppressed, the flow of energy begins to slow down causing disturbances in our energetic field, which can begin to crystallize and create a blockage to the flow of energy. This blockage to the flow of our life force energy can ultimately manifest itself as disease.

In Search of Subtle Energy
– A Historical Perspective

> *The universe is full of magical things, patiently waiting for our wits to grow sharper.*
> — EDEN PHILLPOTTS

The ideas presented in this book are grounded in several centuries of thought, doctrine, literature and scientific discovery. What follows is an overview of that historical grounding.

The concept of subtle energy has been around since the most ancient of times. As far back as 5,000 years ago, this ever-evasive energy that fills us was first described in India and was again identified in China some 2,000 years later. Around 500 BC, in Greece, the Pythagoreans believed in a universal energy that permeates all of nature.

Moving forward in time, Boirac and Liebeault, in approximately 1100 AD, observed that we have a healthy or unhealthy effect on other people's health simply by being in their presence. Additionally, they found that these energetic interactions could also occur at a distance. By the late 1500s, Jan Baptista von Helmont, a physician who devoted himself to the study of chemistry, proposed the existence of a pure vital spirit that permeates all of nature, a "fluid that could not be weighted or measured." He called this energy or spirit "archeus."

By the late 1600s, Gottfried Wilhelm Leibnitz, a German philosopher, mathematician and logician, theorized that all of the elements in the universe are centers of force with localized motion and that this movement is dependent upon the action of spirit. Even Sir Isaac Newton, while commonly remembered for his Laws of Mechanics, which propagated the view of the human body as a biochemical machine, was well aware of subtle energies. In his book *The Principia Mathematica*, which was published in 1697, Newton clearly discloses, "These are things which cannot be explained in a few words, nor are we furnished with that sufficiency of experiments which is required [for] an accurate determination and demonstration of the laws by which this electric and elastic spirit operates."

In the latter part of the 18th century, Franz Anton Mesmer, the father of modern day hypnotherapy, announced that he had found a great universal cure for both physical and emotional problems. He believed that there was an invisible fluid flowing throughout the body, which he called "animal magnetism." He proposed that this magnetism influenced the mental, emotional and physical aspects of our lives.

With the advent of electricity in the 19th century, science took another leap forward in its understanding of subtle energy. James Clerk Maxwell, a Scottish physicist in the early 1800s, was the first to show that visible light was just a small part of the realm of electromagnetic radiation. He predicted the existence of other electromagnetic waves that had yet to be detected. He was right.

By the middle of the 1800s, Count Wilhelm von Reichenbach found that the human energy field, or aura, had many properties that were similar to the electromagnetic field described by Maxwell. He called this field the "odic field." He also found that the odic field could be conducted down a wire, traveling at a rate of approximately four meters per second. In another study, von Reichenbach found that the human aura produces a polarity similar to that found in crystals. When measured along the major axis of our bodies, he found one side of the body to be negative and the other positive. At the Hospital de la Charité in France, Dr. Luys proved von Reichenbach's theory of the human body's polarization, with the right side being positive and the left side negative.

After qualifying as a doctor in 1850, Ambrose August Liebeault experimented extensively with various techniques of mesmerism (hypnosis) and developed a theory regarding mental attention, associating it with a "nervous force." Thus, when we pay attention to some part of the body, the nervous force flows toward it, increasing its activity. Conversely, if there is a lack of attention to a part of the body, the flow of this force would be reduced and the activity of that part depressed. Candace Pert, Ph.D., in her recent study regarding peptides and emotions, confirmed his theory.

Walter Kilner, M.D., while working at St. Thomas Hospital in London around 1911, invented a special kind of screen that enabled anyone to view the aura, or as he called it, the "human atmosphere." With this screen, Kilner found he was able to diagnose illness, because the aura around the sick or affected organ would appear noticeably weaker than the remaining organs. In his book *The Human Aura*, which was at long last published in 1965, he states that the aura appears to differ from person to person depending on their physical, emotional and mental state.

In an attempt to correlate the laws of biology with those of physics, Albert Abrams studied the subtle emanation of life forms and applied them to the diagnosis and treatment of disease. According to Abrams, the body emanates not one, but three different energies simultaneously: physical, psychical and auric energy. He theorized that each disease has a specific vibratory rate, which could be detected by tapping on a patient's abdomen or spine. This information was published in his book *New Concepts in Diagnosis and Treatment* in 1916. Continuing with Abrams' work, Dr. George de la Warr and Dr. Ruth Drown developed an instrument that could be used to detect radiation from living tissues. Called "radionics," this device was reported to work over long distances. W. E. Boyd, also following the work of Albert Abrams, invented his own radionic-type device called the "emanometer." When put to the test by the Royal Society of Medicine, the Emanometer passed twenty-five separate tests with one hundred percent accuracy.

French philosopher Henri Bergson looked to describe the immaterial force he called "élan vita," whose existence could not be scientifically verified. He felt that it provides the vital impulse that continuously shapes all life. In turn, German biologist and master experimenter Hans Driesch felt that the biochemical process found in an embryo could not account for all of the vast complexities of organic life. He proposed that there was a energetic field influencing them. He called this "entelechy."

In his work during the early 1900s, Harold Saxton Burr, Ph.D., discovered that all living things were molded and controlled by electrodynamic fields, which could be measured with a standard voltmeter. Calling these fields "L-fields," he felt that they acted as a blueprint for the development of living organisms. Dr. Burr also believed that by measuring the voltages within the L-field, physical and mental conditions could be revealed. His work led him to conclude that through these fields we are interconnected with one another and the entire universe.

Also in the early 1900s, Dr. Wilhelm Reich, following in the work of Sigmund Freud, theorized that emotional trauma creates muscular tension in the body, which he called "armoring." This armoring inhibited the free flow of energy in the body. He coined the term "orgone" to describe this energy and the human energy field. Reich studied the relationship between the flow of orgone energy in the body and physical disturbances. Using psychotherapy, he found ways in which to release these blockages (armoring) from the energetic systems in the body, thus restoring health.

Dr. Dora Kunz, a clairvoyant and healer, observed in her work that when the human energy field is in health, it vibrates at what she called a "natural autonomous rhythm." With disease, the rhythm and energy levels are changed. She also observed that when there is pathology in a specific organ, thus changing its natural autonomous rhythm, the rhythm of neighboring organs is also affected. In physics, this is called impedance matching.

In 1939, Semyon D. Kirlian, an electrician and founder of Kirlian photography with his wife Valentina Kirlian, a teacher and journalist. He felt that photographs taken with their specialized camera detected our life force energy. Kirlian photography captures of film the coronal discharge around living objects. His work also demonstrated what is called the "phantom leaf effect," in which a leaf, cut in half, shows the coronal discharge of the whole leaf as if uncut. This effect is thought to depict the etheric growth template of the leaf.

In Korea, in the 1960s, Professor Kim Bong Han performed experiments to identify the anatomic nature of the meridian system. His findings suggested that the meridian system was an independent vascular network within the body. He then suggested that the meridian system is formed during embryonic development and may guide the growth and development of the circulatory and lymphatic systems, forming within fifteen hours of conception.

Dr. Hiroshi Motoyama of Japan, specialist in Oriental medicine, presented evidence for the existence of the chakras, the energy centers within the body. Motoyama found that when an individual projected energy from his or her chakras, significant disturbances in the electromagnetic field in and around their chakras could be detected. Itzhar Bentov then duplicated these findings. In the 1970s, Marcel Vogel found that sensitive people could attune themselves to the human energy fields of others and through those fields elicit responses as well as create a climate of healing. His experiments demonstrated that the mind's energies could be focused, received and registered in millivolts.

According to Rupert Sheldrake, Ph.D., a leading scientist in the field of biology, "morphogenetic fields" act as a template for the development, growth and healing of all life forms. He believed that these fields carry information but no energy and are available throughout time and space without any loss of intensity. He believed that this information is used to create the patterns of physical forms. He felt that the DNA in the genes did not carry all of the information needed to shape a system, but instead the organism taps into the morphogenetic field of an earlier form, receiving what could be called "genetic habits." Sheldrake also identifies the morphogenetic field as the location of stored memory and knowledge that was later called the "collective unconscious" by Carl Jung.

Dr. Robert Becker, an orthopedic surgeon and medical research doctor, claims that most living creatures are electrical by nature and are able to assist the regrowth of bone by applying a slight electrical charge to the injured area. He also mapped a complex electrical field on the body that was similarly shaped to the human form and the central nervous system. He also describes what he believes to be a separate nervous system that comprises a series of channels or meridians that are responsible for the flow of energy into the vital organs.

Most recently, the work of William A. Tiller, Ph.D, Professor Emeritus of Materials Science and Engineering at Stanford University, bridges the so-called conventional and non-conventional realms of scientific inquiry. Currently, he is devoting effort to the development of reliable instrumentation for the detection and study of "subtle energy" fields in nature. His experiments in the field of subtle energy suggest that nature expresses itself in many other dimensions than just the physical realm and that these other dimensions interact with the physical domain. Other experiments suggest that when human intention is applied to the unseen forces in the subtle dimensions, it could propel events in the physical domain.

Throughout time, the idea and understanding that we are filled with an indescribable essence has persisted. People have accepted it in the past and are rediscovering it now. In recent years, scientists and researchers are learning to measure this essence, document it and apply their findings to new systems of diagnostics and treatment in the realms of health and wellness. In the words of Isaac Asimov, a biochemist and famous science fiction author, "The most exciting phrase to hear in science, the one that heralds the most discoveries, is not "Eureka," but "That's funny..."

The Physical Body and Beyond

> *Life is a series of sensations connected to different states of consciousness.*
> — REMY DE GOURMONT

In Western society, humanity's view of our existence on earth based is solely on our interaction with the physical plane, where we live in a three-dimensional world. The physical world, however, represents only one dimension of the human experience and embodies only a fraction of the reality of the universe.

If we look back at some of the most ancient religious and philosophical texts, the notion that other dimensions exist beyond the physical plane can easily be found. Sanskrit texts, for example, describe four distinct planes of consciousness that exist beyond the physical world. Called "bodies," they include the etheric, astral or emotional, mental and causal bodies. In Qabalistic texts, these same alternative planes of existence, called "worlds," are identified as Assiah, the World of Matter, Yetzirah, the World of Formation, Briah, the World of Creation and Atziluth, the World of Ability.

The subtle bodies can be equated to the octaves on a piano, with each body vibrating at a different rate or frequency. The etheric body (Assiah) vibrates at the slowest frequency, while the causal body (Atziluth) vibrates the fastest. These bodies move from the gross, dense form of the physical body until they merge again in the world of spirit in the causal body.

It is believed that the four subtle bodies correlate to the four primary ranges measured by an EEG. (An EEG, or electroencephalograph, is a graphic record of the electrical activity of the brain.) Delta waves, for example, operate at a frequency of 1–3.5 Hz and are related to the physical body. Theta waves are associated with the emotional or astral body and operate at 3.5–7 Hz. Alpha waves operate at 7–14 Hz and are related to the mental body. And finally, the causal body is said to operate at 14–30 Hz, where it correlates with beta waves.

Each subtle body has its own distinctive features. For instance, each body contains *chakras* or energy centers. They contain seven separate yet distinct layers and are connected to each other via the *nadis* or energy channels. Through the action of the chakras and nadis the bodies interact with each other as well as with emanations received from the environment.

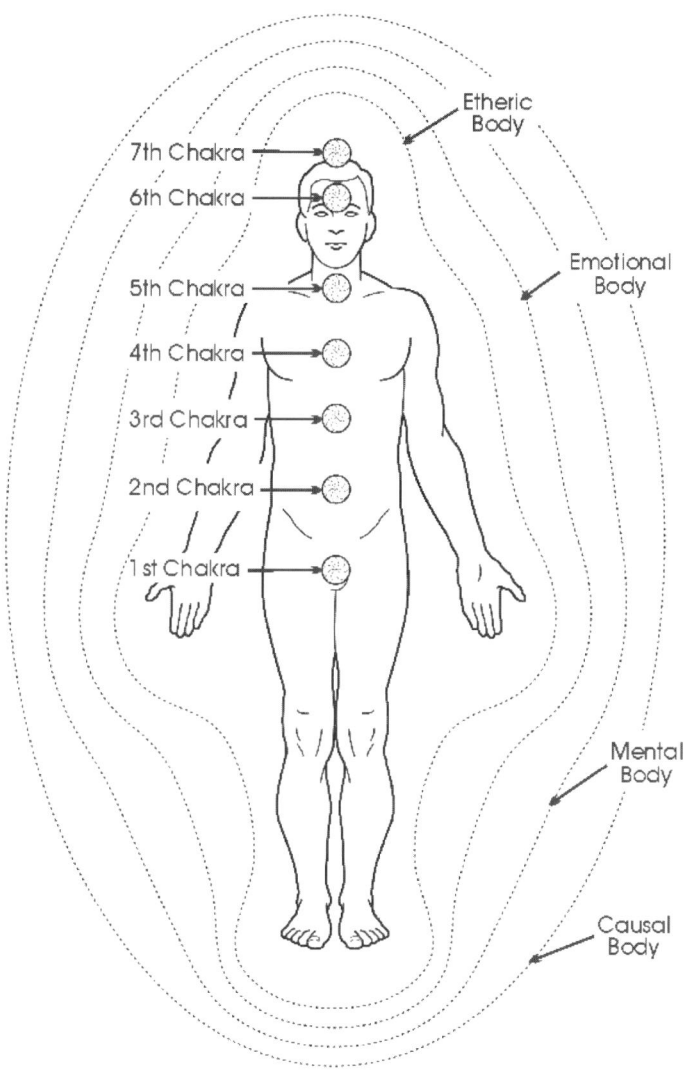

Figure 2
The Subtle Body

The subtle bodies occupy the same time-space continuum as our physical body does in our three-dimensional world. This occurs in the same way radio and television waves pass through the same space without interference.

If you take a moment and think about it, the air around us is filled with the energy of hundreds of radio and television broadcasts in any given moment. It is also filled with thousands of telephone conversations that are transmitted by cordless and wireless phones. We are not aware of the broadcasts because they exist outside the range of our perception. If, however, we turn on the TV, the energy of the television broadcast is translated into our favorite television show. In addition, when we change the channel and tune into another station we don't end up watching channel two on channel thirty-nine. This is because each channel is relayed at slightly different frequencies, which keeps the signals from mixing. This allows them to occupy the same space without interfering with one another.

Each of the bodies has a unique property or characteristic. The chief property of the physical body and physical world is matter. It is expressed as the world in which we live. It is represented by the things we can see, touch, hear and experience. It works to provide us with a basis for our consensual reality. By its very nature matter has no power or ability to move on its own and must always be acted on by some form of energy from an outside force.

We interact in the physical world by the use of our physical bodies. We are all familiar with the physical body. It is made up of two arms, two legs, a head, a torso, organs and glands as well as many other systems and subsystems that function on biochemical levels. The physical body uses the foods we eat and the air we breathe to provide it with energy. It is also fed by our life force energy, which energizes its cells, tissues and organs.

The physical body serves as a foundation for the other bodies and as a way for the soul to express itself on the physical plane. It is often perceived as the shell we inhabit as we interact on the physical plane. It allows us to function successfully in the physical world.

The etheric body vibrates at a frequency closest to the physical body. This non-physical body has the same characteristics as the physical body, such as organs, glands and other anatomical features, but these structures exist outside of our normal perceptual range. Many times the etheric body can be seen by intuitives. It is often referred to as the aura.

The etheric body is concerned with the processes and activities of energy, in and around the physical body. It is believed by some that the etheric body is superimposed upon the physical body. The reality is that physical tissues exist because this energy field supersedes the physical body. It acts as the blueprint of the physical body, providing it with a framework or pattern upon which it is shaped and anchored. It is said to supply information to the body's cells, thus guiding the body through its automated processes such as growth and development, repair and healing.

For example, it is the function of the etheric body to direct the cells of an embryo through the development of the organs, glands and other bodily systems. It is this same energy that supports the growth and development of a newborn from birth to maturation. This energy allows for and guides the repair of the physical body when we break a bone or skin our knees. This innate ability for growth, development and repair is something scientists still can't explain.

The astral or emotional body vibrates at a frequency higher than that of the etheric body. It is often thought of as being separate and independent of the physical body, yet is an inseparable part of who we are. It is shaped by our feelings and expresses itself through our emotions. It is instrumental in our ability to express ourselves.

Feelings are experienced in the physical body as bodily sensations, where they always involve a tangible bodily sense. When we encounter an emotionally charged event we undergo physiological changes in our bodies that result in a bodily sensation or feeling. We may not know or understand what we are feeling, but we feel a heightened awareness of some kind of physical sensation. Throughout the day, we experience a number of different feelings, each of which contains a distinct meaning. When we are able to express these physical sensations they are called emotions.

The mental body is the world of thoughts and concrete ideas. It reflects our ability to think and construct images. It is where our ideas and imagination transition from the nothingness of the causal body and enter into the constructs of the mind. It is through the mind and the mental body that the soul communicates with us.

The mental body should not be confused with the brain. Instead, it represents the energy of our ideas, beliefs and values. Thinking, imagery, perceptions, judgments, creativity, invention and inspiration are all expressions of the mental body, and represent the essence of our inner reality that is conveyed to the world.

The causal body is the world of spirit, the world of pure energy. It is often referred to as the soul body or our higher self. It is where our soul joins with the cosmic conscious, the universe, or God. Whereas the mental body was concerned with the creation of concrete thoughts and ideas, the causal body is involved with the creation of abstract ideas and concepts. It is the part of us that works to guide us to health, harmony and wholeness.

While it is believed that there are bodies that exist beyond the causal body, the causal body represents the part of us that is closest to the source, or God. It is the divine spark around which all of the other bodies are built. It can be seen as a gatekeeper where it sees what is going on in our lives from a higher perspective and attempts to share this information with the conscious mind.

The intrinsic wholeness of a person cannot be considered apart from his or her totality. Although each of the bodies may seem independent and separate from the workings of our physical body, they make up a vital part of who we are. As we move forward, we will be taking an in-depth look at each of the bodies as well as the other components that make up our energetic selves. Only by understanding the workings of our all of our parts and their relationships to each other can we ever hope to create and maintain health, wellness, harmony and wholeness in our lives.

The Chakras – An Introduction

> *The secret of health for both mind and body is not to mourn for the past, not to worry about the future, not to anticipate troubles, but to live the present moment wisely and earnestly.*
>
> — SIDDHARTHA GAUTAMA

Each of our subtle bodies is composed of a number of component parts, which include the chakras. The term "chakra" is a Sanskrit word that means "wheel" or "disk." In Yogic literature, chakras are thought of as spinning vortexes of energy within the subtle body. They are formed where lines of energy or force intersect one another. The role of the chakras is to gather and organize our life force energy, much like acupuncture points are specialized locations that allow energy to flow in and out of a layer of the subtle body. Chakras also work to extend our perception of the world around us.

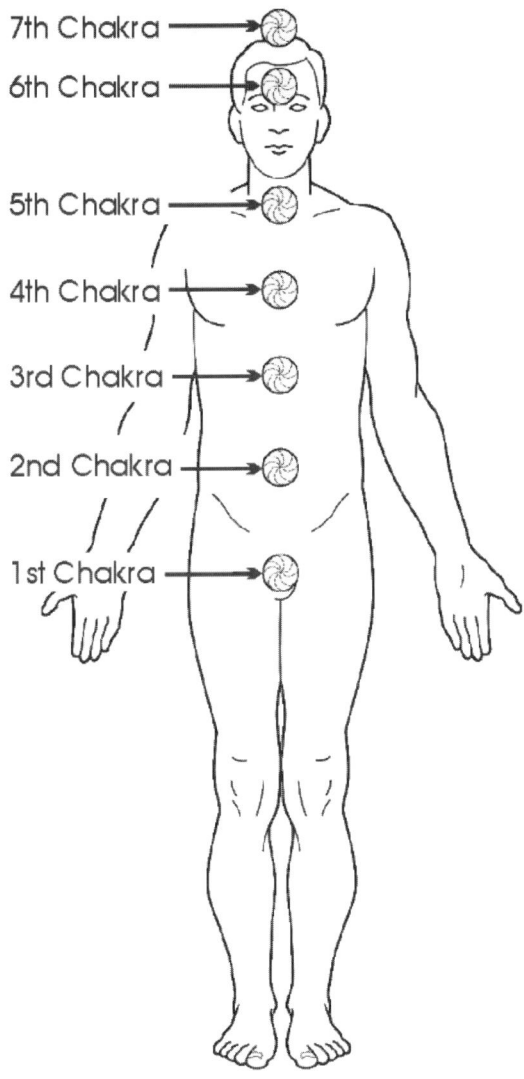

Figure 3
The Seven Major Chakras

Invisible to the naked eye, each chakra allows for the reception, assimilation and transmission of energy and information from our environment. According to Richard Gerber, the author of *Vibrational Medicine for the Twenty-first Century*, the chakras are emotional, mental and spiritual energy processors that act and react to a different patterns or vibrations of energy. Information that is transmitted and received by the chakras can include social, sexual and spiritual energy vibrations.

Each subtle body contains seven major chakras, which transport specific vibrations of energy through our energetic system. They are located in a vertical column up and down the spine. The first three of our chakras appear below the sternum, the last three above the heart, leaving the fourth and central chakra to function the balancing point for all of the chakras. In addition to these seven chakras, other specialized energy centers can be found in the palms of our hands, the soles of our feet and in the crooks of our knees and elbows. Ancient texts state that there are as many as 360 chakras, or points for energy transfer, in the subtle body.

Generally speaking, the first chakra receives, assimilates and transmits energy and information regarding our interaction with the physical world, with the survival of the physical body and our ability to manifest our wants, needs and desires into the physical world. The second chakra receives, assimilates and transmits energy and information associated with our feelings, our creative or organizational energy, and is the seat of our desires. The third chakra is concerned with the regulation of energy within the body as well as how we use our energy as we interact with the world around us.

The fourth chakra, or heart chakra, vibrates at the frequency of love and is responsible for creating balance and harmony within the subtle body. The fifth chakra vibrates with the energy of communication on both verbal and nonverbal levels. Where the fifth chakra can be thought of as the sound that is transmitted and received by a radio, the sixth chakra provides us with the pictures that we see. Associated with our vision and imagination, the sixth chakra is often called the third eye. The last of the major chakras, the seventh chakra is responsible for our connection with spiritual energy. It is said that through this chakra we can communicate with God. (We will explore each of the chakras in later sections.)

When viewed by a skilled intuitive, healthy chakras appear open, unarmored, energetic, free of stagnant energy, spin in a clockwise direction and are about the size of a silver dollar. Energy and information travels easily through the chakras in both directions. Each chakra has two distinct sections, the inner ring and the outer band. The inner ring makes up the majority of the chakra and works to transmit, receive and assimilate information. The outer band runs along the outside edge of the chakra and surrounds the inner ring. Working like a muscle, it controls the opening and closing of the chakra, where it regulates the flow of energy.

Each chakra, in addition to its ability to open and close like the aperture of a camera, vibrates or resonates at a particular frequency or within a specific frequency range. Spiritual texts traditionally associate a specific color to each. The color red vibrates at the slowest frequency and is assigned to the first chakra. The color purple vibrates at the highest frequency and is assigned to the seventh chakra. These colors reflect the ideal energetic vibration associated with each chakra.

The Chakras and Chakra Colors	
Chakra	**Color**
First	Red
Second	Orange
Third	Yellow
Fourth	Green
Fifth	Blue
Sixth	Indigo
Seventh	Purple

The chakras can also provide us with information about the personality or constitution of an individual as well as his or her current state of health and wellness. The colors observed in each chakra, for example, reflect the frequency of energy being metabolized by an individual at any given moment. So while texts ascribe red to the first chakra and green to the fourth, the colors observed in these chakras may actually appear as corn silk blue and mustard yellow respectively.

There is a belief that when a chakra is healthy it should be open 100% of the way. The truth is that in order to interact with the world as we know it, our chakras should only be 75% to 85% open to the flow of energy from the environment. Chakras act as filtering devices, filtering energy from our environment. If we didn't filter or somehow control the influx of energy from our environment we would be overwhelmed by the vast amount of input and stimuli that is constantly available to us.

According to John E. Nelson, the author of *Healing the Split*, at conception we are completely open to the flow of energy from our environment. He feels that at birth, one of the first things an infant does as it learns to interact with the world is to develop a sense of self. To do this, the infant forms what he calls a "psychic membrane" that allows it to filter information from the environment. All sensory information, he believes, undergoes this filtering process.

When we interact with the world around us, we interact with what is called "consensual reality." Consensual reality is based upon a series of beliefs that we, as a society, share. Consensual reality allows us to view the world as a coherent whole, with our day-to-day experiences appearing stable. It allows us to make sense of the world in which we live. Decided upon by our ancestors, consensual reality allows us to feel at ease because we are able to find others who experience the world in similar ways. We agree upon what is real and what is not. Beliefs that fall outside of this agreed upon reality are often seen as being distortions of the real world and are viewed as being abnormal.

In fact, there is no objective reality. The seemingly objective picture of the world that we call reality is in fact a subjective picture in our minds – a picture that is different for every living being. We create this reality so that a constant barrage of sensory input does not overwhelm us. We maintain this reality by paying attention to what is important and disregarding the rest.

We are constantly transmitting our thoughts and feelings out into the world around us. We also have the ability to receive the energies transmitted by others. When we shut down our chakras, we filter out from our awareness much of the information being transmitted by others. This filtering process blocks our innate ability to feel the emotions of others and to receive communications on nonverbal levels, as well as the ability to see the thoughts and ideas of others.

It is not uncommon for someone diagnosed with schizophrenia to have one or more of their chakras open 100% of the way. They often report hearing voices, seeing invisible forces in and around them and having experiences that would be considered outside the norm. The ability of these individuals to filter "reality" is somehow impaired. Spiritually advanced individuals, on the other hand, work consciously to open their chakras to a level above the norm. By bringing in additional "sensory" information, these individuals exhibit abilities such as clairvoyance, clairaudience and clairsentience. While these skills could be thought of as schizoid tendencies, spiritually aware individuals maintain a firm grip on consensual reality.

Each chakra processes information within a specific band or range of energetic vibrations. They function much like a typical AM/FM radio. On a radio, you can tune in to any FM station when your tuner is set within the range of 88 to 108 MHz. Let's say for this example that your fourth chakra processes information within this frequency range. The fourth chakra is the chakra of affinity. One of its functions is to process the vibration of love, which in this instance we'll say vibrates at a frequency of 92.8 MHz.

If your fourth chakra is healthy, open and functioning you would be able to receive energetic vibrations from any station on the dial, including the vibration of love. If, on the other hand, your fourth chakra is not fully awakened or if there have been issues that have affected the flow of energy through it, the number of stations that could be tuned in may be lessened. This decrease may affect our ability to tune into the frequency of 92.8 MHz and thus to send or receive love. When we do try to tune in to the vibration of love we may experience a lot of static or interference. Depending on how much the chakra has been affected we may not be able to tune in or access this energetic vibration at all.

When we are in the midst of a traumatic event, we block the natural flow of energy moving through the chakras. This is normal and natural in the short term. Over time the unpleasant events that have affected us throughout our lifetime can take their toll on our chakras' ability to function, causing them to shut down.

Chakras typically don't close all at once. Instead they shut down gradually due to the repetition of hurtful or disturbing events. For example, we may find ourselves stuck in an unhealthy relationship, a job or habit. Over time, the chakras can become blocked, clogged, congested or distorted. These repeated patterns of action can keep us from growing and could be identified or characterized by the chakra that is under-energized, has a reduced vibratory rate or is unable to transmit fully. In the end, the flow of our life force energy through our chakras becomes inhibited.

Anodea Judith, in her book *Wheels of Light*, theorizes that a dysfunction in a specific chakra can be seen as a dysfunction in the body, where they reflect or record every fear and every hateful, sorrowful, self-pitying event in our lives that we choose to hold on to. For example, a person with a constriction in the fifth chakra may have physical symptoms such as a sore throat, tight shoulders or even hypothyroidism. These physical symptoms may manifest in someone who is afraid to speak their truth, express themselves or their feelings or even cry. As the flow of energy into the fifth chakra diminishes, the throat constricts and over time the associated organs begin to break down.

Each chakra acts as a receptor, transformer and assimilator of energy and information at within a specific frequency range. They also process and store information regarding events that have affected us throughout our lifetime. It is through the chakras that we experience the world and in turn our world may be reflected in them. As we delve further into exploring our subtle nature, we will be investigating the specific function of each chakra in greater detail.

Energy Flow and the Subtle Body

> *There is a vitality, a life force, an energy, a quickening, that is translated through you into action, and because there is only one of you in all time, this expression is unique. And if you block it, it will never exist through any other medium and will be lost.*
>
> — MARTHA GRAHAM

In order to fully understand the function of the chakras and the nature of the subtle bodies, it is important to understand how energy moves through them individually and as a whole. All energy and information is transported through the subtle bodies via energy channels called nadis. The function of the nadis is to transfer or funnel energy into and out of the chakra. There is a nadi connected to each side of the chakras in each of the bodies where they transport energy and information from the world around us through the subtle body to nerve ganglia (bundles of nerve cells that lie outside the central nervous system) in the physical body.

The nadis are made up of fine threads of energetic matter that exist purely on subtle levels. These energetic structures connect one chakra to another and work to direct and transfer energetic vibrations in the same way our veins and arteries direct and carry blood through our body or like a phone cord carries our conversations over its copper wire. Yogic texts have described up to 72,000 nadis in the subtle body.

The seven major chakras are connected to each other via a vertical column of energetic matter that runs up and down the spine, which according to Yogic traditions is called the Sushumna. The Sushumna's function is to transport energy through the subtle bodies, which provides power and energy to each of the chakras. Whereas the nadi can be thought of as functioning like an electrical wire or like an individual nerve that runs through our body, the Sushumna can be regarded as a major electrical power bus or as functioning much like our spinal cord, which acts as an electrical highway for nerve transmission.

By means of a nadi that extends out of the seventh chakra, energy is funneled into the body and transported through the Sushumna to the first chakra. Energy exits the Sushumna through a nadi that is connected to the first chakra, where it is ultimately grounded. The flow of this energy can be thought of as functioning like a DC or direct current circuit. A DC circuit is an unbroken path through

Energy Flow and the Subtle Body / 47

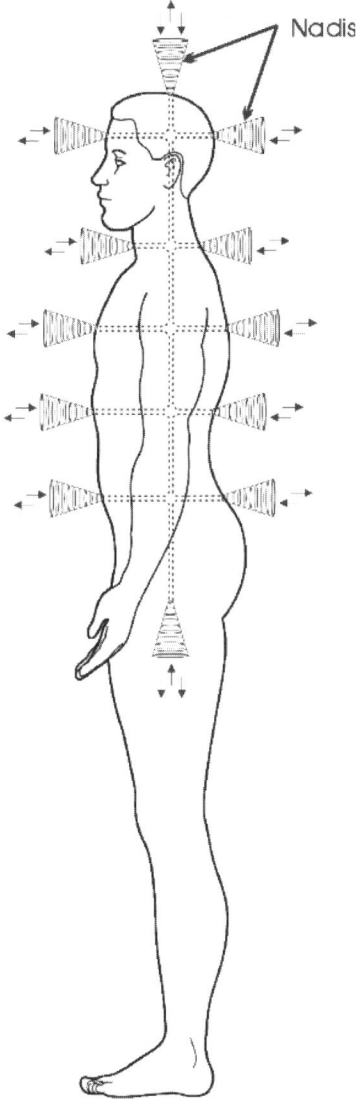

Figure 4
Chakras and Their Associated Nadis

which an electric current flows from positive to negative. That is, it moves from a power source such as a battery to an output or to ground where the excess electricity has dissipated.

When a circuit is complete, that is, when all of the connections are made properly, current flows. If the connections are not made properly and the circuit is broken, the current cannot flow. Likewise, if the circuit that makes up the Sushumna is broken, the flow of energy through the chakras stops. Like the electrical circuit, if there is no power or energy coming in via the seventh chakra, or if the circuit isn't grounded by means of the first chakra, energy will not flow as well.

Also moving up the spine and intertwining the Sushumna are the Ida and Pingala nadis. The Ida is located on the left side of the spinal column and is associated with the feminine, negative and yin aspects of our being. The Pingala in turn is located on the right side of the spinal column and is associated with the masculine, positive and yang aspects of our being. These nadis move upward from the first chakra, alternating from left to right as they travel up the spine, where they surround and activate each chakra. It is believed that when these two aspects of ourselves are balanced, our spiritual energy or Kundalini can unfold.

Attached to each side of our second through sixth chakras are nadis as well. Each of these chakras has both a front and a back extension where energy flows in, perpendicular to the stream of energy through the Sushumna. Barbara Brennan, in her book *Hands of Light*, has identified

Energy Flow and the Subtle Body / 49

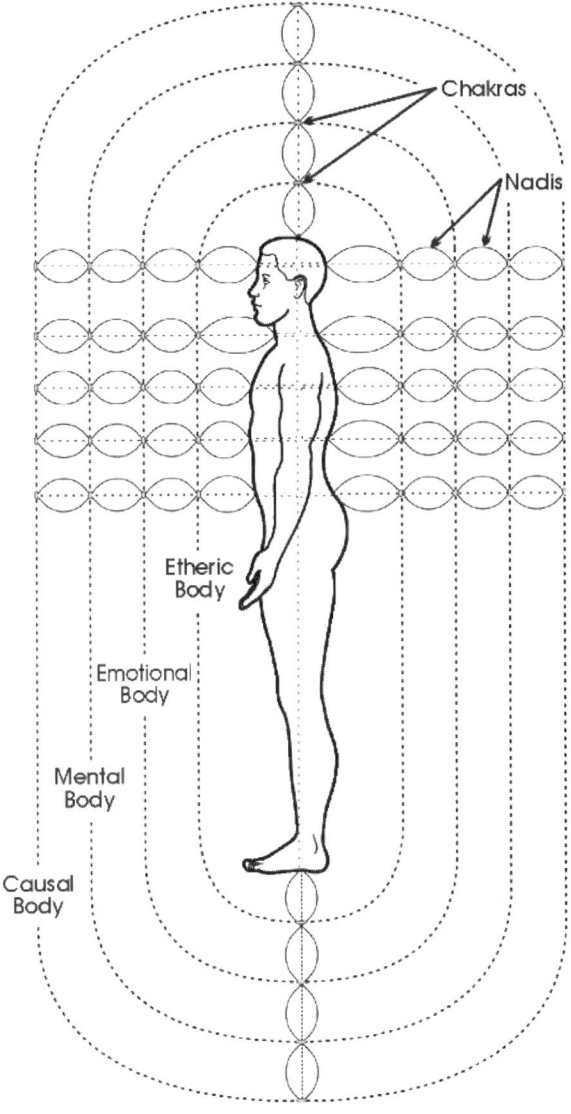

Figure 5
Movement of Subtle Energy Through the Bodies

the functioning of the front of each chakra as being related to our feelings and the rear of each chakra as being related to our wills. Another way to look at the dual nature of the chakras means that the front of the chakra relates to things we are processing on a conscious level, while the back correlates to things we have pushed behind us or are processing on an unconscious level.

Physically, we are able to look at or see what is in front of us, but are unable to see, or have difficulty seeing, what is going on behind our backs. The same holds true on energetic levels. Typically, we carry the information that we are actively processing in the front of the chakra and energies and issues that we are unable or unwilling to process in the back. It does not mean that we aren't experiencing the effects of this energy; it is just that it is outside of our conscious awareness. "Why couldn't I see that" is a phrase we use to reflect this idea. When we are hurt, we "push it behind us," or at times find ourselves feeling as if we were "stabbed in the back" when something hurtful is done to us in a sly, sneaky or deceiving way.

Now that we understand how energy moves within each of the subtle bodies, let's move on and take a look at how energy and information are transported, received and assimilated by and between each of the subtle bodies.

The chakras play a critical role in the movement of energy between the subtle bodies. According to Richard Gerber, author of *Vibrational Medicine: New Choices For Healing Ourselves*, they can be thought of as functioning like electrical transformers. An electrical transformer reduces or amplifies the voltage of an electrical current. Chakras, like their physical counterparts, step down or increase subtle energy from one frequency to another or from one dimension to the next. Energy is transported via the nadis, with the chakra functioning as a sort of relay station. Incoming energy is slowed down until it reaches a vibration or frequency our subtle bodies can assimilate. In essence, the chakras regulate the flow of energy into our bodies, providing it to us in a form or vibration we can process.

The chakras of the mental body, for example, reduce the vibrational frequency of the energy it receives from the causal body. From here it is either disseminated into the mental body, or is passed on and slowed down even farther as it travels on to layers of a slower vibratory rate. This continues through each of our subtle bodies, until it reaches the physical body, where a physiological or hormonal response occurs.

This is easily illustrated when you look at the flow of energy through the four worlds of the Qabalah. It shows energy and information as it comes in through the seventh chakra of the causal body, where it travels through the causal body to its first chakra. Like a transformer that increases or decreases the current in a circuit, the first chakra interfaces with the seventh chakra of the mental body, where the energy is transformed into the appropriate frequency required by this body. The energy then moves through the mental body until it reaches its first chakra, where it interfaces with the seventh chakra of the emotional body. The same pattern holds true of the emotional, etheric and physical bodies,

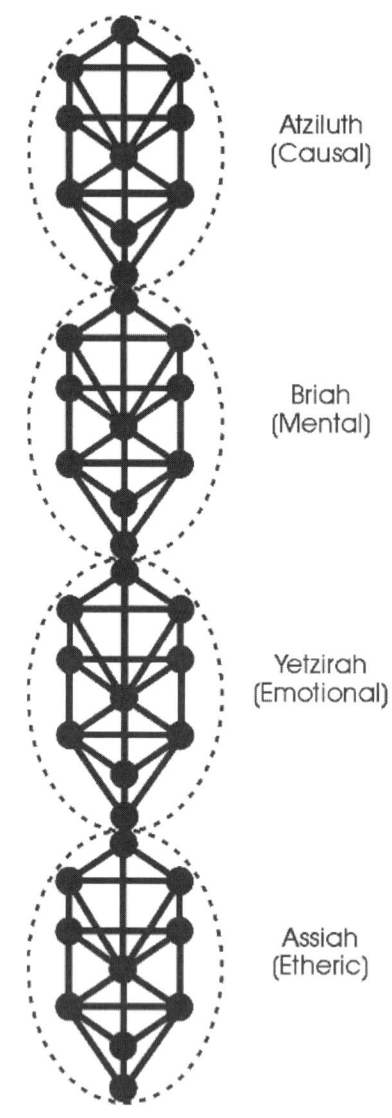

Figure 6
Qabalistic View of Subtle Energy Flow

where energy is transformed into the next lower energy vibration until it is manifested in the physical world.

Another way of looking at the movement of energy through our chakras from one subtle body to the next may be reflected in the physics of black holes. Generally speaking, physicists believe that black holes are areas of space that are densely filled with matter in a very small space. Created by a collapsed star, this concentration of matter is thought to have such an immense gravitational pull that nearby objects, including light, are pulled in and are unable to escape.

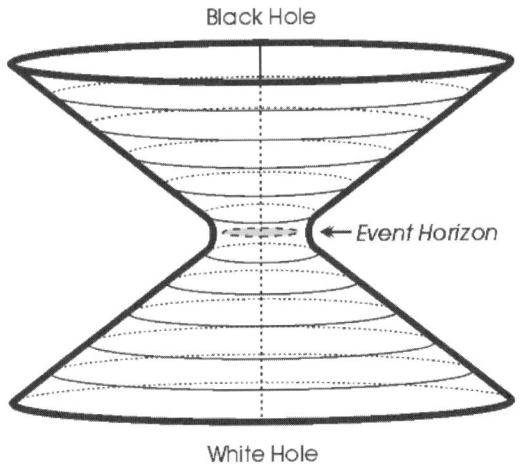

Figure 7
Black Holes and White Holes

Based on mathematical models, using Schwarzschild Geometry, it is theorized that once you cross the event horizon of a black hole, time and space are distorted. It is believed that some black holes connect to what are called white holes via a funnel of energy called a wormhole. It is thought that wormholes may be pathways into other universes or dimensions. While it is too early to speculate upon the relationship between black holes and the movement of energy and information from one layer of the subtle body to another, it does leave you something to ponder.

Each of our thoughts, feelings, ideas and emotions vibrates at a specific frequency, which we transmit and receive from the world around us. Joy, for example, vibrates at one frequency, while fear vibrates at another. (It is interesting to note that every disease also has a specific vibration.) When we receive the vibration of joy, we always interpret this energetic vibration as joy and when we receive the energy of fear, we always recognize it as fear.

This energy and information is transmitted and received by the virtue of resonance. In the natural world, resonance occurs when a vibrating object forces a second object into motion. It is easily seen when discussing the action of tuning forks. Suppose a 256 Hz tuning fork, mounted on a sound box, is set upon a table and a second 256 Hz tuning fork is placed on a table nearby.

When the first tuning fork is struck, it begins to vibrate at its natural frequency of 256 Hz. The energy of its vibration is carried by soundwave through the air. In essence, the air is now "tuned" to the frequency of the vibrating tuning fork. Since both tuning forks share the same natural frequency of 256 Hz, when the soundwaves strike the second tuning fork it begins to vibrate as well. In essence the first tuning fork forces the second tuning fork into vibrational motion.

For example, when we are excited, enthusiastic, joyful, hurt or upset, we transmit the vibration of these emotions through the subtle bodies, via the chakras, out into the environment where we essentially "tune" the environment. Once transmitted, the vibration of these emotions can be received by the nadis and chakras of others and are filtered down through their subtle bodies until they reach their physical body creating a feeling, a sensation or biochemical response.

Energetic vibrations are constantly being transmitted, received and assimilated by the chakras and nadis of each of the subtle bodies. These vibrations travel from the causal body through each successive body until it is manifested in the physical body as a physiological response. We experience a physiological response when the energy we receive interacts with the nerve ganglia and stimulates a biochemical response. The energy of this physiological response, which can include our corresponding thoughts, feelings, ideas and emotions, is then transmitted back through the subtle body and out into the world around us.

The Qabalah

> *You cannot acquire experience by making experiments.*
> *You cannot create experience. You must undergo it.*
> — Albert Camus

So far, we have explored how energy and information flow through the subtle body and how they are transmitted, received and assimilated by chakras and nadis. Before we move on, it is important to digress here slightly and discuss some basic concepts and tenets of the Qabalah. Like the chakras, the Qabalah provides a defining pattern for the growth and development of the soul and provides a valuable key when looking to understand the function of the subtle bodies and the chakras.

Scholars have identified the study of the Qabalah as being the Yoga of the West. The Qabalah forms the basis of Jewish Mysticism. Its foundation, beliefs and tenets echo those of the Yogic system, including the chakras. It has been theorized that the ideas and methodology used in the chakra system represent abstract ideals that are to be achieved. The Qabalistic system, on the other hand, expresses itself through the use of specific notions and concrete symbols that bring unconscious thoughts, ideas and behaviors into our conscious awareness.

In ancient times, the meaning of the word Qabalah was "the law." Today, the word Qabalah is often translated as meaning "that which is received." While it is not clear exactly where the mystical traditions of the Qabalah originated, some texts claim that this mystical system originated with Moses on Mount Sinai, while others say it was provided by the angels to Adam as a means of returning to grace after the fall of man. Regardless of its origin, the Western Mystery Tradition of the Qabalah began to emerge around the second century AD and is used as a guide for exploring our inner truths.

Pictorially, the beliefs and principles of the Qabalah are represented in the Tree of Life. The goal of the Tree of Life is to help one find integration and wholeness within oneself and is a symbol that is used to describe the unfolding transition from God to Man. The wonderful thing about the Tree of Life is that it provides us with a road map to follow as we venture into the realm of the unconscious.

The Tree of Life is broken down into seven distinct levels that directly correlate to the seven chakras found in Yogic traditions. In addition to these seven levels, the Tree of Life is also made up of ten spheres or sephiroth (the plural

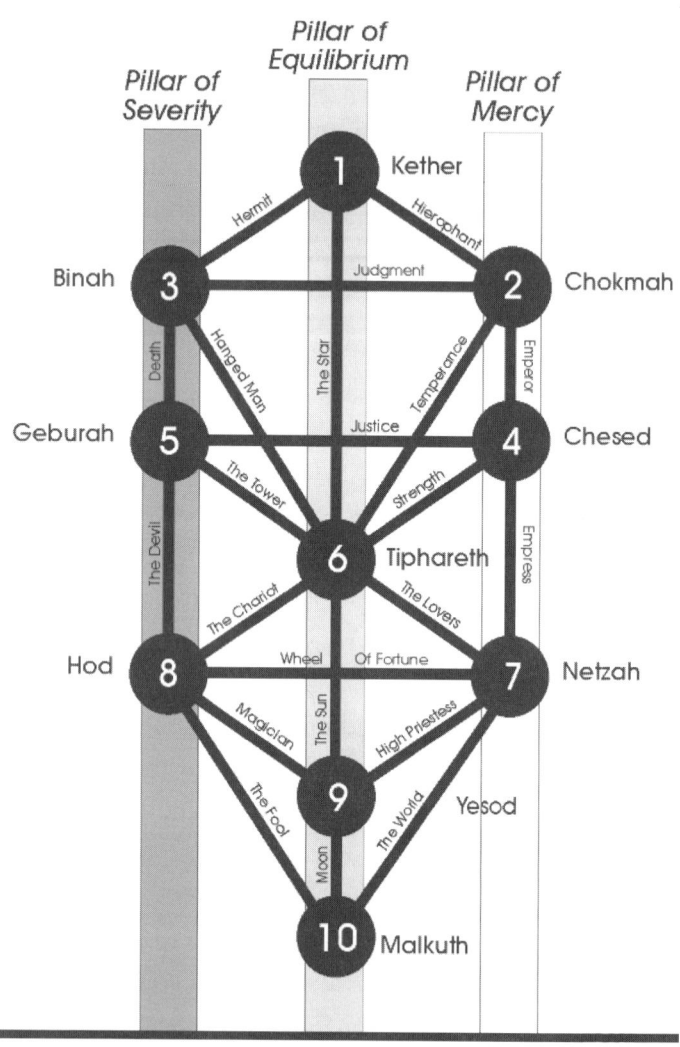

Figure 8
Tree of Life

of sephirah) that symbolize objective energy centers and discrete states of consciousness that are available to us. Represented by both title and number indicating its sequence in creation, each sephirah acts as a distinct phase in the evolution of the soul.

Sephiroth on the Tree of Life		
Number	Name	Meaning
1	Kether	Crown
2	Chokmah	Wisdom
3	Binah	Understanding
4	Chesed	Mercy
5	Geburah	Strength
6	Tiphareth	Beauty
7	Netzach	Victory
8	Hod	Splendor or Glory
9	Yesod	Foundation
10	Malkuth	Kingdom

In addition to the energies of the sephiroth, the Tree of Life is also made up of twenty-two lines that connect one sephirah to another. These connections are called "paths." The paths represent our subjective conscious, the experience we have as we pass from one sephirah to the next. A path also acts as a channel of divine influence, providing equilibrium between the two sephiroth it connects. Collectively, the sephiroth and paths are called the Thirty-two Paths of Wisdom.

Each path corresponds with one of the twenty-two Hebrew letters, an astrological correspondence and one of the twenty-two major arcana or "trump" cards of a standard tarot deck. The tarot is made up of seventy-eight cards that are used for "fortune telling," divination, contemplation and meditation. They are divided into four suits of fourteen cards, ace through ten, then page, knight, queen and king, plus twenty-two trump cards such as the Death Card, the Hanged Man and the Lovers.

The four suits, commonly referred to as the Minor Arcana, are representative of the energies of the sephiroth as they act in each of the four worlds, with each suit, pentacles, swords, cups and wands representing the worlds Assiah, Yetsirah, Binah and Atziluth respectively. It is interesting to note that a standard deck of playing cards developed from this rich philosophical tradition.

The Tree is also made up of three pillars: the Pillar of Severity, the Pillar of Mercy and the Pillar of Equilibrium. The outer pillars symbolize polarities of energy similar to those found in the eastern concepts of yin and yang. The Pillar of Mercy is positive, kinetic, active, constructive and the bringer of force. The Pillar of Severity, in turn, is negative, static, passive, destructive and the bringer of form. The three pillars can also be equated to the Sushumna, the Ida and Pingala nadis that run up the spine.

Paths on the Tree of Life

No.	Hebrew Letter	Astrological Correspondence	Path No.	Major Arcana
1	Aleph	Uranus	0	The Fool
2	Bayt	Mercury	1	The Magician
3	Ghimmel	Moon	2	The High Priestess
4	Dallet	Venus	3	The Empress
5	Hay	Aries	4	The Emperor
6	Vau	Taurus	5	The Hierophant
7	Zany	Gemini	6	The Lovers
8	Chayt	Cancer	7	The Chariot
9	Tayt	Leo	8	Strength
10	Yod	Virgo	9	The Hermit
11	Khaf	Jupiter	10	The Wheel of Fortune
12	Lammed	Libra	11	Justice
13	Mem	Neptune	12	The Hanged Man
14	Noon	Scorpio	13	Death
15	Sammekh	Sagittarius	14	Temperance
16	Ayn	Capricorn	15	The Devil
17	Phay	Mars	16	The Tower
18	Tsadde	Aquarius	17	The Star
19	Qof	Pisces	18	The Moon
20	Raysh	Sun	19	The Sun
21	Sheen	Pluto	20	The Judgment
22	Tav	Saturn	21	The World

Like the movement of energy through the Ida and Pingala, subtle energy zigzags from positive to negative and then balanced as it travels through the Tree of Life, where it moves along the "Lightning Path." Following the numerical order of the sepiroth, the Lightning Path identifies the route of manifestation, where subtle energy moves from a

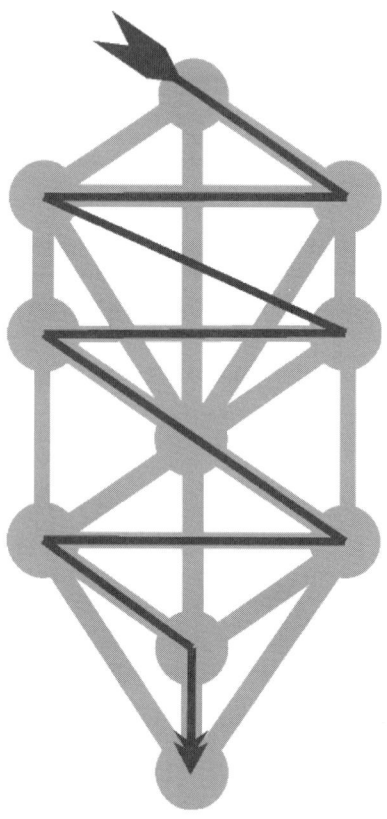

Figure 9
The Lightning Path

state of nothingness, through the subtle planes, finally to condense as matter in the physical world.

The Tree of Life holds that all of manifestation is based on duality. So, for example, at the third chakra we find the energy of Netzach and Hod. Netzach, at the base of the Pillar of Mercy, is our creative imagination, while Hod, at the base of the Pillar of Severity, personifies concrete goals and objectives established in our minds. If there is too much Netzach and too little Hod present, we might be highly imaginative but impractical. On the other hand, if too much Hod is present and not enough Netzach, we may be good at passing an exam, but possess very little imagination. It is believed that when the sephiroth found on the outer poles are balanced, the chakra, the energy center, opens.

The Tree of Life gives us a tool that enables us to explore all aspects of our inner and outer selves. The Tree is not static, but is filled with concepts of movement, change and relationships. It helps us to recognize that no aspect of our life can be explained devoid of its relationship to our other parts. With that, no sephirah can be described without reference to the other sephiroth. It also shares with us the complex relationships life holds and helps to remind us that attention must be paid to all of our parts.

Section 2

From Spirit to Self: The Nature of the Subtle Bodies

The Causal Body

> *The body, mind and spirit constitute together the human entity… Action, awareness and being are the threefold aspects of human life, which have to be properly understood. Although they appear to be distinct, it is the unity of actions, awareness and being which make for the fullness of human life.*
>
> — SATHYA SAI BABA

Of the four subtle bodies, the causal body vibrates at the highest frequency. Called Atziluth in Hebrew, it is the first world to be created out of negative existence. It is the place where all originates and is the source of our uniqueness and the foundation of our individuality. It is the central point of our consciousness and interfaces directly with the collective conscious, the universe or God. It is at the causal body that the vibrational pattern our lives is established. It is where energy first takes form and is separated or individuated from the collective wholeness of the universe, where our unique skills, abilities, path and potential derive.

Often referred to as the soul body, the causal body expresses itself through our higher self or the soul. Ever present, the soul is impersonal and objective. It has no judgments, nor sets any standards. It doesn't operate based upon "have tos," doubts, pressures, anxiety or fears. It recognizes our perfection, our wholeness and accepts things as they are because "it is all right just the way it is." According to Christian Mysticism and Carmelite Spirituality, the soul is the first principle of life. It is what animates us and is often regarded as being immortal. It is the unseen force that fills us from the point of conception and leaves the body at death.

Through the soul we can gain access to an infinite supply of information. It is the source of our inspiration and holds the answer to all of our questions, including how to achieve happiness, balance and wholeness. Our soul communicates with us through our intuition. It also speaks to us though images and feelings as well as through our desires and longings, each of which come from deep within us.

The soul's goal is to bring us back into wholeness. Motivated by its desire for wholeness, our soul guides us as we develop our individuality, our authenticity. The soul can be thought of as an inner guide that works to help us identify what we need to do to bring the personality back into alignment with the soul. The personality, an aspect of the mental body, is a part of us that has splintered off or fragmented from the whole. It sees itself as being separate and alone. It can be thought of as a part of the soul that is looking for healing, completeness, balance and harmony.

Over the last two hundred years many members of Western or industrialized societies have lost their connection with their souls. This happened when we began placing a greater value on personal gain and worldly possessions than on inner peace and harmony. Ambition, achievement, mental desires and pleasure have overshadowed our identification with the inner promptings of our soul, where we acknowledge only those things that can be seen, felt, tasted or touched. We have been taught to seek contentment from these earthly delights. We think, "If I can only find that elusive golden ring I will be happy, content and whole." But these things can only bring us temporary pleasure.

As human beings we were given free will to choose the paths our lives take. We can choose to follow the guidance provided by our soul or we can reject it. When we follow its lead, life tends to take on a more effortless quality. When we follow the promptings of the soul, it doesn't mean that our life will be great. We learn through our pain and pleasure, our successes as well as our failures. When we reject these promptings, however, life can become difficult. For many of us it is through struggle and adversity that we learn some of our greatest lessons. These lessons work to build inner strength and a strong sense of self. It is through these lessons that God works with us, helping us to recognize and follow the promptings of the soul. This will ultimately bring us back into wholeness.

Wholeness is achieved when the personality, our outward expression, coincides with our inner world, the world of our soul. Everything we say or do is an expression our inner and outer selves, of who we are and what we think. If we think one thing and say another, or feel one way and act another, internal conflicts arise, creating imbalances within our system. It is a conflict between our personality and our soul. When the expressions of our inner and outer selves are balanced, we cannot see where the personality ends and the soul begins. It is only when our inner and outer worlds are congruent that we can be authentic to others and ourselves. In other words, this congruency allows us to be whole.

The Mental Body

> *Every principle is a judgment, every judgment the outcome of experience, and experience is only acquired by the exercise of the senses.*
> — Marquis de Sade

Briah, or the mental body, is the realm of the mind. It houses our thoughts, ideas, concepts and viewpoints. It reflects our ability to think and construct mental images, which characterize our existence into definite categories. These categories provide definition and identity to our experiences and act as patterns by which we relate to God, the world and others.

The mind is not the brain. The brain is the instrument through which the mind works on the physical plane. The mind is fluid. It can take you to any place on earth, from the peak of the highest mountain to the depths of the deepest sea. It can instantly propel you out into the vastness of space or allow you to focus on the components of our subatomic world. It allows you to explore any period of time or any point in history, both past and present, and allows you to travel into the future where you can venture into realms unknown and then return, without ever moving a muscle.

The mental body is made up of two separate but equal parts, the conscious mind and the unconscious mind. Thought to be a byproduct of the brain, we associate the workings of the conscious mind with our mental chatter and our everyday waking life. We use the conscious mind when we think and perceive the world around us. It involves mental processing that is within our immediate awareness and under our direct control. Its function is to record our experiences, process this information and come up with logical conclusions.

The unconscious mind, on the other hand, involves mental processes that operate outside of our immediate attention and exist beneath our waking consciousness. Not under our direct control, it functions based on the information it stores, including everything we see, feel, hear and experience. The subconscious mind inspires and guides as well as influences the conscious mind. Ever alert, the subconscious mind also controls the vital processes of our bodies such as our heartbeat and breathing.

Associated with the mind and the mental body is the ego or personality. The personality is the way in which we express ourselves in the physical world. Our identification with the physical world and material possessions is an aspect of our personality. The workings of the personality are typically based on our reaction to or an expectation of something. These reactions are formed and maintained by our perceptions, both good and bad, including our interpersonal relationships, life experiences, learned knowledge and beliefs. Like the workings of the soul through the causal body, our personality strives to guide us as we move through life. The guidance it provides, however, is finite because it directs us based on information that it receives from our past experiences and then calculates logical conclusions based upon it.

According to Christopher Wynter and Fiona Tulk, authors of *Transpersonal LifeStreams*, our personality is an expression of the mind on either conscious or unconscious levels. It can be viewed as a conditional expression of the soul. It creates an illusion about who we are, where it believes we are distinct individuals: unique and separate. This divides the world into two parts – what is me and mine and what is everything else.

The personality reflects who or what the mind thinks "I am." René Déscartes coined the phrase "I think, therefore I am." If we think we are beautiful, intelligent, sexy, rich, funny or creative the personality accepts this as being true. On the other hand, if we think we are fat, dumb, klutzy, unimaginative, ugly, poor or unlovable, the personality sees these ideas as being true as well, even if they are not. Then we look outside ourselves in order to validate this self-image we have created in our minds. We do things we feel necessary in order to maintain the role that we have created for ourselves. Over time we often end up believing *we are* our personality and forget about or repress our inner self.

The nature of the personality is survival: survival of itself, its views and the reality it created about who we are. It works at all cost to preserve this continuous thread of consciousness that has always existed. At times the image projected by our personality conflicts with our inner self or other people's view of who they "think" we are or should be. To minimize any threat to our self-identification, the personality creates strategies and survival mechanisms so that it can remain intact. Any threat brings about an immediate reaction as it works to maintain control and avoid any changes.

Sometimes the illusions we have created about ourselves are so embedded and ingrained that we even deceive ourselves. We learn to accommodate others, enforce rules of behavior upon ourselves or do what is expected. We willingly stay in challenging or difficult situations, suppressing our true self rather than changing it. This is because underneath every negative expression of the personality there is an emotion, either recognized or denied, which acts as the impetus for the personality's expression. Many times this emotion is based in fear. In fact, the thought of potential change can often cause us to cling to this illusion so that we don't have to face what is inside.

The personality is formed around our beliefs. A belief is anything we decide is true or real. Our beliefs are based on conclusions we make about life including our assumptions, judgments, ideas and opinions. They form an image of who we are and what our life should be. They give us a sense of identity and help define us as individuals. We use our beliefs to analyze, categorize and interpret every event that occurs in our lives. They are the basis of the habits, routines, ambitions, rationalizations, justifications and limitations we have in our lives.

Our beliefs dictate our experiences. They can be perceived as crystallized or habitual thought forms. These unconscious influences impact our conscious and unconscious thoughts, where they impact the way we think, the way we act and the way we feel. Our beliefs create barriers that interfere with our ability to be whole. They are boundaries we create and impose upon ourselves; as such, they can distort our perception of reality, preventing us from being and experiencing who and what we really are.

There is a myth that we are all created equal, that we all share the same beliefs, needs, desires, drives and instincts. The truth is that we are all different. In the same way that we all have different genetic strengths and weaknesses, we all have different views, ideas, opinions and beliefs. We experience the world based on our varying personal, social and political backgrounds. The majority of our beliefs come from others, from friends, family members and society. Others are formed as we go through life. These include our ideas of right and wrong, and our ideologies, manners and customs. Many of these beliefs are handed down generation to generation and work to support the consensual reality we have collectively created.

As we go through life, our beliefs can change. We are constantly creating new beliefs or validating existing ones.

Some of our beliefs are helpful to us, while others may be ultimately hurting us. Our beliefs can be positive and uplifting, while others can be negative or restrictive. "I belong," "I can do it" or "people like me" are all examples of positive beliefs, while "something's wrong with me," "I'm not good enough" and "nobody likes me" are negative ones.

Our perceptions of events in our lives endeavor to keep us congruent with our beliefs. Our perceptions are selective and differentiating and typically focus on one thing excluding all others. They tend to reinforce our beliefs, because they reflect the truth we choose to see. So if you believe that life treats you unfairly, then you will pay more attention to all of the bad things that may happen to you during the day rather than acknowledging any of the good. Then at the end of the day you can say to yourself, "Just like I thought, life sucks!"

Many times, what we perceive as being real is only a small portion of the whole, and if we don't perceive something we often think of it being unreal or imaginary. Reality, however, exists whether we are cognizant of it or not.

The programming of our personality can cause us to ignore our interests, drives and passions and instead blindly follow the dictates established by man and society. As we try harder and harder to be in control and maintain our sense of self and our chosen beliefs, we block the promptings of spirit and the workings of our soul. Ultimately, the personality may conflict with the directives of the soul and work its way into manifestation upon the physical plane.

It is believed that the mental body plays only a small

role in our ability to maintain health. According to Alice Bailey, the author of *Esoteric Healing*, most illnesses and diseases are the manifestation of some unwanted condition in the mental and emotional bodies. She feels that the cause of 90% of all diseases can be attributed to the emotional and etheric bodies and only 5% in the mental body, with the remainder being caused by direct physical means such as accidents, injuries or gross excess. This is because our thoughts in and of themselves do not create disease.

Everything we want or need, however, starts out as a thought or idea in our mind. It precedes all of our actions. We would do nothing or create nothing if we didn't think about it first. Thinking underscores all of our joys as well as all of our sorrows and provides input into all that we say and do. Our thoughts work to direct the flow of energy through our systems, yet do not have any energy of their own. It is only when we energize our thoughts by adding a feeling or emotion to them that the flow of our life force energy moves through them, activating and propelling them toward manifestation. Without the movement of energy through our thoughts they would just be wishes, hopes or possibilities.

We are often warned to watch out what we ask for, because we just might get it. Our thoughts can become very powerful forces that affect our lives and can act like self-fulfilling prophecies. Any idea that we hold steadily and clearly in our mind will be acted on and brought forth into manifestation by our unconscious mind. Nothing comes to us except what we ask for. It may not come to us in the way we want or think it should, but it will come to us in a way that will help us grow as spiritual beings and become more aligned with our souls.

Frederick Bailes, in his book *Your Mind Can Heal You*, believes that illness and disease are distorted ideas or thoughts that have crystallized into physical or visible form. Our thoughts and ideas are the product of the conscious mind. They are transmitted or impressed upon the subconscious mind. Intelligent and creative in its function, the subconscious mind has no preferences of its own. This non-reasoning intelligence communicates our thoughts and ideas to the emotional body in literal terms. In return, the emotional body provides the etheric body with a pattern or plan for manifestation.

Bailes gives a wonderful example of this process as he discusses the case of a man suffering from severe arthritis.

> *The subsequent discussion brought out that his wife's sister lived about a mile away in the same city. He detested his sister-in-law and her husband, but his wife insisted upon their walking there every Sunday afternoon. He had tried every subterfuge to evade these weekly visits, but they had gone on for some years since his wife was an extremely strong-willed woman.*
>
> *The inner conflict and his hidden rage, plus his very strong desire to find a way out of going, became the dominant thought-pattern until it had become a controlling factor.*

> *After about twelve years of this, he began to develop arthritis. It was a very gradual process, and finally he could not take the weekly walks. They had no car; so he stayed at home.*
>
> *I pointed out to him the possibility that his mental experience had a direct connection with his physical condition, and that his desire not to walk to his relatives' home had been taken up by Universal Mind so that he had attracted this physical condition – even asked for it.*

In this example, the thought his client held clearly in his mind was that he didn't want to visit his in-laws. The net result was that he manifested arthritis to resolve the conflict that existed between his personality and his inner world. It is not that he thought about getting arthritis, but in the end, his prayers were answered.

Other examples of conflicts manifesting on the physical plane between our inner and outer worlds include pride, which can be thought of as rigidity of the mind and can ultimately produce stiffness in the body. Denial, or the refusal to see the truth, can manifest as impaired vision or hearing. Those who labor to control others may find themselves slaves to their own bodies, with their desires and ambitions curtailed by their disorder, while those who are angry or irritated may find inflammation and irritation of their bodily tissues.

The mental body forms the basis of what we experience in our lives and our reactions to it. It sets the stage for its expression in the emotional body. Mental conflicts are an indication that the mental body is in need of healing. It is an indication that we are out of harmony with ourselves and the laws of nature. This includes our beliefs, judgments, opinions, prejudices, assumptions, expectations and perceptions of the world, each of which can have an effect on our subtle energy. They act as resistors in the mental body, where they inhibit the flow of our life force energy and reduce the amount of energy that is available to the subsequent energetic bodies.

The Emotional Body

One must marry one's feelings to one's beliefs and ideas. That is probably the only way to achieve a measure of harmony in one's life.

— Etty Hilsum

Shaped by our feelings, the emotional body, or Yetzirah in Qabalistic texts, plays a vital role in our ability to express our emotions and our emotional state. It represents an aspect of our life force energy as it flows through us. Our emotions form a bridge between mind and matter. When we perceive an event, our mental body analyzes and interprets it. It is filtered through our personality where it is compared to our thoughts, ideas, beliefs and values to determine if the event was positive or negative. Based on the result, energy is transmitted to the emotional body, where we react to it. This reaction is then sent to the physical body, where we respond and experience a physical sensation or feeling.

Feelings unite the body and mind and provide integrity between our inner world and our outer experience. Feelings, however, are not emotions; feelings are the precursor to emotions. Emotions can be thought of as the labels we put on our feelings. They operate on a much higher level of human cognitive functioning. Happy, sad, angry and enthusiastic are words that we use to describe the actual physical sensation we are experiencing, that is, the feeling.

Feelings are closer to the body's experiences. They are those indescribable sensations we have in our bodies. They are less formed, less tangible than what we think of as emotions. They are a reflection of the quantity and quality of stimuli that we have been exposed to throughout our lives. If you think about it, our feelings change all of the time. Week by week, day by day, hour by hour and even over the briefest period of time, we can experience a wide variety of feelings.

Feelings are the result of our reaction to physical sensations or stimuli – good and bad, pleasant and painful. Every feeling we experience creates specific biochemical reactions in the body. They can be likened to currents of electricity that pass through us and activate cellular signals within the body. These signals, once turned on, transform our emotional information into a physiological response. These biochemical changes are not experienced in only one part of our bodies (such as in our heads, arms or torsos), but in every one of our cells.

Each of our feelings vibrates at a different rate or frequency. Feelings that are typically identified as being negative, such as hate, anger and grief vibrate at lower frequencies, while feelings that are thought of as being positive such as joy, love and happiness vibrate at a higher frequency. Negative feelings constrict the flow of energy through the subtle body, leaving us feeling tired, depleted or fatigued. Positive feelings accentuate the flow of energy through the subtle body, thus leaving us feeling relaxed and energized.

All feelings are important and necessary as long as they are coming from a place of wholeness. This includes feelings that are typically identified as being negative. It's normal and natural for us to have negative feelings. Negative feelings are vital to our survival. We use anger to help us define our boundaries and fear to protect us from danger.

Elmer Green, Ph.D., a pioneer in the use of biofeedback for the treatment of disease, stated, "Every change in the physiological state is accompanied by an appropriate change in the mental emotional state, conscious or unconscious, and conversely, every change in the mental emotional state, conscious or unconscious, is accompanied by an appropriate change in the physiological state."

The flow of energy from our mental body, through our emotional body and finally to our physical body can be experienced when we think about doing something as simple as drinking lemon juice. Imagine a cool fresh juicy lemon sitting on a table in front of you. Next to the lemon rests a serrated knife and a small clear glass. Envision yourself picking up the knife and cutting the lemon in half, a small spray of its bitter juice caressing your fingers as you cut into its yellow skin. Taking one of the lemon halves in your hand, gently squeeze its sour juice into the glass. When you are done, imagine yourself lifting the small clear glass to your lips and taking a sip of the freshly squeezed lemon juice.

As you read these words did you find your mouth watering? Perhaps you could almost taste the tartness of the lemon in your mouth. Your body may even have shivered slightly with the thought of drinking the juice. So while only words were used here, the image created in the mental body was transmitted via the emotional body to the physical body, where the drinking of the lemon juice was felt and experienced by our bodies.

Over the years, a number of theories about how our emotions work have been proposed. William James and Carl Lange proposed some of the earliest theories on this topic. They suggest that when a threatening situation is experienced, our perception of the event creates a specific physiological response in the body, such as an increase in blood pressure, heart rate or breathing. Their theory assumes that each of our feelings creates a specific biological response, which is then sent to the brain and the relevant emotion is subsequently displayed.

Another theory was proposed by Walter Canon in 1929 and was later modified by Philip Bard. Their theory, known as the Canon-Bard Theory, suggests that sensory information first moves to the thalamus of the brain, where the message is divided. Part of it goes to the cortex, where we experience the conscious subjective experience of the emotion or feeling, while the other part goes to the hypothalamus, which triggers physiological changes in the body.

In 1964, Stanley Schachter proposed that our thought processes as well as our environment are contributing factors in the type of emotions we experience. He believed that when something happens in our environment, the event triggers bodily changes. Based on these physiological changes, we evaluate the situation and identify what emotion we are feeling. He felt that our assessments are based upon our life experiences as well as our interpretation of the event, which triggered the emotion we experience.

American Psychologist Robert Plutchik, in 1980, proposed that we experience eight primary emotions: sadness, disgust, anger, anticipation, joy, acceptance, fear and surprise. Like the primary colors red, blue and yellow, which can be mixed together to create green, orange and purple, Plutchik suggested that our basic emotions can be mixed together to create secondary and tertiary emotions. To him, emotions such as fear combined with surprise equaled the emotion of alarm, while joy mixed with acceptance produced love. By including additional factors such as intensity and duration, he felt that the number of potential emotional combinations was unlimited.

Candace Pert, Ph.D., has proposed the most recent theory on how emotions work. She believes that emotions happen in both the mind and the body simultaneously. Her theory identifies peptides and other chemical messengers in the body as being the basis of emotions. When we are happy, specific peptides are released in the body, resulting in the feeling of happiness. When we are sad, different sets of peptides are released, producing these feelings in the body. It is her belief that each peptide has its own emotional tone or mood that is sensed by the body and when released alone or combined with others, produces an array of emotions.

Many of us don't know how to properly express our feelings. However, our ability to honor and express our emotions is critical to our overall health and well-being. Western societies place little value on feelings and instead place an emphasis on logic and other aspects of the mind. We are taught to suppress our feelings and are left with the underlying belief that when we express them we are being foolish or weak.

In the end, we can choose to express what we really feel, think, want, need or desire or we can choose to internalize it. Emotions that are not expressed or remain unresolved influence our behaviors and our physiological processing, causing us emotional pain. They inhibit the flow of our life force energy, which causes them to manifest somewhere else or in another form. Inhibited emotions often appear as sulkiness, whining, sarcasm, envy, cynicism or even cattiness.

There is a strong connection between our ability to express our emotions and the functioning of the personality. As you may recall, our personality is made up of all our life experiences, including our hopes and dreams, our conflicts, our self-imposed restrictions, our inner pains and distress as well as our expectations and disappointments.

When we choose not to express a feeling, based on the input of the personality, the flow of its energy through our bodies is inhibited, causing us to experience inner conflicts or resistance. This resistance creates blockages in our subtle energy.

The personality utilizes a number of coping devices in order to maintain our belief structures and provide us with a sense of well-being. Devices such as self-deception or a distorted view of reality protect us from emotional discomfort. They shield us from experiencing or re-experiencing uncomfortable feelings such as pain, anxiety, sadness and anger. Many times these coping devices or defense mechanisms are learned in early childhood, and over time and through repetition end up operating on automatic or habitual levels.

Defense mechanisms we utilize to deal with emotional conflicts can include:

Defense Mechanisms
Acting out – where we respond to an event through our actions before we reflect on our true feelings. **Anticipation** – where we experience an emotional reaction in advance or in anticipation of a future event. **Avoidance** – where we avoid specific situations, objects or activities.

> **Defense Mechanisms (continued)**
>
> **Denial** – where we fail to recognize the obvious implications or consequences of our thoughts, actions or situations.
>
> **Intellectualization** – where we use abstract thinking or generalization to minimize feelings.
>
> **Passive Aggression** – where we indirectly and unassertively express aggression towards others in the form of resistance, resentment or hostility.
>
> **Rationalization** – where we offer a logical or socially acceptable explanation for an act or decision.
>
> **Reaction Formation** – where we become the opposite of what we fear.
>
> **Repression** – where we exclude painful or conflicting thoughts, impulses or memories from awareness.
>
> **Suppression** – where we intentionally exclude our thoughts and emotions from our consciousness. Suppression is conscious, while repression normally occurs unconsciously.

Of the defense mechanisms available to us, repression and/or suppression are viewed as being the primary coping devices we utilize. Freud was the first to identify the phenomenon of repression. He thought that, in the case of trauma, we often choose to forget, deny or ignore the experience and remove it from our conscious mind. This saves us from the pain, discomfort or anxiety it may produce.

Repressed emotions are the result of experiences that have been forgotten or suppressed because they could not be consciously faced. Fixed or habitual patterns are good indicators of repressed past experiences. Many times, events in our lives trigger or activate the memories of repressed past experiences, causing us to react to these experiences. These reactions are based not upon what is happening now, but on the reality of the original experiences.

It has been theorized that all negative emotions, emotional responses and coping devices are associated with fear in one form or another. Shame, sorrow, regret, guilt and resentment are all expressions of fear: fear to face the original trauma and release it. It was once said that if you look under depression you'll find anger and if you look under anger you'll find sadness. If you look under sadness you will find fear.

Fear is defined as an emotional response to an unknown or impending danger or as an expectation of evil. Fear can create feelings of apprehension, anxiety, alarm, dread, fright or terror. When you are in fear, you are scared of someone, something or a potential outcome. Fear has a limiting effect on our thoughts and behaviors. It keeps us from putting our hand on the hot burner of the stove and from jumping from high places. It also makes us tentative when going into a darkened room. These types of fear are good. They keep us safe. They make us think before we act, not knowing the potential outcome and repercussions of our actions.

According to H.P. Lovecraft, "The oldest and strongest emotion of mankind is fear." We experience fear when we venture into uncharted ground, especially when the outcome is unknown. We can also experience fear when we lose our jobs, look to end a relationship or even when we try to express our needs and desires.

Fear can impact us in many ways. When we are in fear, we are hesitant to take steps forward. Our minds are filled with thoughts of a traumatic experience, a negative outcome or the potential repercussions of our choices and decisions. We may manifest these fears as procrastination, where we choose to do nothing. Sometimes we demonstrate resistance, digging in our heels and holding on tightly to our current position or situation. Some of us go into denial about our fears, choosing to blame others or the situation for our choices. Others just avoid putting themselves into scary situations, thus eliminating any possible threat.

The bottom line is that fear takes away our choices. Because of fear, we end up dwelling on our imperfections, limitations, difficulties, barriers or delays. These thoughts can end up dominating our attention and restricting our behavior. Fear can keep us from doing the things we want or need to do for ourselves. It limits us, constrains us and can end up ruling our lives. It consumes our energy and enjoyment of life, leaving us experiencing additional unexplainable stress, fatigue, frustration or feeling just plain stuck.

We are constantly being affected by our desires, longings, irritations, delights or suppressed impulses. It requires a lot of our energy to suppress our emotions. The more the flow of our energy is suppressed, the less there is for us to use in our daily lives. Emotions that do not flow through our energetic system can become toxic. The more we deny them, the greater the ultimate toxicity, which can manifest itself in the form of an explosive release of the pent-up emotion or in physical disease.

The Etheric Body

> *Each cell of our body, each organ, the brain and the mind – all the "elements" of our being – are interconnected at a physical and subtle level which allows us to think, talk, act and exist in a balanced, coherent and synchronic manner, when each part acts for the benefit of the other parts.*
>
> — Horia Cristescu

As we move closer to the denseness of the physical body we encounter the etheric body. In Qabalistic texts this body, or world, is referred to as Assiah. It is here that patterns that are established in the mental body and activated in the emotional body become formalized in order to manifest as form or substance in the physical world.

The etheric body, commonly called the aura, is defined as the field of energy that surrounds living things and every material object. It acts as our first line of defense as it insulates the physical body from the environment. It is said that the etheric body reflects the subtle energy of the physical body, where it changes in color, shape and size according to the thoughts and emotions being experienced at any given time.

Our life force energy flows through the etheric body as it works its way towards the physical body. So while the etheric body does not add any causal factors to the manifestation of illness and disease, as the blueprint of the physical body, it guides the working of bodily processes and repair. If disturbances or imbalances in the etheric body occur, thus distorting the etheric template, abnormal cells and tissues can be created. Disease and illnesses can be detected in this body, days, weeks, months and even years prior to their manifesting in the physical body.

The etheric body is the part of our subtle energetic system that is readily perceived by intuitives. Based on highly sensitive equipment, scientists are now able to identify and validate the existence of the etheric body, moving it from the realm of theology into the realm of science. Harold Saxton Burr of Yale University, for example, found an electric field on the surface of living organisms, including worms, salamanders, mammals and even, significantly, humans.

In a separate investigation, the etheric body has been photographed and measured through the use of Kirlian photography. Kirlian photography is a photographic process that captures the etheric body of people or other living things. The technique involves the use of a high frequency, high-voltage, low-amperage electrical field to photograph its subject. The resulting image displays a glowing, multi-colored emanation that surrounds the subject. This emanation is known as its aura. It has been proposed that variations in the strength and intensity of these emanations are an indicator of health.

The Meridians

> *We are shaped by our thoughts; we become what we think. When the mind is pure, joy follows like a shadow that never leaves.*
> — Buddha, The Dharmapada

The meridians, as described in Chinese medicine, are channels that lie beneath the skin's surface and transport our life force energy from the etheric body down to cellular levels. There are twelve main meridians in the physical body that function in a way similar to that of the nadis found in Yogic literature.

Energy is said to enter the body through the acupuncture points, which correlate to the chakras. It then travels through the meridians and into an organ or other body structure. It is believed that the meridians provide an interface between the etheric and the physical body and may provide a guide for the growth and development of the body, particularly the arteries, veins and lymphatic vessels.

The meridians have been found to have a physical counterpart. In the 1960s, Dr. Kim Bong-han of North Korea's National Meridian Research Institute discovered the presence of meridians as a component of our physical makeup. Dr. Kim injected radioactive p32, an isotope of phosphorus, into an acupuncture point. The radioactive p32 moved along a fine duct-like channel of approximately 0.5 to 1.5 microns in diameter. He found that the p32 followed the same path as classical acupuncture meridians. He then injected this same material into nearby tissues and discovered the concentrations to be insignificant.

In a separate study, to evaluate the importance of the meridians to tissues and tissue growth, Dr. Kim severed the meridian going to the liver in a frog. Shortly after severing the meridian he began noticing changes in the liver tissue. Within three days, serious vascular degeneration was noticed throughout the liver. In a different experiment, Dr. Kim found that the meridians were formed within 15 hours of conception in chickens. This occurred long before even the most elementary organs were formed. Dr. Kim also found that the fluid in the meridians contained elevated concentrations of DNA, RNA, amino acids, adrenaline and hormones. The levels that he found were much higher than what is normally found in the blood.

The work performed by Dr. Kim suggests that the meridian system is an independent network within the body that functions through a series of unique and separate structures. His work also indicates that the channels that make up the meridian system reach all the way down to the individual tissue cell. It can then be concluded that the meridians provide the body with some type of information, which influences bodily function.

The Physical Body

> *Over the years your bodies become walking autobiographies, telling friends and strangers alike of the minor and major stresses of your lives.*
>
> — MARILY FERGUSON

So far, we have discussed how our thoughts and emotions trigger physiological responses in our bodies. It is now known, for example, that certain emotional upsets can cause the stomach to secrete the hormone gastrin into the bloodstream. Gastrin signals the stomach to produce hydrochloric acid. If an excess of hydrochloric acid is found in the stomach, it can cause irritation and inflammation of the stomach lining.

One of the most deeply investigated of all our psycho-biological states is the effect of stress on our bodies. By looking at the cascade of neural, hormonal and biochemical changes that even a small amount of stress produces in our bodies, we are provided with an example of how emotional responses are manifested on physical levels.

We incur stress in direct relationship to how we react physically, mentally and emotionally to the challenges and changes in our lives. Not all stress is bad. Stress can challenge us to act in creative and resourceful ways, such as when it motivates us to do our very best. However, sometimes the stress we experience can become so great that it overwhelms us and can become harmful to our bodies.

For example, let's say something happens to us – our boss reprimands us, our husband, wife or lover tells us they want to end our relationship or we get pulled over by the police for speeding. If, based on our life experiences, this situation is perceived as a threat, our unconscious mind responds by triggering an emotional response and we experience stress. Deirdre Davis Brigham, in her book *Imagery for Getting Well*, provides a wonderful play-by-play description of what happens next.

> *When a decision has been made by our unconscious Supreme court that the situation is a threat to survival, the message is conveyed to the hypothalamus (considered a part of the "brain"), which chemically communicates with the pineal or pituitary gland (generally considered the master control center for the "body").*
>
> *The pituitary begins mobilizing the body for what it understands to be a threat to its survival, releasing*

adrenocorticoptropic hormones (ACTH) as well as activating hormones for the adrenal medulla. The adrenal medulla pumps adrenaline, noradrenaline, and other catecholamines into the bloodstream, increasing heart rate and blood pressure as well as shifting blood flow from the smooth muscles of the digestive system to the skeletal muscles (to enable fight or flight). Plasma glucose, triglycerides, and free fatty acids increase, so they may be used by the body as fuel; platelet aggregation increases (aiding blood clotting); and kidney clearance is reduced.

With the activation of the adrenal cortex by ACTH, cortisol is poured into the bloodstream. Cholesterol production is increased for its fuel value and cortisol causes the pouring of glucose into the bloodstream, starting the process of gluconeogenesis, which is the creation of glucose for energy fuel to be used after the stores in the liver have been exhausted. Most frequently, glucose is created by breaking down the body's protein (muscle tissue, bones and organs), which causes floods of insulin to allow the muscles to use the glucose. This, in turn, desensitizes the insulin receptors of the cells so that more and more insulin is required for the body to effectively use sugar fuel.

While our body is designed to handle the occasional flood of chemicals that stress produces, it was not intended to handle them on an ongoing or prolonged basis. There is now evidence showing that prolonged stress impacts the functioning of our bodies, thus opening the door to chronic disease. As stress becomes a part of our everyday lives, the body tries to adapt to this overload of chemicals in an effort to maintain homeostasis. These adaptations may take the form of high blood pressure, increased blood sugar levels and lowered immunity, which over time can cause more permanent and chronic issues.

It is my hope that by now you recognize the fact that the physical body is not just a biochemical machine. It has a consciousness unto itself in the same way the etheric, emotional, mental and causal bodies do. Each cell, tissue and organ possess a level of consciousness that works to carry out the mind's instructions. This unison of body, mind, spirit, material and immaterial working as a whole and acting through a system of relationships and interrelationships is referred to as the psychosomatic information network. It links our energetic systems together and coordinates its interaction with the organs and cells in our bodies in an intelligent and organized manner.

Information is transmitted, received and assimilated by our tissues and organs in the form of chemical messages. For example, our nervous system is the mechanism for sending and receiving sensory information in our bodies. It is concerned with the correlation and integration of our bodily processes and our ability to adjust to our environment. Nerves transmit information as electrical impulses from one area of the body to another at speeds of more than 100 meters per second. Our nerves do not touch each other, but are instead separated from each other by a narrow gap called the synaptic cleft. For information to cross the synaptic cleft, special chemical messengers called neurotransmitters are released at the end of one nerve cell and bind to receptor sites on the next nerve cell.

Neurotransmitters are all part of a group of messenger molecules that are classified as information substances. Information substances distribute information throughout the body. They form the basis of biological communication, a kind of organic language. They relay information across the different functional systems including the endocrine, neurological, gastrointestinal and immune systems. Information substances produced by neurons are called neuropeptides. Those produced by the endocrine system are called hormones and those produced by the immune system are called immunotransmitters.

When information substances are released in one part of our body they travel through the extracellular fluid and are received by receptor sites on the cell walls of tissues in another part of our body. Receptors and receptor sites are single molecules of proteins that interface with the cells in the body. Receptors sit on the membrane of a cell and have roots that reach deep into the interior of the cell. They function as chemically activated switches that turn on or off specific chemical reactions. It has been found that the average cell has hundreds of receptors on it that respond to specific chemicals within the body.

Like a lock and key mechanism, receptors act like keyholes waiting for the right type of chemical key to come up and bind to them. Binding occurs as a result of "receptor specificity," meaning the receptor ignores all but the specific key or ligand that fits it correctly. For instance, the opiate receptor can only receive ligands that are members of the opiate group which includes endorphins, morphine or heroin. Once a ligand binds to a receptor, it activates the receptor molecule causing metabolic and biochemical change to occur in the cell.

Scientific evidence now shows that this chemically based system is much older and far more primitive than originally thought. This process, although relatively slow in comparison to neural transmission, has been found in some of the simplest forms of life on the planet. This chemical messaging system even exists in a primitive single-celled animal called the tetrahymena, where it manufactures many of the same information substances our bodies do.

In her book *Molecules of Emotions*, Candice Pert, Ph.D., provides a more dynamic description of this process. "[Imagine] two voices – ligand and receptor – striking the same note and producing a vibration that rings a doorbell to open the doorway to the cell ... The receptor, having received a message, transmits it from the surface of the cell deep into the cell's interior, where the message can change the state of the cell dramatically." This biochemical change can activate cell division, the manufacture of new proteins and a number of other cellular activities. (It is interesting to note that Pert also describes the communication of information into the cell in terms of vibration and resonance.)

In her groundbreaking work on the role of information

substances within the body, Pert has identified seven major nodal points which have high concentrations of receptor sites. There are striking similarities between the locations of these nodal points and the traditional location of the chakras, an implication so strong that it cannot be overlooked. Pert also found that the entire lining of the digestive tract, from the esophagus through the large intestine and colon was lined with cells that are receptor rich. She believes that this may be why we experience "gut feelings."

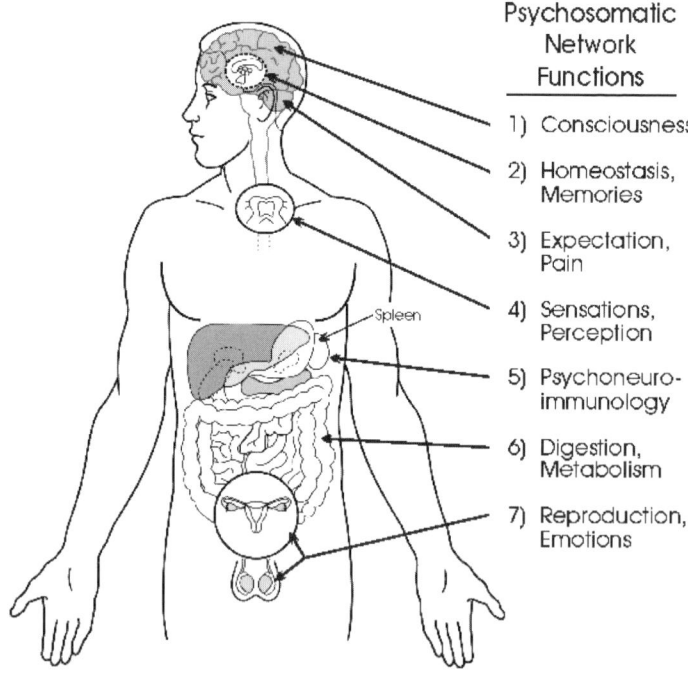

Figure 10
Nodal Points in the Psychosomatic Network

These recent discoveries of the role information substances play in the body are important for understanding how memories are stored. Researchers are finding that memories may not be stored only in the brain as was once thought, but as part of our psychosomatic network that includes the physical body. It is believed that some memories are linked to a specific set of biochemical conditions in the body. For instance, a traumatic event typically elicits a major physiological response. The memory of this event often ends up becoming biochemically attached to the chemistry of the traumatic physiological state in what is called a "state-dependent memory."

During periods of emotional crisis and physical stress, specific information substances are released in the body, creating a specific internal chemistry. It has been found that when our inner chemistry returns to its normal condition, memories of the event are not readily accessible by the conscious mind. It is theorized that this information is encoded at deeper levels in the body and is only accessible when we recreate this chemistry in our bodies.

For example, if we experience a traumatic event such as being in a serious car accident, the limbic-hypothalamic-pituitary-adrenal system suddenly releases information substances into the body. All of the events, both external stimuli and internalized impressions of the accident are encoded in this special state or condition of consciousness. We may feel a bit dazed or perhaps be in a state of shock. After a few hours or days we may find that the details of the accident, which were clear at first, now seem hazy or almost forgotten.

The memories of the event, however, are not forgotten. They are imprinted in the muscles and tissues of our bodies.

State-dependent memories explain why the smell of chocolate chip cookies baking in the oven can take us back to specific childhood memories or why a particular song allows us to relive an experience. These cues not only stimulate vague memories, they can trigger a full recall of the event, which includes feelings, images, smells and sensations. When the biochemistry of a memory is triggered and recreated in our bodies, it is not that we remember a past experience; we relive it.

Some of the emotions we experience cause our muscles to contract along with each and every cell in our bodies. Wilhelm Reich, in his book *Character Analysis*, believed that unreleased traumas are stored in the body's tissues and are reflected in muscular tensions within the body. He believed that the physical manifestation of illness is not merely the result of the psychological process, but of the psychological process manifesting itself in the physical realm. He felt that all of our life experiences find expression in the physical body, taking on the form of defense mechanisms, reaction patterns and body postures.

He deemed that muscular tensions are a reflection of psychological tension we are experiencing and can be considered to be synonymous with psychological dysfunction. He felt that both chronic muscular tension and repressed emotions serve the same defensive function and both influence our self-perception, self-esteem, self-image and our interactions with others and our environment.

When we choose to not communicate an emotion, either consciously or unconsciously, we suppress it in our bodies by tightening the muscles that would normally express it. If the muscular tension becomes chronic, the associated muscles can become rigid, reducing their mobility and flexibility. We use muscular tension or armoring to dull feelings in the body. It inhibits the free flow of our emotional energy.

Muscular tension or body armoring protects us from experiencing or re-experiencing painful or threatening feelings. In turn, our spontaneity and creativity are also effected. As a result, we are also unable to experience joy, happiness, love, sadness, fear, sensuality or anger. Elsworth F. Baker, M.D., in his book *Man in the Trap*, stated that "Armoring may be divided into natural or temporary muscular contraction and permanent or chronic contraction." Temporary muscular contractions occur in every living animal that is being threatened. With continued and maintained threats, real or perceived, they can become chronic and eventually become permanent.

Fixed or chronic muscular patterns are an indicator of repressed past experiences because, when we hold this energy in, our bodies create a series of unique muscular patterns. It has been found that a person's mental and emotional character can be described based on the pattern of chronic muscular tension in his or her body. By understanding the specific patterns of muscular tension, our psychological history and defense structure can be assessed. For example, take an individual who is afraid. He covers his feeling of fear by pretending that he is brave or courageous.

Body Armoring Segments	
Ocular	
Includes:	**Eyes, ears, forehead and cheekbones**
Symptoms:	Expressionless eyes, rigid forehead and eyelids, masklike expression
Expression:	Mask we present to the world: cover-up for the true inner self; conflict between inner and outer world
Oral	
Includes:	**Jaw, tongue, chin, larynx and mouth**
Symptoms:	Clenched jaw, tight or closed mouth
Expression:	Used to stop ourselves from making sounds/crying, being forced to "swallow" anything from others
Cervical	
Includes:	**Neck**
Symptoms:	Neck stiffness or pain, headaches
Expression:	Self restraint, inaccessibility and conformity to rules and standards; conflicts between head and heart
Shoulder	
Includes:	**Deltoids, chest, pectorals and muscles between shoulder blades**

Symptoms:	*Expression:*
1) Shoulders pulled back	Holding back
2) Rounded shoulders	Being burdened
3) Hunched shoulders	Vulnerability or self-protection
4) Raised shoulders	Fear

Body Armoring Segments (continued)	
Chest	
Includes:	Chest
Symptoms:	Chest tension, suppressed breathing, high blood pressure, asthma, respiratory problems, palpitations, anxiety
Expression:	Grief, sadness, heartbreak, restraint and self-control; inability to experience love or compassion
Diaphragm	
Includes:	**Diaphragm**
Symptoms:	Impaired breathing
Expression:	Tension in response to anxiety or fear, repression of pleasure impulses, repression of anger or rage
Abdominal	
Includes:	**Rectus abdominis muscle and lower back**
Symptoms:	Abdominal tightness or back pain
Expression:	Fear of sexual feelings – cuts feeling from the heart to the genitals, irritation and crossness
Pelvic	
Includes:	**Pelvic muscles and legs**
Symptoms:	Pelvis pulled back, anal sphincter contracted
Expression:	Lumbago, sciatica, constipation, urinary problems, sexual problems

He compensates for this with fixed postural attitudes; his shoulders may be squared off, his chest inflated or his belly sticking out.

According to Reich, the body armors itself in horizontal segments. Each segment comprises a group of muscles or organs that work together to express a particular emotion. These segments include the ocular, oral, neck, shoulders, chest, diaphragm, abdominal and pelvic segments. The preceding pages show a table that describes each of these segments as well as their physical and emotional manifestation.

Our psychosomatic network, like our physical body, needs to be balanced. It operates through a series of ongoing checks, balances and feedback loops. When something interferes with the functioning of this system, disease ensues. Distortions to our energetic system often originate in the mental body. In order for our thoughts to have an effect on our health, a cascading effect must occur.

Filtered by our beliefs, our perception of an event generates either a positive or negative response within us. Our unconscious and conscious minds, out of a desire to not re-experience a traumatic event, react in order to protect us. They do this by engaging our defense mechanisms, which work to inhibit our natural response. This inhibition occurs through the use of our emotional defense mechanisms such as denial, repression or suppression in the emotional body, and through body armoring and disturbances to the flow of information substances in the physical body.

Our psychosomatic network then begins to collapse, resulting in an inability of our body to respond correctly to stimuli. This inability can impact our autonomic systems and cell functions such as breathing, blood flow, immunity, digestion and elimination. In turn, the physical body transmits the energy of this suppressed response back to the mental body, where it supports our judgments, beliefs and perceptions of reality.

As our energetic system works to compensate for the imbalances in each of the bodies, each suppressed response works to knock us further out of balance and wholeness. On physical levels the chemistry produced by the repressed emotion gets trapped in the cells of the body, where it can be stored indefinitely. It is believed that over time this toxic chemical overload trapped in the cells precipitates many physical diseases.

Section 3

Experiencing the Power of the Chakras

Before We Get Started ...

Previously, when we discussed the nature of the chakras, we spoke about them in a singular, almost anatomical way. As we move forward, we will examine the chakras on a totally different level. In order to fully understand them we must experience them, not just on an intellectual level but from the depth of our being.

We act and interact with the energy and information that is provided to us by the chakras all the time. They are always open. They are always turned on, providing us with information from our inner world and the world around us in kind of a full-blown multimedia production. If only one chakra were working at a time, or if we could only access the data being processed by one chakra at a time, it would be like watching television with just one eye open and the sound off. Our chakras provide us with stimuli in the form of images, words, feelings and sensations, all at the same time. This information is always there, ever present, for us to access and use.

As our life force energy moves through the subtle bodies, we don't recognize it in the terms of "I am having a mental body experience," or "an etheric body experience," but instead in terms of the experience we have on chakra levels. For instance, we could talk endlessly about having a clairvoyant experience (a function of the sixth chakra), but until you recognize what it is like to have one, you will never fully understand how you interact with energy and information that is provided on this level. It is only by understanding and experiencing the flow of energy through our chakras that we will be able to fully understand their function, thus providing us with additional insights into ourselves.

In the pages that follow, we will be exploring each chakra one by one in a linear fashion. The chakras, however, are anything but linear. By understanding, experiencing, recognizing and validating their actions as they move through us, our ability to act and react to the information they provide will increase tenfold.

My goal, as you journey into the realm of the chakra, is to create a framework for understanding them, not only on an intellectual level but also on an emotional and bodily level as well. Through this, you will be able to recognize how the flow of your life force energy manifests itself in your world.

The First Chakra

> *You gain strength, courage and confidence by every experience in which you really stop to look fear in the face. You are able to say to yourself, 'I have lived through this horror. I can take the next thing that comes along.' You must do the thing you think you cannot do.*
>
> — ELEANOR ROOSEVELT

Located at the base of the spine, the first chakra is associated with the physical body and the world of matter. Called Muladhara in Sanskrit, this energy center is referred to as Malkuth in Qabalistic literature, in which it is the tenth sephirah on the Tree of Life. More specifically, the first chakra is located at the perincum, which can be found midway between the anus and the genitals. Affiliated with the color red, the first chakra is considered the densest and the slowest moving of all the major chakras.

The first chakra relates all things that are solid, earthy and grounded. According to Qabalistic texts, the first chakra permits "God's will" to manifest. It allows consciousness to manifest and spiritual patterns, which were conceived of in the seventh chakra, to be expressed in physical form. On physiological levels, the first chakra is associated with the adrenal glands, the coccyx and the coccyglelganglion as well as the large intestines. As the center of manifestation into the physical world, its association with the large intestines only makes sense. It is through the large intestines that solid matter is passed out of the body and into the world around us.

The first chakra is responsible for the generation and identification of our needs. We are all motivated by our unsatisfied needs. Our needs, particularly our need to survive, can exert an enormous influence over our actions. According to Abraham Maslow and his "hierarchy of needs," there are different levels to our needs, with our basic needs wanting to be satisfied before more our more complex needs can be identified and ultimately met.

Our base needs can be so compelling that they can lead a person to lying, cheating, stealing and even violence. Abraham Maslow believed that humans aren't inherently evil. Instead, he felt that people who are deprived of their base needs are driven to getting them met by whatever means necessary. This is especially true when it comes to our most basic needs including the need for air, food and water.

Our need for physical survival, that is, our need to keep our bodies alive, is vital. We witness this need for physical

> ### Maslow's Hierarchy of Needs
>
> **Physiological Needs** – our need for air, food, and water. These needs can be very strong and if we are deprived over time, we will die.
>
> **Safety Needs** – our need to have stability and consistency in our lives and our environment.
>
> **Social Needs** – these include our need to escape loneliness and have a sense of belonging.
>
> **Esteem Needs** – these include our need for self-esteem and respect from others.
>
> **Self-Actualization Needs** – at this level, all of our lower needs are met and we are able to be our authentic selves.

survival when we see a tree bent over to one side in order to stay in the sunlight or when we hear stories of animals that, when caught in a hunter's trap, are compelled to chew off their own limbs in order to escape. We also encounter a need for physiological survival when we hear of someone in distress fighting for his or her life.

Our ability to have our base needs met has changed as we have grown as a society. We are no longer hunters and gatherers concerned with what we will eat. Nowadays, we have jobs, bank accounts and credit cards that allow us to buy food and pay for shelter. It is through these means that we are able to satisfy our basic need for survival. When our ability to take care of our basic needs becomes threatened, we experience the same reaction as our ancestors.

Jamie is a 35-year-old woman who worked her way up through the ranks at a local paper manufacturing company. Jamie started working for the company just out of high school. Now a project manager, she feels as if she has finally arrived at the point where she is working to her potential and earning a sizable income. Recently, however, the company has begun downsizing, with layoffs occurring weekly. Having no formal training or education, Jamie is fearful that she will be next. Going to work, which was once a joy, has now become a burden for Jamie. She feels as if she is walking on eggshells and questions every decision she makes.

Without another paper manufacturing company nearby, she does not know what she will do when the axe finally does fall. She is constantly worried about finding another job and earning a comparable income. She has become tense and irritable and has started counting pennies as well as watching each of her expenditures. Plagued with acid indigestion, she has also been having problems sleeping, eating and concentrating.

Needless to say, Jamie is "in survival."

Jamie's ability to satisfy her physiological needs is being threatened. While she has not been laid off, the potential is certainly there. Spurred on by the belief that she does not have the pertinent skills to get another high-paying job in her hometown, she begins worrying about what her future may hold. In response, her first chakra has become contracted and fear has become the prominent emotion in her life. We typically experience fear when our survival is threatened. As Jamie's first chakra begins to contract, disrupting the flow of energy through this center, she is left feeling afraid, hopeless and hanging on for dear life.

The flow of life force energy through her body is also being affected, causing her to keep unwanted mental and emotional energy bound in her body. If Jamie could only believe and trust in her skills and abilities, the flow of energy through her first chakra would be restored. While the outcome of her employment dilemma wouldn't necessarily change, at least she would be able to address it calmly, rationally and most importantly, not from a place of fear.

Fear activates the "fight or flight" mechanism in our bodies. It is our body's natural response to real and perceived danger and threatening situations. On a very base level, we identify and react to each of our encounters based upon whether a situation is pleasurable or painful, safe or harmful, good or bad. If an encounter feels pleasurable or safe, we go about our business as usual. If, however, there is a feeling or inkling of pain or danger, our fight or flight mechanism activates, stimulating our adrenal glands and creating a series of biochemical and physiological changes in our bodies.

Our fight or flight mechanism can easily be seen when we look at examples from the animal kingdom. Imagine a small herd of gazelles gently grazing in a grass-filled plain on the Serengeti. Small bushes dot the terrain and the hot noonday sun is shining down on them as they calmly nip the green tips off the wild grasses.

Unbeknownst to them, fifty yards downwind is a lioness that hasn't eaten for several days. Momentarily the wind shifts. One of the gazelles' noses twitches as she takes a whiff of the air around her. She notices something different in the air and recognizes that she is no longer safe. Instinctively, her fight or flight mechanism activates and she takes off running from the impending danger, alerting the rest of the herd who follow behind her.

We have this same instinctual response. After work, Margaret decided to go out for a quick dinner with some friends. When she arrived at 6:00 P.M., the sun was still out and Margaret decided that it would be okay for her to park her car a couple of blocks away. It was the middle of the summer and she figured that by the time she finished eating it would still be light out and she would be able to get back to her car safely. Time slipped by and before she knew it, it was already midnight. With an 8:00 meeting in the morning, Margaret decided she had better head on home and get some sleep. With that, she said goodnight to her friends and headed out of the restaurant.

Walking out the door and heading down the block to where her car was parked, Margaret heard a peculiar noise coming from behind her and became immediately uncomfortable. Turning, she noticed three unsavory-looking men walking down the other side of the street. Her perceptions, based on cultural beliefs and programming, left her feeling unsafe. In response, Margaret's fight or flight mechanism kicked in. Instead of contracting, her first chakra expanded. Her visual and auditory acuity increased. Her adrenal glands activated, releasing adrenalin into her bloodstream. Her heart rate increased, her breathing quickened and her steps hastened. It was not until she had gotten into her car and driven away that she finally felt safe enough for her body's biochemical and energetic systems to come back into alignment.

In this situation, the perceived threat Margaret experienced may well have saved her life. The fear it elicits in us, however, if left unchecked can end up controlling our lives. When we are in fear, our minds are often filled with thoughts, images and negative beliefs of what could or might happen. Regardless of the reality of these thoughts, our fears can keep us caught up in a dysfunctional pattern of behavior, leaving us hesitant to take steps forward.

Carol and Frank got married in the mid-fifties, just after high school. They were high school sweethearts and were very much in love. In the beginning, Carol felt that her relationship with Frank was wonderful. They were both young and carefree but this quickly changed after Carol had their first child. She was twenty at the time and determined to be a good mother, so she stayed at home to care for their baby. Two more children soon followed, and with each child her relationship to Frank grew colder and more distant. As time passed, Frank began drinking. He would often go out "with the boys" after work and not get home until late. While this bothered Carol, she would often make excuses for Frank and worked to shield both her children and herself from the discord in their marriage.

One day, Carol learned that Frank was having an affair with a woman at work. Carol wanted to confront Frank about his illicit tryst, but she was afraid that Frank would leave her for this other woman. The thought of being a single mother with three young children was paralyzing. The idea that she could end up on welfare or worse was more than she could imagine. She would often lie in bed pondering the idea of saying something to Frank, but her imagined outcome was always the same: he would leave her and she would be alone, destitute and helpless.

While Frank did end the relationship with the woman at work, it was only a few years later that Carol found out that he was seeing someone else. Hurt and distraught, Carol again said nothing. She rationalized to herself that she was "keeping the family together." The years went by and Frank's behavior only changed for the worse. His drinking and womanizing was obvious to their friends and family. No one could understand why Carol stayed with Frank. When someone would try to say something about what they saw going on, she would protect and defend Frank, their relationship and their marriage.

It was not until Carol turned sixty-five that she realized that something needed to change. It was then that she came to see me. Her youngest child had just married. She had finally recognized or at least admitted to herself that she had been in denial, making excuses for her husband for over forty years. At sixty-five, however, she was unsure of how to change or even if she was capable of it.

On some levels, it is easy to empathize with Carol's decision. In the fifties and sixties it was frowned upon to be a single parent, especially of three children. I explained to Carol that ultimately, the decision she made to stay with her husband was based on fear, fear of being single, fear of raising three children alone. Since she was unable or unwilling to address this fear, she ended up being feeling trapped. The reality of her situation was that she really didn't know what would have happened to her and her children if she had left Frank in the beginning.

While some fears are good and essential for our basic survival, many of the ones we face daily have nothing to do with any real physical threat or danger. Many times they are based upon a belief that has no bearing on reality. For Carol, she believed that she would not be able to make it on her own. She also believed that she would end up alone and live her life as a single mom. The only real peril she actually experienced was the thoughts and ideas she fabricated in her mind. No one really knows what would have happened then or will happen now if she makes the decision to leave. The possibilities are endless; the ones she conjured up in her mind only a few.

I explained to Carol that fear can be like sitting in a dark room with a scary black and white poster of a werewolf or Dracula hanging on the back of the door. As we look ahead, the only thing we can see is this terrifying creature obstructing our passage and forward movement. What we don't realize, as we sit in the darkness, is that the threat isn't real. Once we turn on the lights, we can easily see that it is only a poster and no danger exists at all. What's more, as we sit in this darkened room, unable or unwilling to either turn on the lights or step through that door, we will never know what is on the other side. We will be forever trapped by our own reservations, worries and uncertainties and will never come to know the freedom and sense of power that is experienced after stepping through their limitations into the light of a new day.

About six months later I received a call from Carol. She had decided to leave Frank. Since our meeting, she had found a part-time job and was in the process of finding a new place to live. She sounded happy and determined. She also shared with me that she had not felt so empowered in years. Good work, Carol!

Grounding is another aspect of the first chakra. We are grounded when we are energetically connected to the physical world. We do this via the nadi that connects to our first chakra. This nadi is often referred to as our grounding cord. When we discussed the flow of energy through the bodies, we talked about how energy and information flows in through the seventh chakra, travels through the body and out the first chakra. When energy exits out of the first chakra it travels down our grounding cord where it is dissipated in the earth. When we are grounded, the electrical circuit of our subtle body is complete and our life force energy can flow freely though us.

Our grounding cord acts like a release valve where stagnant energy found in the body can also be eliminated. Like the large intestine that eliminates material waste from the body, our grounding cord works to eliminate energetic waste from the subtle body. Our grounding cord also protects the body. In the book *Wheels of Light,* Anodea Judith explains the function of our grounding cord in this way: "Just as a lightning rod protects a building by sending its voltage into the ground, so too our grounding protects the body from becoming overloaded by the tensions of everyday life. Grounding allows us to transmute the impact of the stressful vibration."

Grounding also allows our subtle energy to solidify and condense. It can be thought of as the birth canal of the physical world. It is through grounding that consciousness manifests on the physical plane – where ideas conceived in the seventh chakra become reality. From a Qabalistic perspective, man's task on earth is to gain mastery over the physical plane. Once mastered, man will then evolve beyond the necessity of inhabiting bodies made of cellular materials. It is through the first chakra and our grounding cord that man is in direct contact with the physical plane. Without this connection, our ability to control, manipulate and manifest our needs into the energetic vibration we call the physical plane would be lost.

Martin came to see me one bright summer morning. His chief complaint was stomach issues. He stated that he was having a hard time digesting foods. Whenever he ate, he felt as if the food just sat in his stomach. Along with the ongoing feeling of fullness he also complained of excessive burping and a few bouts with acid reflux. On physical levels, Martin was expressing classic gallbladder symptoms. I believed the flow of bile through his gallbladder was hindered and was backing up into his liver. Upon further investigation a much deeper level to Martin's gastric complaints was uncovered.

Martin was a very creative man who was always filled with ideas for a new and better widget. When asked if he experienced difficulty manifesting his inventions in the physical world, a weak chuckle and eye roll was Martin's reply. Martin explained that as a child he didn't have permission to manifest his thoughts, ideas, needs and desires. He felt that whenever he expressed an interest in something, it would be taken away from him and brought to fruition by someone else.

Energetically, Martin had no grounding cord. Energy and information were still coming in through his seventh chakra. This is what provided him with his creative ideas and inventions. This energy, however, wasn't being released or grounded back into the earth or consolidated into a form that could be manifested into the physical world. Basically, it had nowhere to go.

By the time Martin came to see me, his energy, especially the energy of his thoughts, ideas, needs and desires, could only travel as far as his third chakra where he would labor to digest them. The energetic imbalance, which started in his first chakra, was now impacting his third. As the unexpressed energy started overflowing his first chakra, it began working its way up his energetic system. This blockage was causing not only his digestive issues, but also problems with goal setting and decision making, both classic third chakra issues. Not until Martin reconnected his energetic body to the physical world via a grounding cord would he truly begin to heal.

Grounding involves opening the first chakra and allowing gravity to do its thing. It plays a critical role in the maintenance of our subtle body and our energetic selves. By feeling the energy flow in our bodies, we enhance our ability to ground and release blockages. If we are not grounded, nothing is working. Our energy isn't flowing, our ability to manifest in the physical world hindered. We may also find ourselves feeling paralyzed in fear, or as if nothing in our lives is moving forward. By being grounded we create an escape valve for our bodies that allows the stresses and strains of our daily lives to drain. So no matter what your issues are, learning to keep your energy moving and flowing is the foundation of health, healing and well-being.

Here is an exercise you can use to help you connect or reconnect your energy to the earth:

- *To begin this meditation, close your eyes and take a deep breath.*
- *Take a moment to notice what's happening around you.*
- *Where are you in the room?*
- *What is with you in the room?*
- *Take a moment to orient yourself to your surroundings.*
- *Listen to your heart beat.*
- *Say hello to your body.*

- Breathe in again and allow yourself, as spirit, to rest back into your body.
- Now that you're relaxed, it's time to create a grounding cord.
- A grounding cord is a line of energy that runs from the first chakra down to the center of the planet.
- What do you want in a good grounding cord?
- It must be solid, and it has to conduct foreign and excess energy out of your body and aura.
- It must be free of any resistance so you can easily and effortlessly release energy through it.
- It must also stay free of other people's energy and those who may want to ground through you.
- The first Chakra is located at the base of the spine. Direct your energy and attention there. You may find this chakra tingling, vibrating or feeling warmer as you focus your attention there.
- In your mind's eye, visualize the center of planet.
- The center of the planet can look any way you want. It can appear as a hollow ball or a solid sphere. It can be made of molten rock or like the insides of a baseball. It can even appear as a ball of light.
- Whatever you want the center of the planet to look like, have that appear in your mind's eye now.
- Create a line of energy that goes from the first chakra down to the center of the planet.
- Let this line of energy appear as a Redwood tree.
- Allow this Redwood tree to form easily and effortlessly.
- When it reaches the center of the planet, allow your

Redwood tree to form roots, hooking you firmly into the planet.
- *Imagine your body releasing energy down your grounding cord, your Redwood tree, all the way down to the center of the planet.*
- *Take a nice deep breath.*
- *Notice how this feels to your body.*
- *Did you notice any shifts in your energy?*
- *Do you feel more relaxed with your grounding cord in place?*
- *Do you feel more centered, clearer or more at ease?*
- *Continue to release energy down your grounding cord for one to two minutes.*
- *When your body feels complete, bend over and stretch out your body, opening your eyes when you feel ready.*

When our energy has stagnated or is not flowing freely through this center, we tend to lack confidence or feel weak or self-destructive. We may find it hard to get grounded, achieve our goals or interact with the physical. In contrast, when our life force energy is flowing freely though this energy center, we feel grounded, safe and alive. We are able to manifest our needs and trust in the world around us. We feel humble, safe and in control. We are able to feel connected to life and to experience a sense of stillness within ourselves.

The Second Chakra

> *There is a delicate balance of putting yourself last and not being a doormat and thinking of yourself first and not coming off as selfish, arrogant or bossy.*
> — CINDY L. TEACHEY

Moving up the body the next energy center we come to is the second chakra. Called Svadhishana in Sanskrit, this energy center is referred to as Yesod in Qabalistic literature where it occupies the ninth sephirah on the Tree of Life. It is located between the navel and the genitals and is identified as the controlling agent that "gives birth" to our creations upon the physical plane. Physiologically speaking, the second chakra is associated with the sacral vertebrae and the sacral plexus nerve ganglion. It is also associated with the reproductive organs and in particular the ovaries and testes. These endocrine glands produce the hormones needed for reproduction and birth.

Associated with the color orange, the second chakra is perceived as being less dense than the first chakra. It is often seen as the interface between the world of energy and the physical world. The second chakra controls the energy of integration, creativity and our ability to feel. It is the seat of our desires.

The second chakra is intimately connected to the Moon in both Yogic literature and Qabalistic texts. The Moon is associated with the physiological cycles of women and is connected with the growth of plants and other life on our planet. The moon produces the never-ending movement of the tides on Earth. Like the unceasing cyclical movement of the Moon, energy flows in and out of the second chakra, ever in motion.

In the previous section on the first chakra, we discussed the instinctual responses we experience as we interact with the world around us. This is typified by our fight or flight response, the physiological reaction we have when our survival is threatened. The physical body, however, only recognizes rudimentary sensations such as pain, fatigue and discomfort. The second chakra works to organize the sensations we experience. This organization results in feelings.

Feelings are the result of our reaction to physical sensations or stimuli; both good and bad, pleasant and painful. The vibration of feelings exists all around us. As you may recall, each of us transmits, receives and assimilates information from the world around us. Feelings vibrate at a frequency that can be received by the second chakra. So like the tides that flow in and out in their continuous cycle, so too does energy flow into and out of our second chakra.

Our feelings have the ability to communicate our current state of being. Our bodies assimilate our feelings and let us know how we feel in any given moment. Feelings may also be transmitted out into our environment where we can share our experiences with others. Interestingly, this subtle form of energy exchange has been recognized as the primary way in which animals communicate with each other.

In man, these subtle feelings are often ignored. Many times we may feel that something is amiss, but instead of acting on this information we suppress it. We do this because we either cannot understand its promptings or because it doesn't agree with the thoughts, opinions or judgments of our mind, which can easily override our feelings. Many people never recognize that their feelings provide them with important perceptual information.

Our ability to recognize energy on feeling levels is called *clairsentience*. The term is often associated with psychics. Nonetheless, we all possess the ability to feel the energy around us. We all have clairsentient abilities. The ability to feel energy is innately built into each of us. Whether we act on the information provided to us on conscious or unconscious levels is another story altogether.

Think about how may times you've walked into a room and had an uncomfortable feeling or noticed a strange "vibe." This is your second chakra at work, providing you with information from your environment. Or what about the times when you had a strong feeling, a strong notion, one that you experienced deep in your gut that told you something was going to happen. Or perhaps you felt as if someone were looking at you, only to turn your head to see someone in the car next to you staring. You were receiving this information on second chakra, clairsentient levels.

As with the energy of any of our chakras, some people are more open to this energy vibration than others. It is not that they have some special gift, but instead they have learned to acknowledge, validate and act upon the feelings they are experiencing. They are thought of as listening to their gut feelings, of trusting their instincts or of being sensitive, empathic or intuitive.

There are times when it is difficult for us to separate our feelings from those being broadcast around us. This is especially true for individuals who find themselves sensitive to energy from their environment. We experience this when we get caught up in the excitement of a great sales pitch or the anxiety and tension we feel when going to a crowded shopping mall on Christmas Eve. We may find ourselves angry for no reason at all or upset over something that has nothing to do with us.

When the predominant energy vibration of our environment dominates our own feelings, we are "mirroring" the vibration. Our body is resonating in response to our surroundings. Mirroring can be seen in the dynamics of a mob and can explain the mentality of those who participate in a riot. Once we are out of the energetically overwhelming situation and back into a neutral setting, our true feelings come back to the surface. Upon reflection, we often wonder why we felt or acted a certain way, or made certain choices or decisions.

As we mirror a vibration, we allow our energetic self to resonate at the same frequency as the world around us. The feelings we experience often confuse us into believing that they are *our* true feelings. Inadvertently, we accept them as if they are our own. As a society, we do not talk about the interchange of energy. It is never explained to us that we can pick up feelings from our environment and those around us. For that reason, we assume that the feelings we are experiencing are ours, so we act and react to them.

Our needs, as you may recall, are an energy processed in the first chakra. But we all aspire to have a life filled with love, joy, financial and physical security, meaningful relationships, inner peace, self-esteem, as well as fulfilling employment. Each of these things is an expression of our desires. When our needs for food, air, water and shelter have been met, we are able to access the energy of the second chakra. In the second chakra, our needs are transformed into desires through the addition of feelings.

Our desires help us identify and express our needs. They set the stage for getting our needs met and achieving satisfaction in our lives. Our desires are typically expressed as wants rather than needs. We want a new pair of shoes, a new car, a meaningful relationship or a new job.

Our desires, however, can be a dual-edged sword because it is only when we work to satisfy our true or deepest needs that we will ever experience a feeling of genuine satisfaction. Only then will our desire for a particular item or experience subside. So, while we may "want" a new car, we may find that, after buying it, the underlying need has yet to be met or satisfied. Our genuine or true need will then manifest as another desire looking for fulfillment. This is often the case in our work. We work hard because we desire financial security and success in our endeavors. However, the underlying need that seeks to be fulfilled may be recognition, achievement, respect or approval.

Our desires can be thought of as the fuel that fires our needs and provides us with a motive or motivation for getting them met. Our desires prompt us to identify our choices and make decisions. Our desires compel us to take action, because without any action, our needs will never be met or satisfied. Without the driving force of our desires, we would do nothing and, not attending to our most basic needs, we would die.

Like our needs, our desires can exert a strong influence on us. If strong enough, they can cause us to use every ounce of our power and energy in obtaining or accomplishing our heart's desires. Robert Collier, in *Riches Within Your Reach*, writes, "Moreover, the degree and the intensity of your work, mental or physical, is determined by the degree of desire manifested in you concerning the object or end of such work ... The degree of force, energy, will, determination, persistence and continuous application manifested by an individual in his aspirations, ambitions, aims, performances, actions, and work, is determined primarily by the degree of his Desire for the attainment of these objects – his degree of 'want' and 'want to' concerning that object."

Justin, a sixteen-year-old high school student, was enrolled in all Honors courses. At the time I met Justin's mom, Fran, Justin was failing the majority of his classes and would possibly have to repeat the tenth grade. "It isn't that Justin isn't smart enough to handle the work, it's that he just isn't doing the work in the first place," Fran explained. Wanting to help her son, Fran felt as if she had tried everything in the book. She talked to him, rewarded him and even punished him. Nothing seemed to get through.

Fran felt confused about what was going on. She had seen Justin show great motivation in the past. When he wanted a TV and then a stereo for his bedroom, he worked hard, putting in every ounce of his energy to obtain them. With school, however, Fran felt that she was the one who had used every ounce of her energy in trying to help him pass. Frustrated and at her wits' end, Fran hoped that perhaps I would be able to provide her with insights into her son's behavior.

When I looked at Justin's energy, he seemed like a good natured, intelligent teenager. As I started to probe deeper into what was going on, at first glance I thought that Justin might be having a problem manifesting his needs and desires into the physical world. When I looked at his first chakra he had a grounding cord and his energy was flowing. Obviously this was not the issue. Then I thought, perhaps Justin had a third chakra issue where he was having difficulty identifying goals and completing tasks. This wasn't the issue either.

The fulfilling of "tasks," however, wasn't the appropriate

energy or energetic vibration to tune into when looking at Justin. When I reframed the internal question and asked to see the vibration of homework or other school related activities, this was when Justin's difficulty became crystal clear. When faced with homework, Justin's first and third chakras all but shut down. It was intriguing because the issue wasn't in either of these chakras but instead originated in his second.

Getting right to the point, I told Fran that energy and motivation weren't Justin's problem – *desire* was. I felt that once Justin put his mind to something, once he wanted it, once he desired it, he always followed it through to completion. I felt as if Justin had plenty of desire; desire to do the things he wanted – watch TV, play computer games, socialize with his friends and even lie around and do nothing.

School, however, wasn't on the list of things he *wanted*. It wasn't that he wished to fail school, it just wasn't fun. It was low on his priority list. This lack of desire affected his ability to create goals and engage his energy (an aspect of the third chakra). He did direct his energy toward how he could avoid doing schoolwork so that he could have what he desired, which was more time to do what he wanted. In Fran's mind it appeared he wanted nothing.

I felt that no matter how hard Fran tried to motivate her son, it was really up to him. Only he could light the fires of his desires. I told her that until he wanted to do better in school she would remain unsuccessful despite her best efforts. Sad as it seemed, perhaps being held back in school was what it would to take to help Justin reprioritize his life.

There is the adage that you can lead a horse to water, but you can't make it drink. As a parent, teacher, spouse or friend, we can only present others with thoughts, information and concepts with the hope that it may spark the fires of their desires. If there is no desire, then there is no corresponding need that wants to be satisfied. In Justin's case, the need to pass school just wasn't there.

As we work to get our needs met, it is also critical to first know what our souls really want. This opens the door for our needs to be satisfied. By identifying the essence of what we desire, we can ensure that our real needs are met. It is the difference between thinking you want a new car and identifying the essence of your need, which might be a more reliable form of transportation. As we open ourselves to having our needs met, we also open ourselves to receiving answers in whatever way, shape or size they may come.

Barbara really wanted a new relationship. She had lived alone for the past five years, dating on and off, but hadn't met Mr. Right. She was searching for a relationship that was healthy, committed and long term. She explained that the men she had been dating had all turned out to be "jerks" for one reason or another and after a short period of time she would end the relationship.

When asked what she wanted in a relationship, "breathing" was her only reply. When I looked energetically at what she really wanted, what she truly desired in her intimate relationships, there was nothing concrete, only some vague ideas, if that. I sensed it wasn't that Barbara didn't know what she wanted in a relationship, but that she had never taken the time to identify what she needed.

I asked Barbara if she had ever made a list of what she wanted in her relationships. Many women do this when they are teenagers. The list typically consists of four items: tall, dark, handsome with lots of money. I explained to Barbara that we transmit our needs and desires into the world through our second chakra. If "breathing" was the only need or desire she transmitted regarding her relationships, then she had achieved that by inviting in any Tom, Dick or Harry that happened to pass by. Accordingly, she should be happy and satisfied.

I told her that in order to meet the man of her dreams, to meet her soulmate, she would need to be a bit more specific. By being more specific, she would be able to update what was being transmitted through her second chakra. Instead of broadcasting the requirement of "breathing" she would now be able to transmit her true needs and desires out to the world. Consequently, instead of having an open door for anyone to walk through, she would admit only those who were looking to have similar needs satisfied.

Now, while it was important for Barbara to identify her basic physical and monetary requirements, for her to truly get her heart's desire she needed to identify details of what she really wanted in her intimate relationships. So I asked Barbara if she would want her partner to hold her hand as they walked through the mall? Would she want to snuggle with him in bed or have him wink at her across a crowded room? Was it important to her to be able to share her thoughts and feelings with him? Did she want her partner to be someone she could rely on? How often did she want to see him? How often did she want him to call her?

Our question and answer period went on for about twenty minutes. With each question, I tried to get Barbara to think about what she really wanted, what she really needed and what was most important to her. I suggested to Barbara that she go home, find a quiet place to work and write down each question that came up about her relationship needs. As she answered them, I suggested that she try to feel the answer in her body, to let the feeling engulf her. If she wanted her partner to hold her hand as they walked down the street, I wanted her to visualize it or feel it with all of her being.

Barely two weeks had gone by when I received an excited call from Barbara. She had just started dating someone new and as if like magic, her new friend possessed all of the qualities that she had hoped for and dreamed of. Ah, the universe is a wonderful thing.

When our needs and desires are met we are left feeling satisfied. We feel nurtured. Nurturing is a quality of the second chakra. Nurturing implies that we not only work to have others' needs and desires satisfied, but to have our own fulfilled as well. Nurturing requires that there is a give and take, that there is an equal exchange of energy, so if you give energy to others, you should be open to receiving some in return.

Energy is exchanged in the form of goods, products or services. In most countries of the world, the primary instrument used to exchange energy is money. We exchange our labor for a paycheck. We take our paycheck and use the money to buy a television set or pay to have a cavity filled. But the exchange of energy occurs all the time in ways we don't often think about.

We give our energy when we provide a dry shoulder to cry on, pick up a friend because his car is in the shop and even when we smile at a stranger we pass on the street. In turn, we receive energy when we let a friend help us out of a financial bind, when we let our husbands, wives, children or significant others cook us dinner because we aren't feeling well, or when we are encouraged, praised or complimented. Our ability to give and receive energy helps to fulfill our desires and satisfy our needs.

This give and take of energy is important to maintain, not only in the second chakra, but in all of the chakras. It creates a balance within us. When we give of ourselves, our energy goes out and hopefully satisfies the needs of others. In turn, when we receive energy, our needs can be satisfied as well. There are no specific rules regarding the exchange of energy; we just need be open to receiving it and be happy to give. If there were a continuous give and take of energy on this planet, all of our needs could easily be met. Our society would be in balance and we would all experience the satisfaction we deeply desire. But that is not how our world operates.

Sometimes we invalidate our needs and desires. At times, we use our energy to satisfy other people's needs while ignoring our own. This energy dynamic is often seen in women. From an early age, women are taught to invalidate their needs and desires. They are often expected to ensure the satisfaction of others as they prepare for their roles as wife, mother and caregiver.

The flow of energy from the second chakra of these types – men or women – always flows in an outward direction as opposed to flowing in and out. On second chakra levels, I call these individuals Givers. They are always willing to help out and will always lend a hand when asked. They are supportive with their time, money and energy, give it away happily with no expectation of repayment or reciprocation, and often feel guilty when they are presented with the opportunity to take something back for themselves. Givers aren't open to receiving energy.

On the other hand, there are those who are very good at getting their needs met. I call these individuals Takers. Takers do just that – they take and take and then many times they come back and ask for more. The flow of energy in and out of their second chakra is also impaired, except that the flow of energy is always going into the body. Many times the "taking" that Takers do isn't to satisfy a genuine need or desire, but because it makes their lives easier, because it is offered or even because it makes them feel more powerful or in control. Takers aren't willing to give energy.

Interestingly, while these individuals are not internally balanced, many times Givers and Takers attract one another unconsciously to help balance out their energy or to help them learn a life lesson. The Giver is always happy to give, while the Taker needs to take. Although dysfunctional, each compensates for the imbalanced need of the other – that is, until the Giver looks to get his or her needs met or the Taker finds some reason to give. Then the delicate balance of this polar relationship begins to wobble.

Often it is hard for Givers to open themselves up to receiving. As the old saying goes, "it is better to give than receive." A Giver often has to learn how to put his or her guilt aside and allow energy to flow in. While there may be issues in other chakras that interfere with their ability to receive, it is important for Givers to recognize the value of getting their needs met. As the Givers work to have their needs met, this shift in their energy may interfere with the Takers' ability to take. It is not uncommon for these "friendships" to quickly fade as the Giver learns to balance his or her second chakra. It is sad to say, but until a Taker decides to put his or her own needs and desires to the side and chooses to give, this person will just move on to the next person from whom to take.

The second chakra can also be thought of as the organizer and houses our creative energy. It is said that the second chakra establishes the final form of manifestation and sits on the threshold between energy and matter. It can be thought of as the mold, pattern or template that creates the final appearance of energy before it reaches the physical world. It manifests not only in our ability to create a new life, but also in our ability to plan, arrange and manipulate the world around us into a new entity that better serves our needs.

At conception, the egg and the sperm unite, thus beginning the development of a new life. At the end of gestation, the baby is born into the physical world. During gestation, the molecules and cells of our bodies are coordinated and structured into a cohesive organism. If it weren't for the actions of the second chakra we would be nothing but a collection of independent cells. So too do our thoughts and ideas gestate until they are structured and "born" into the physical world via the second chakra.

Andrea is a bright and active twenty-nine-year-old woman. Prior to meeting her, we talked on the phone, and Andrea shared with me her chief complaints: bloating and weight gain. When we met in my office the first time, it was apparent that the weight gain to which Andrea was referring centered primarily in her lower abdomen. In fact, it looked as if she were four or five months pregnant.

Andrea stated that she first noticed that she was putting on weight about three years ago. What concerned her most was that in the last year she had gained over twenty pounds. She was upset because the weight seemed to come on all at once, and no matter what she did to try to lose the extra weight, she was unable to shed a pound.

Andrea did admit that she was eating more fast foods than she had in the past, but this did not explain the sudden explosion of weight. In an attempt to get to the bottom of her dilemma, she had gone to her doctor and received a full physical examination and blood work evaluation. Her doctor didn't find anything wrong, but did recommend a diet and exercise program for her to follow. Even though she followed the plan diligently, she experienced little to no success. It was then that she began to think there might be an energetic cause to her weight gain.

Since the majority of her weight gain centered in and around her lower abdomen, that was the first place I tuned into. In terms of her energy, I felt as if Andrea was a very creative individual who derived much pleasure and satisfaction in working on large-scale projects. She loved to put things together. It wasn't that she was crafty in the artistic sense, but I felt she had a strong need to organize and create.

I asked her if something in her life had changed in the year prior to our meeting. I told her that this change had set the energy, or lack thereof, into motion. I felt as if this deviation was interfering with her ability to create. I felt as if her creative energy, instead of flowing as it had in the past, was being suppressed and was trapped inside her body with nowhere to go. I also felt as if there were a number of projects that she had started or wanted to work on, but the suppressed energy was interfering with them as well.

Almost with embarrassment, Andrea realized what had happened. A year ago to the day she had started a new job as an office manager. In all of her prior work positions, in addition to her regular assignments, she also took on the responsibility of organizing the holiday parties, the company picnics, the potlucks or any other events the company sponsored. This was not the case in her current position. So while the day-to-day work was the same, the part of her job she really loved, that which got her creative juices going, was no longer part of her daily routine. She also realized that it wasn't until after she started in this new position that her desire to work on projects at home had diminished as well.

Energetically, Andrea's body was still working on overtime, trying to create. In her previous positions, she'd had an outlet for her creative energy. In her new position, it had no place to go. Instead of being channeled into her work, it was stagnating in her body and backing up in her energetic systems, where it finally manifested on the physical plane as weight gain.

Like a woman in labor, I suggested to Andrea that she push, that is, push a project to completion. Since she had primarily utilized her creative energy at work, it was important that she find a different outlet for it to be channeled, such as in one of her personal projects. I felt that by pushing a project through, it would help her reopen the pathway between the world of energy and the material world, thus allowing her creative energy to flow again. I felt that once she was able to redirect the energy flow, her weight would soon diminish.

Since her issue had manifested onto the physical plane, she also needed to incorporate a diet and exercise plan to assist her physical body in releasing the weight. But with the energetic changes she was going to make, she would now experience success instead of failure. For Andrea, the first few months were the hardest. She started working on a cookbook that had been sitting as fragments on her desk for months. Like a set of gears that had frozen, Andrea began to set the energy of her second chakra in motion. By the end of six months, her cookbook well underway, Andrea had dropped a good twenty to twenty-five pounds.

The dynamics of the second chakra are great and varied. If not enough energy is flowing through this chakra we may invalidate our needs and desires, negate our feelings or have difficulty bringing forth our creations. When our second chakra is in balance and energy is flowing through it, we are creative, imaginative and intuitive. We are in touch with our feelings and are able identify what we want. We are also able to give of ourselves as well as receive from others.

The Third Chakra

If passion drives, let reason hold the reins.

— BENJAMIN FRANKLIN

There is only one word to describe the energetic nature of the third chakra: Power. Called Manipura in Sanskrit, the third chakra is located in the solar plexus just below the sternum and is said to vibrate at the color yellow. On the Tree of Life, the third chakra is the first energy center to appear split into two equal yet opposing parts. The two halves of this energy center rest on the two outer poles of the Tree of Life. By this representation of this energy center we are provided with a deeper understanding of its dual function. On the left, the active, positive, creative, masculine, yang aspect of this energy center is called Netzah, which occupies the seventh position on the Tree.

On the right is the passive, negative, receptive, feminine or yin aspect of this duality called Hod, which holds the eighth position on the Tree.

Physiologically, the third chakra is associated with the solar nerve plexus, the adrenal gland and the organs of digestion, where matter is converted into energy. Thus the function of the third chakra is to produce and provide energy and power for all of our endeavors. It is the fire of combustion and is responsible for all movement and activity that leads to manifestation in the physical worlds. We use this energy to satisfy the desires established in the second chakra.

There are two types of energy produced in the third chakra. One is the fire of our passions. The other is represented by our determination or will. Without either or both of these types of energy, nothing could or would be accomplished. Accomplishment and completion of goals is a critical function of the third chakra. In order to set a thought or idea into motion, energy must be applied to it. Without an initiating or propelling force on one level or another, we would be unable to get our energetic motor running and to manifest into the physical world.

Fred came to me at a health fair wanting to know when he would get a new job. When asked questions like this, the first thing I do is reframe the question by asking myself, "What's keeping Fred from manifesting a new position?" Or, "What energies are blocking him from satisfying his desire?" As I looked at his energetic body to evaluate what was thwarting him, I didn't see any needs or desires that he was seeking to satisfy by getting a new job. I didn't see the energy of desperation or survival because he was out of work. I didn't see any images of what he was trying to create or issues that he was trying to escape. In fact, I didn't see any movement at all.

Based on my observations, I asked Fred if he had done anything to further his job search such as sending out resumes or making phone calls. Based on his energy, I couldn't tell if he actually was looking for a new job or if he was just asking an outlandish question. I didn't feel as if he had put any effort into it at all. It was as if he were waiting for someone to hand him a new job or as if it would somehow be magically provided.

Fred shared with me that he hadn't done anything in his quest to secure a new job – including updating his resume – yet he had the expectation that he would find one regardless. Now, while it is possible to manifest our needs and desires without a lot of effort, there still needs to be a clear idea or goal in mind. This acts as a guiding post for our needs and desires to be manifested. Our goals give us something to work for, someplace for us to apply our energy. They provide us with a guideline we can use. They present us with a formula or a way of satisfying our desires. This was not the case with Fred.

I still shake my head when I think of Fred. It's easy to see in this case that without some energy being put into satisfying his needs and desires nothing would happen.

When we access the energy of Netzah, our inner drive takes the form of passion. When we are passionate about something, we are filled with emotional energy and are working to satisfy a desire that burns deep within us. Tasks we are passionate about seem effortless. We feel inspired, and the heat and power of our passions propel us forward. We experience this when we sit down to work on a project. While it may seem as if we have been only working for a few minutes, in truth, hours may have passed.

Sometimes our passions can lead us astray, creating an imbalance in the third chakra. We can get so caught up in the excitement of a project that we end up losing sight of the end product, the achievement, the goal, the elusive golden ring. So, while being caught up in the emotional, passionate energy of Netzah may feel wonderful, upon reflection we may find that what we were working on was not what we wanted in the first place. In hindsight, we may feel as if we had been spinning our wheels or wasting our time. We may also wonder how or why we got involved at all.

If we allow our passions to get the best of us, they can create an imbalance within our energy fields. Lust, jealousy and revenge are just a few words used to describe passionate states that, when taken to an extreme, can cause us to go over the edge. How often do we hear stories of husbands killing wives in a fit of jealous rage or stalkers who lustfully follow unsuspecting victims or angry drivers who seek revenge in a fit of road rage? Each of these expresses an imbalanced third chakra at Netzah.

The energy of Netzah, our emotional, passionate energy, is balanced by the energy of our will at Hod. Hod is the energy of our will or willpower. Goals and the completion of goals are key and critical. They are tasks of the intellect, logical and structured. Here, the mind rules over emotions. It is through the energy of Hod that we find ourselves saying, "I need to get this or that done."

For all of us, there are countless things we have to or need to do. Each of these tasks engages the power of our wills in order to complete it. Personally, when I think of this energy, balancing my checkbook and doing laundry always come to mind. They are things that I know I have to do, but there is rarely any passion or emotional energy propelling me forward to get them done.

Sometimes we identify goals that intellectually make sense but aren't what we really want, need or desire. We may find that what we are working on and the goals we have set for ourselves require us to engage all of our willpower to get them done. It is the sheer force – the unbridled energy of our will that pushes us forward, moving us toward the achievement of these tasks. We end up making ourselves work even though we may be tired, frustrated or just not enjoying it. Over time, if we continue to force ourselves to work, we can create an imbalance in the third chakra in the opposite direction.

When we use too much willpower (Hod) to get a job done and not enough passion (Netzah), we can end up feeling tired, burnt out and even depressed. Depression is an imbalance of the third chakra. It is commonly seen in individuals who have unsatisfied needs and desires. Instead of using the energy of their passions to propel them forward, they use their will and willpower to accomplish things that they have little to no desire in having or achieving. These individuals are uncertain of what their true needs are or are afraid that their need and desires are wrong. Sometimes it is discovered that these individuals are working to satisfy the needs and desires of someone else. Once they begin to satisfy their own needs or desires, their depression often lifts miraculously.

Bright and imaginative, Amy had a job doing accounting work, a position she had held for the last ten years. She started in this field just after college. She stayed with it because it was sensible, at least according to her parents. At first, this line of work seemed okay to Amy, but after a few years she was no longer feeling satisfied by her work. She rationalized to herself that it was a good job, she made good money and it would be a shame to throw it all away.

Now at thirty-two, Amy was finding that she was having a hard time getting out of bed in the morning. The level of fatigue and exhaustion she experienced was also interfering with her work. She found herself taking naps at lunch and sometimes found herself so tired that she was unable to get out of bed at all.

Amy went to her doctor, and after a series of tests, she was ultimately diagnosed as being depressed. Her doctor immediately put her on Prozac, which she took for a few days and then stopped. She didn't like the way the pills made her feel and was worried about taking a prescription medication for an extended period of time. Searching for the cause of her depression as opposed to wanting to mask it, Amy came to me for help.

When Amy first came to my office, she looked worn out and much older than a woman of thirty-two. Evaluating Amy's energy, it was easy for me to see that there was little if any passion in her life. I asked her if she also experienced the same level of fatigue and exhaustion when she took time off of work or went on vacation. She explained that after a day or so she would start to feel pretty good and be able to go out and enjoy herself, rarely needing to take a nap during the day. Soon after getting back to work, she explained, the symptoms would start up again.

Her answer validated my thoughts. Amy was having issues with her work. I didn't feel as if the issue was where she worked, but instead in the kind of work she was doing. I shared my suspicions with her, asking what really interested her – if given a choice, regardless of money, what would she really want to do? It only took a second before Amy started to excitedly tell me about her lifelong dream: to become a yoga instructor. As a child, yoga had always fascinated her. I watched years drop off her face and the light twinkle in her eyes as she shared her dream with me.

As she continued her story, she told me that her parents weren't very helpful or supportive of her dream. They didn't feel as if there could be a future in yoga instruction and suggested that she should take some business classes instead. Complying with their wishes, Amy started working in accounting and has been there ever since. It was interesting to observe Amy's energy shift back to its original state as she thought of her current work situation.

Amy was in conflict. Deep inside her body, her soul

was trying to communicate to her that she would find real joy and happiness through yoga. I explained to her that I felt the reason she was depressed was because she had been forcing herself to do something she really didn't want to do, namely accounting. It seemed obvious to me that Amy really didn't want to be an accountant. Based on false beliefs, she felt as if she had no choice but to comply. Internally, her passions were pushing her in one direction, yet she forced herself to go in the other. No wonder she was depressed.

I asked her to consider the possibility that she was acting on a belief that said, "You have to have a real job in order to be successful." Then I asked her to consider that perhaps this belief wasn't hers, but had been instilled by her parents. I then asked if she noticed how her emotions shifted when she talked about teaching yoga and how she appeared lighter, freer and more complete. She had. I strengthened my case by mentioning the fact that she always seemed to feel better when she wasn't at work. I suggested that she seriously evaluate her career and perhaps look at doing something else, something more fulfilling for her.

Amy was a very quick study. Within weeks she found a yoga school that had instructor training and immediately signed up. After attending an intensive training program, Amy contacted gyms, schools and even retirement centers in hopes of teaching classes. By the end of six months, Amy was teaching five yoga classes each week. This work provided her with enough income, and more importantly, enough confidence in herself that she quit her job. I had never seen Amy look so happy.

In addition to the energy we use internally to drive and invigorate our bodies, there is another kind of power that manifests itself in the third chakra: personal power. This is the energy we use in relation to others. As with all the chakras, energy and information should flow effortlessly and easily into and out of our energy centers. In the second chakra we talked about Givers and Takers to describe the dynamics of an imbalanced second chakra. On third chakra levels, an imbalance in this energy leaves us with what I call Controllers and their energetic counterparts, Doormats.

Controllers like to be in control all of the time. They need to be in charge. Controllers do things by force, and function by making things happen. They are leaders as opposed to followers. They set the stage and make all the rules and then try to control the outcome of every event or encounter.

From the outside, it appears as if Controllers expect to be followed. Sometimes it may seem as if what they think and feel is the only thing that could possibly be important. They use the energy of their third chakra to ensure that what *they* think should be completed or accomplished is just that, completed and accomplished.

Controlling makes Controllers feel safe. It lets them think that they can influence the outcome of events and situations in their lives, but the reality is that they do this in order to maintain control over a world that was created by their personalities. "Allowing" is not a word in their vocabulary, because if they allow, then the outcome is uncertain, and that might put a crimp into their well-contrived plans.

In Controllers, the dominant flow of energy into and out of their third chakra is in an outward direction. In Doormats, it is just the opposite. The energy into and out of their third chakra primarily flows in an inward direction or is somehow inhibited.

In health, we use our personal power to propel us forward so that we can get our needs and desires met. Doormats are unable to do this. Many times they give away their power and control of themselves and their environment to the person who wields the greatest power. They allow these individuals to dominate, choosing instead to follow. They are unable or unwilling to engage their power and risk conflict. This is what makes them feel safe.

What's interesting is, if you put two Doormats together and ask them what they want or need, they will tend either to "not know" or they will defer the question to the other person. For these individuals, deciding where to go out to dinner or what movie to see can be difficult.

On the flip side, if you put two Controllers together, watch out! With both of them trying to lead and neither of them willing to follow, conflict is sure to ensue. The simplest way to describe this dynamic is in one word: competition. Competition occurs when two people project their energy and neither is willing to receive. Competition is all about power, control and winning. In our world, this is how most wars are started. One side thinks it is right, while the other side thinks it is also right. Neither side is willing to back down and instead of resolving the issue, more energy, that is, more power is applied and the situation only escalates. In the final chapter, war erupts.

It is only when one person projects and the other receives that a balance can be maintained. To achieve balance, there will be times when we are required to lead. In the same way, there will be times where we must relinquish control and follow. This may mean that we will have to leave our ego at the door or summon up every bit of courage we can muster. As we saw in the second chakra, it is only when the give and take of energy in the third chakra is equalized that it will be balanced.

When we experience an imbalance in our third chakra, we can be depressed, angry or frustrated. We may allow others to control our lives or may be the ones trying to control. Imbalances can cause us to be demanding or workaholics or have trouble relaxing. When the third chakra is balanced, we are passionate, responsible, flexible and relaxed. It is easy for us to identify and achieve our goals. We have found our personal power. This allows us to be the controllers of our lives and our destinies.

The Fourth Chakra

> *Love's way of dealing with us is different from conscience's way. Conscience commands; love inspires. What we do out of love, we do because we want to.*
> — ARNOLD JOSEPH TOYNBEE

The fourth Chakra vibrates at the energy of compassion, balance and harmony. When we are in the energetic vibration of the fourth chakra, we can evaluate the goals we established in the third chakra and reflect on our achievements. Located in the center of the chest, this chakra is called Anahata in Sanskrit, and Tiphareth as you move up the Tree of Life to the seventh sephirah. Associated with the color green, the fourth chakra is linked to the thymus gland and the heart plexus and is often called the heart chakra or heart center.

The fourth chakra occupies a unique position within

our energetic makeup. In this point of balance, we find that there are three chakras below it and three chakras above. The primary functions of the lower three chakras revolve around our interaction with the physical world and our external self, where they focus on the satisfaction of our needs and desires and our ability to respond to external stimuli. As we move to the fourth chakra and above, our focus shifts from the physical to the mental and spiritual realms that make us whole.

The fourth chakra acts as an integrator or synthesizer, providing unity to all our parts, be they physical, emotional, mental or spiritual in nature. According to Gareth Knight, author of *A Practical Guide to Qabalistic Symbolism*, the fourth chakra can be thought of as our nucleus and the center of our being. If you look at its placement on the Tree, each sephirah, each aspect of our being is connected to Tiphareth, with the exception of Malkuth or the first chakra. Malkuth is excluded from this dynamic relationship because Malkuth exists only in the world of matter, while the other nine sephiroth exist in the world of energy.

The fourth chakra is the place in which balance and harmony can be established and maintained. It is from this central point that all life radiates, connecting all of our parts to each other. It acts as a master controller, where it provides a pathway for stress to be released. This includes not only emotional stress, but any stress that is placed upon our energetic system. It is the fourth chakra that assists us in equalizing our energy.

When we experience the balance and harmony the fourth

chakra offers, there is a sense of inner wholeness where our bodies and mind are one. When we are in wholeness, we feel as if we are one with ourselves. This wholeness can only be experienced when the different aspects of ourselves are in harmony with one another. It leaves us with a sense of integrity and a connection with our inner self. It is where we can come into contact with our deepest wishes, hopes and dreams. In this state the self, that is, our inner self or soul, can be easily identified as being separate from the ego or personality.

Some of us may experience the energy of wholeness for a brief moment or for extended periods of time. Others may never have or recognize this experience at all. Wholeness isn't achieved through money, social standing or power. These are aspects of the lower three chakras. It can only be achieved by going deep inside ourselves and opening ourselves up to experiencing our true inner nature. When we are in this state, we find ourselves in a place of inner peace, where we are able to rise above the pettiness of our egos and experience altruism, compassion and love.

When we speak of love on a fourth chakra level, it is not a sexual kind of love, but instead a love that is felt toward all things. We are able to rise above our own needs and desires and our attachment to the material and social world. We feel united with the world around us, an inseparable part of the whole.

Before we go on, I want to convey the importance of experiencing this part of yourself. It is only through the experience of being in this state that we can recognize the depth, breadth and contentment this chakra has to offer. Looking to re-experience the peace, harmony and wholeness that can be found when balance is achieved on fourth chakra levels is the reason many people choose a spiritual path or begin their spiritual journey. Below is an exercise that can be used to help you find that place within yourself.

- *To begin, first close your eyes and take a nice deep breath, inhaling through your nose and exhaling though your mouth.*
- *Take another deep breath and allow yourself as spirit to relax gently and easily into your body.*
- *From the base of your spine, at your first chakra, allow a line of energy to drop effortlessly from your first chakra down to the center of the planet.*
- *This is your grounding cord. We discussed grounding and grounding cords when we explored the first chakra.*
- *How does it feel as you reestablish your connection with the earth?*
- *Pause.*
- *As you may recall, our grounding cord acts as a release valve for the physical body, so imagine that you have opened the valve of your first chakra.*
- *Now, allow gravity to work on your behalf.*
- *Allow any unwanted or stagnant energy to flow down your grounding cord.*
- *Let go of any issues that may be going on in your life.*

Perhaps there are problems at work or at home with a spouse or a child. Let go of any stress, frustration, tension or anger you may be experiencing.
- *That's right, just let it all flow down your grounding cord in the same way water flows through a hose or down a drain.*
- *Take a nice deep breath, exhaling slowly.*
- *Pause.*
- *Now, bring your attention, your consciousness to your fourth chakra.*
- *As you may recall, the fourth chakra is located in the center of your chest.*
- *Notice what it feels like to have your energy and attention there.*
- *The fourth chakra vibrates at the color green.*
- *Draw your breath into this chakra, and observe as it is filled with green energy, the energy of self-love.*
- *Watch as your fourth chakra is filled with this healing green energy.*
- *Notice how good it feels to be able to love yourself unconditionally.*
- *Take a moment to validate how open this chakra is to the flow of energy.*
- *Pause.*
- *As we did with the first chakra, imagine that you can also open the valve to your fourth chakra.*
- *Imagine that there is a small knob or dial to the side of your fourth chakra that controls how open or closed this chakra is.*

- *Turn the knob to the right and let the flow of your life force energy increase as it flows through this center.*
- *Notice what it feels like as you allow more energy to flow through this center.*
- *Enjoy the experience of balance and harmony that is yours for the asking.*
- *Take another deep breath, allowing yourself as spirit to rest even further in your body.*
- *Pause.*
- *Take a moment and shift your attention from your body to the world around you.*
- *How are you experiencing it? Are you still feeling separate and alone? Or are you feeling connected, one with the world around you?*
- *Notice how good it feels to be connected, united, one…*
- *Allow yourself to sit in the energy of wholeness for a few minutes.*
- *Long pause.*
- *When you feel complete, bring your energy and attention back to your body.*
- *Take a nice deep breath, open your eyes and stretch out.*

Qabalistically, the sephirah Tiphareth sits on the middle pillar, the Pillar of Equilibrium. This central placement on the Tree of Life lies directly below Kether, the first sephirah. Tiphareth has been described as being the "reflection of God's will in the hearts of man." To fully understand the concepts of balance, harmony and wholeness from this perspective, it requires that we take a fresh look at the Tree of Life.

The Tree of Life is a symbol that represents the ever-changing relationships that take place within our being. This two dimensional representation of the interchange of our life force energy can only rudimentarily describe the forces and dynamics at work. If, however, we view this diagram from a slightly different perspective, it simplifies the dynamics taking place in this chakra as well as dramatically represents the complex interactions that take place within our energetic system.

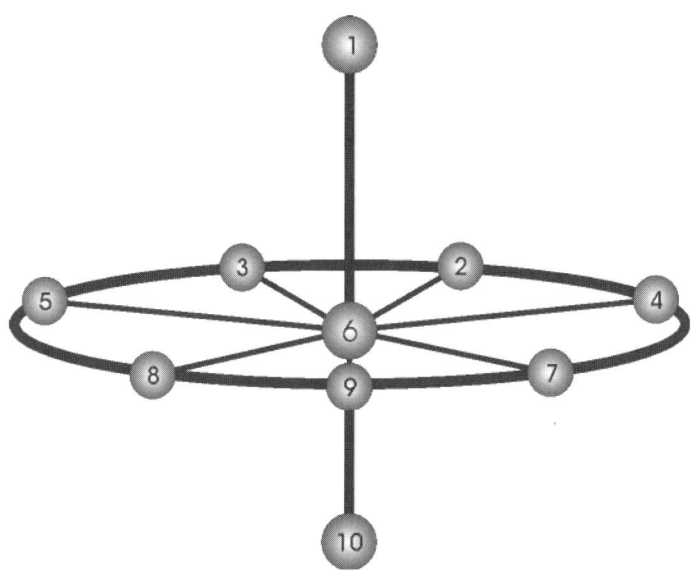

Figure 11
Illustration of Balanced Energy

Imagine the Tree of Life in the shape of a spinning top with Kether, the seventh chakra, functioning as the handle. On the opposite end Malkuth, the first chakra, functions as the tip or point of the top that touches the ground. These two points represent the flow of energy through our bodies. Next, imagine Tiphareth, the fourth chakra, resting midway between these two points. Now, circling at a right angle to the line created between Kether and Malkuth at the location of Tiphareth are the seven remaining sephiroth, with each one connecting to Tiphareth.

From this perspective it is easy to envision our life force energy coming in to our body through Kether, our seventh chakra, where it radiates out equally to all of our parts via Tiphareth, the fourth chakra, and exits the body via Malkuth, the first chakra. Harmony is maintained when all of our parts are balanced in relation to the others. We can achieve this delicate balance when we evaluate our thoughts, ideas, needs and desires in relation to our inner self, our soul. This includes our beliefs, our judgments, our needs, our desires and our fears. This delicate balance within ourselves can easily be thrown off balance, causing problems in our lives.

Prior to getting sick, Ben was the head of the computer department for a multi-billion dollar corporation. In this position, he was under constant pressure and non-stop stress, and he loved it. This was the game he loved to play, regardless of how it left him feeling physically. Ben was at the top of his game for years, but one day it all caught up with him, leaving him with a liver that was all but shut down.

It was years after Ben started down the road to recovery that I met him. He came to me to get some insights and validation regarding his work plans and choices. He was finally starting to feel better and was thinking about going back to work. Ben's energy at first glance seemed calm and mellow. I imagined this calmness was something he learned over the years he had been sick.

I was amazed at the shift his energy took as he started to talk about the kind of work he was looking to pursue, which was in essence the same type of work he had been doing in the past. This energetic shift provided me with great insight into why he had become sick in the first place and the repercussions he would experience if he chose to go down that path again.

Ben ran his life on third chakra energy. He loved what he did. His life was filled with passion and he put all of his energy into his work. At first, this worked well for Ben. His need for achievement and recognition in his workspace was satisfied and this satisfaction fueled the fires of his desires. It kept him going for years. Ben was always on top of the tasks at hand. He always knew what he needed to do in order to excel at his job and worked hard at setting and achieving goals, regardless of the personal cost.

Over time, Ben's need to achieve began to override the other needs his body tried to express. So instead of listening to what his inner self endeavored to communicate, he kept going relentlessly, ignoring the guidance offered. Ben's third chakra was out of balance. So while he may have felt tired and fatigued, he used his willpower, the energy of Hod, to force his body to maintain his frantic work pace.

As time went on, the imbalance grew and grew, yet Ben chose to continue ignoring the warnings he was receiving until one day the need for balance exerted itself into the physical world, where his liver shut down. This one act forced him to stop and rest, which was something he desperately needed.

If we chart Ben's energy based on the following illustration, it would look something like this, just prior to the emergence of his health concerns.

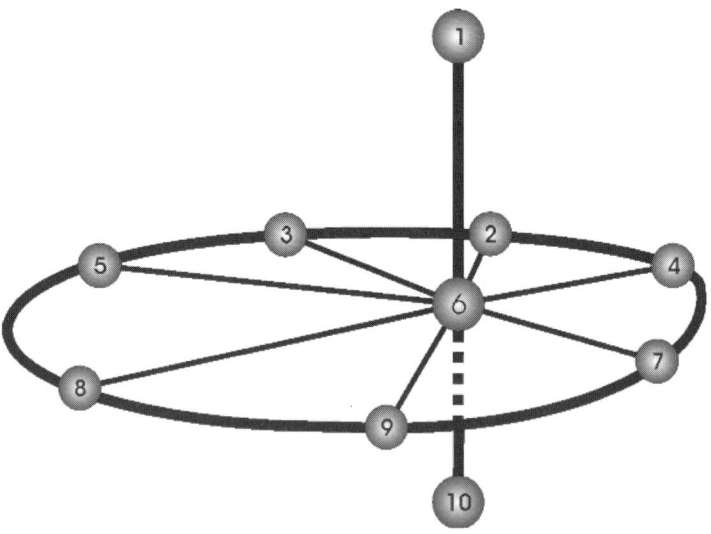

Figure 12
Illustration of Imbalanced Energy

The further out of balance Ben became, the more stress was added to his energetic makeup. From this illustration, it is easy to see how the third chakra imbalance of his life put so much pressure and stress on the overall functioning of his energetic system that something finally had to give. So while the fourth chakra didn't initiate the re-establishment of equilibrium of Ben's energy, it did provide a pathway for balance to be restored.

Needless to say, I did not recommend to Ben that he pursue the same type of work he had done in the past. It seemed clear to me that if he did, he would find himself in the same situation that had caused his health issues in the first place. In that type of environment, his third chakra would again start running amok. It would not take long before all the work he had done to restore his health would be undone. My suggestion to him was to find something that would nurture the calm, balanced, mellow person he had become through this life lesson.

We all experience moments of imbalance and disharmony in our lives. The fourth chakra, however, functions to maintain harmony on all levels. To restore inner harmony, it is important to reflect upon where we are and what we are doing. This evaluation process forces us to look into the depths of ourselves. We do this when we ask ourselves questions such as "How does this feel to me?" or "Is this right for me?" with "me" being the operative word, meaning in the depth of *myself, my soul*.

It is through this reflective process that we achieve congruence, balance and harmony. On one level, it allows us to access the Godhood within us. In addition, from the central positioning of the fourth chakra, we have access to all of our parts. From here we can check in and verify if there is harmony and agreement within all of them. If it doesn't somehow feel right, if there is a hesitation, an uncomfortable feeling associated with it, then it must not be "right" for us. If something feels good to us, to the depth of our being, we experience what I like to call the "warm and fuzzies." The warm and fuzzies are a great indicator that what we are thinking, feeling or doing is in congruence with all our parts. It is a sign that we are on the right track, because it feels good and right to us.

Here's one thing that I would like you to notice: at the fourth chakra a question is being used to access information. In the lower three chakras, this questioning or reflective process was not necessary. This is because those chakras operated based upon an input and response mechanism whereby we experienced some kind of input and our body responded. As we move into the higher chakras, we are unable to access this information directly. To jump the bridge from bodily sensations to consciousness, we need to reflect.

We reflect by asking questions of ourselves such as "How am I feeling now?" "Is this the right move for me?" or "What should I be doing now?" On fourth chakra levels, the answers we will receive will always be about what we need or what feels good or right to us.

As we begin to reflect upon how something feels to us, we are given the opportunity to recognize and validate our affinity. Affinity is our ability to love others and ourselves unconditionally. When we are in affinity with ourselves, we like ourselves. We are able to love and accept all of our parts, thus allowing us to be who we are or want to be, that is, until such time as we choose to change it.

We are in affinity with ourselves when we value our thoughts, ideas, needs and desires. This is not to say that there is no room to meet someone else's needs or desires, but when we are in affinity, we require that our needs be met as well. Like our second chakra ability to receive, when we love ourselves, we open ourselves up to having our needs met or making a conscious choice to defer them. All parents experience this as they raise their children.

Receiving is important. It isn't that we are being greedy or Takers, but instead because it works to create and maintain balance through an equal exchange of energy. In the fourth chakra we place a value on ourselves which includes our time and our energy. We also place a value on getting our needs and desires met because they are important *to us!*

I met Connie at a healing clinic where I volunteered my time. In our first session, it was easy for me to see that her energy was really scattered. Having no grounding cord, she was having problems connecting with the physical world as well as manifesting her needs and desires onto the physical plane.

At the time, I was teaching classes on how to work with our energetic bodies. One of the topics covered in class was how to ground the body, where students learned a technique similar to the one we discussed when covering the first chakra. I suggested to Connie that she come and take my class. I felt that it would help her begin the process of healing and help her bring wholeness back into her life.

She said she was unable to afford the cost of tuition. After much prodding and reassurance, I talked her into coming and taking the class anyway. It was about two years later that I again saw Connie. She stopped by a wellness fair that I organized and sponsored. After saying hello, she timidly handed me a small item wrapped with tissue paper. Opening the package, I found a refrigerator magnet in the shape of an angel. With a smile on her face, Connie told me that she thought I was an angel for letting her take the class. Though she felt it wasn't much, she had hoped it would in some way repay me for my kindness.

It is hard to describe the plethora of feelings and emotions that flooded in. With that small token, I felt that I had been repaid the cost of the class one hundredfold. With this small gesture on her part, Connie more than reciprocated the energy I had given to her. When we talk about an equal exchange of energy, it doesn't necessarily mean penny for penny, dollar for dollar, hour for hour. Instead it refers to the value it has *for us*.

Similar to affinity is the energy of compassion. Through the reflective process of the fourth chakra, we are able to stand in someone else's shoes. We are able to recognize and validate someone else's feelings and experiences. It is as if we are asking ourselves, "How would this feel if it were happening to me?" From this position we are able to match their energetic vibration and recognize how we would feel if given the same circumstances or situation. From this space, we are able to make conscious choices about what action, if any, should be taken.

Since we are no longer struggling for the power and control of the third chakra, we can consciously choose to sacrifice ourselves for the betterment of another. When we act selflessly, there is no expectation of an energetic return. There will always be times where we have to put our own needs and desires to the side. There will also be times when what we need to do may not be pleasant or comfortable. We do it, not because their needs and desires are more important than our own but because it is "the right thing to do."

If the energy flowing through our fourth chakra is imbalanced, we may feel unworthy or find ourselves worrying about others. When the fourth chakra is balanced we feel whole and one with ourselves. We are in touch with all aspects of ourselves and look to nurture others as well as ourselves. We have the ability to be empathic and compassionate and surrender ourselves in the name of doing what is right.

The Fifth Chakra

Without words to objectify and categorize our sensations and place them in relation to one another, we cannot evolve a tradition of what is real in the world.

— RUTH HUBBARD

Located in the cleft of the throat is the fifth chakra. The fifth chakra is the energy center of communication. It controls our ability to express our thoughts, ideas, feelings and emotions. It is also here that we "communicate" with our inner self and with God.

Called Visuddha in Sanskrit, this chakra is made up of the sephiroth Geburah and Chesed. Chesed sits on the positive Pillar of Mercy, while Geburah rests on the negative pillar, the Pillar of Severity. Associated with the color blue, on physiological levels the fifth chakra is related to the cervical ganglia medulla as well as the thyroid gland. Based on its physical location alone, it is no wonder that this chakra vibrates with the energy of communication.

When we think of communication, we traditionally think of our ability to use words. Our words are thoughts expressed that convey the message of our intentions. They can be thought of as a reflection or external manifestation of our inner programming. The words we use can tell a lot about how or what we think. They are a mirror of our thoughts, beliefs, judgments, assumptions and opinions. Our words can be charged with the positive energy of love, which helps us to expand and grow, or they can be charged with a negative energy, such as fear, which causes us to shrink away from who we truly are.

Our words and our speech have the power to set the energy or the direction we choose in our lives. If we say good and positive things, good and positive things (experiences) happen to us. Our words give us the opportunity to experience life from a positive or optimistic point of view. If, on the other hand, we come from negativity, saying negative things, negative things will happen to us or we will end up seeing life as one big problem or disappointment.

Our ability to communicate verbally can cause some of us difficulty. When I talk about self-expression, especially our ability to verbalize our thoughts, ideas, opinions, feelings, needs and desires, there is an underlying implication – that we are expressing ourselves to someone else. The fifth chakra houses our beliefs and belief systems. Our beliefs or our perception about an event or situation can play a significant role in our ability to communicate our feelings about it.

If we believe we are not important, then anything that we may want to say would likewise be unimportant. If we believe our communication will create a negative or adverse response in the person we would like to talk to, many times we simply choose not to say anything. When we hold back our communication with others, the flow of energy through the chakra is diminished.

Verbal communication is only one small aspect of the fifth chakra. This is the chakra of formulation or information transduction. It is here that we are able to transform our thoughts, concerns, creative ideas, opinions, feelings and even emotions into a set of symbols that we collectively understand. We then use these symbols to communicate, to share our experiences with others.

In mathematics, symbols are constantly used to express mathematical operations and variables. When we see the "=" symbol, we recognize this symbol as meaning "equal to," as in 2+2=4. Through learning, we have all come to understand its meaning and implication. The same is true when we are driving. A red light tells us symbolically to "stop," while a green light tells us to "go."

Our words are symbols as well. As we develop language skills, we learn to associate a representation of a physical item, a concept, a feeling or an emotion with a specific word or word groups. These representations are based on our direct experiences as well as on learning. When someone shares an experience with us, we take and process their words through our databank of symbols. Through this set of symbols we are able to recreate their experience within ourselves.

This inner recreation of their experience, however, is based upon our knowledge, judgments, fears, needs and desires. In the sixth chakra we house our ability to visualize. In order to communicate a visual image such as a memory to someone else, it has to be transformed into a set of symbols – in this instance, words. Let's say, for example, that I want to buy a new car. I can see the image of my perfect car in my mind's eye. If I were to describe this car based on my knowledge, understanding and experience, I would say that it was a small car that has a V-8 engine. This car is a two-seater and red in color.

Could you guess what kind of car I wanted based on my description? In my mind, I know exactly what kind of car it is. There is, however a specific word that elicits a total understanding of the kind of car I want. If I told you that I wanted a red Mercedes Benz 450SL, would an image of this car come to your mind immediately? Perhaps you have seen Mercedes Benzes in the past. Maybe a friend or a relative owned one or you just remember seeing one driving down the road or in a television commercial. However, if I said I wanted a Corvette or a Porsche, would the image in your mind's eye change? With each of these symbols I am able to communicate completely different things, even though they are still small two-seater cars, in red.

Communication can take the form of more than just words. We can also express ourselves through modalities such as art, music and dance. In the picture *Starry, Starry Night* by Vincent Van Gogh we get to share his impression of a star-filled evening. In the hula, the traditional dance of Hawaii, complex stories and myths are shared via the dancers' rhythmic movements. When we hear our national anthem, the bravery and heroism of our forefathers is recalled.

On fifth chakra levels, we also have another voice that we work and interact with daily. This is our inner voice. Although we may at first ask, "What inner voice?" we are all familiar with its subtle promptings. Our inner voice is often confused with the ramblings of our conscious mind. However, it's not the nonstop conversation that goes on in our heads all day long and sometimes well into the night.

Instead, our inner voice speaks to us in small utterances that come from deep within. The role of our inner voice is to provide us with guidance along the path we call life. Whether we know it or not, we are always being provided with guidance by which to live our lives. It is here that God communicates with us through the functioning of the causal body and the souls. This communication works to guide us down a path of health, harmony and balance.

In metaphysical terms, the communication of our inner voice is often called *clairaudience*. The promptings of our inner voice can be soft and delicate, gently reminding us to pay a bill or call a friend. Other times our inner voice can be more insistent, where it may seem as if it is nagging us, reminding us over and over of some unfinished business for days, weeks or even years.

In Qabalistic terms, the fifth chakra, in the form of Chesed and Geburah, provides us with two different types of inner communication. The first is our ability to communicate with God, which is the function of Chesed. The other is there to let us know when we are out of balance. This is the function of Geburah. Let's take a moment to look at each of these.

Chesed, the fourth sephirah, sits on the Pillar of Mercy. Positive in nature, the operative words used when describing the action of Chesed are *obedience* or *surrender*: that is, surrender to the will of God. We do this by listening. Geburah, on the other hand, sits on the Pillar of Severity in the fifth position. Negative in nature, its actions are those of adjustment and assessment, and it is the bringer of unmitigated truth.

Chesed is the open door of possibilities, for under God, everything is possible. It is the energy of brainstorming, the creation of options and configurations of an idea. Geburah is the side of us that says this is what we can do or achieve from a realistic, reflective perspective. It works to warn us and keep us in our integrity. It defines our limits.

When I think of the actions of Chesed and Geburah, I always think of Evelyn. I have known Evelyn for the past two years. We see each other regularly and often spend time visiting and sharing the exploits of our day. Although she is not a client, she does provide a perfect example of how God works to communicate to us even if we choose not to listen. This is what I have observed.

Evelyn smokes two or three packs of cigarettes a day. God in Chesed says to Evelyn, "You need to quit smoking." Evelyn, as she takes another drag off of her cigarette, says "You know, I really need to quit these things." Days and weeks go by, giving her the time and opportunity to quit. Does she? No.

So God in Geburah says, "Hmmm ... I guess you didn't get my message," and Evelyn starts having coughing fits, fits so severe that she pulls the muscles in her sides, causing her problems when walking, sitting and even breathing. In her discomfort, Evelyn, working through the energy of Geburah, asks for guidance. "What's causing me to have this pain?" The answer she receives, via Chesed, is, "It's the cigarettes. You really need to quit smoking." In turn, Evelyn says, "You know, I think my smoking is somehow related to these coughing fits. I really need to quit."

Again, she is given the time and opportunity to listen/obey/surrender to the will of God, but she doesn't. So God, in Geburah, says again, "Still didn't get my message?" and Evelyn starts to cough up phlegm mixed with blood. Now she is really frightened that something is truly wrong. In this moment of reflection God, via Chesed, again tells her, "You need to quit smoking." Like clockwork, Evelyn turns around and says, "You know, I really need to quit smoking." Does she quit? No. Oh, she cuts back on the number of cigarettes she is smoking, that is, until she stops coughing up blood, but then she is right back to smoking two to three packs a day.

What will happen to Evelyn is anybody's guess. In the end, only Evelyn can choose her fate.

It is thought that all disease experienced in the world today originated in the same way – because we have deviated from God's will. Not only physical or mental illness, but anything that pulls us out of the state of balance found in the fourth chakra. Greed, war, pollution, abuse, judgment, racism, pride, arrogance – all are the outcome of man deviating from God's will.

In the end, our inner self must ask and seek advice. So, as in the fourth chakra, we must take the time to request guidance and reflect. As it is said, "If you ask a question, you always get an answer." Through Chesed, an answer is always delivered. This answer is always the will of God. God will always provide us with answers to our deepest questions and concerns, even if they are not what we want to hear.

Man, above all other species in the animal kingdom, has been blessed or perhaps cursed with the ability to choose, so as with any kind of advice, we can choose to listen or not. We can make up our own minds, ethically and morally, leaving us personally responsible for the path we follow.

When studying the Book of Genesis, biblical scholars have alluded to the fact that in eating from the tree of knowledge Adam and Eve were the first to deviate from the will of God. They chose to eat the forbidden fruit and with it lost paradise. It was their regrettable choice, their arrogant decision not listen to the will of God that caused the fall of man, from which we are still recovering. Regardless of the truth or accuracy of the story of Adam and Eve, their fate is a classic example of what happens when we deviate from God's will.

The choice is always ours. We can choose to listen, aligning our will with the will of God, and experience harmony in our lives, or we can choose not to. We can go into denial or simply ignore the advice given. We can choose to do whatever we want regardless of the outcome to others and ourselves. We can allow our power, authority, bigotry, hypocrisy or fear to pull us away from our center and leave us unbalanced.

It is here that we encounter the work of Geburah. Its action can be thought of as a kind of spiritual steering. That is, when we are out of balance, when we are deviating from the will of God, God will always send us subtle prompts to help guide us back on track. The further we deviate, the louder the promptings become. If we still choose not to pay attention, we will ultimately manifest something into our lives that will grab our attention and hopefully help us to choose to change. When we don't pay attention, we put stress on our energetic system until it reaches a point where our need for balance exerts itself and looks to be restored. This restoration of balance can be done the easy way or the hard way.

Our spiritual steering can be likened to driving a car. Imagine you are driving your car down a busy interstate or expressway. You are not paying attention and your car starts to veer off in the direction of oncoming traffic. If your attention is returned to your driving quickly, the correction you would need to make may be insignificant. If, however, you choose to not pay attention, your car may continue veering off to the side, right over the double yellow lines, leaving you driving right into oncoming traffic. The amount of correction required to get you back into your lane would be much greater than before. If a correction isn't made at this point, and your attention still isn't on the road, it may be only a matter of time before you collide with oncoming traffic.

Geburah is the bringer of Karma. It operates based on the laws of cause and effect and works to keep balance. In physics, the third law of motion states: For every action, there is an equal and opposite reaction. Karma can be thought of in the same way. When we experience Karma, it is not because we are good or bad. Karma is an impersonal energy dynamic that works to help restore balance.

Michael Star, in his article *What is Karma*, describes it as the following: "Karma is just the consequences of old choices – old beliefs and old attitudes, which unconsciously create and recreate similar consequences, until we become conscious of them and choose to change them." The actions of Karma are not meant to punish us; rather, they are there to provide us with an opportunity to make changes in our lives by correcting old mistakes. They work to break down our old negative thought patterns and break up any resistance we are experiencing. Karma acts as a persistent reminder. It challenges us to reevaluate our truths and will keep reminding us until it becomes too painful not to.

Personally, I like to think of the actions of Geburah as the cosmic 2×4. We can always choose to not listen, but it is only a matter of time before we get the proverbial 2×4 up the side of the head. For some, this can be a big wakeup call. For others, it's not. If we choose to continue not listening, the amount of energy needed to correct the deviation escalates. It is as if we have been knocked down into the street and someone comes by and kicks us. And if that weren't enough, just wait, because here comes a car down the street that runs our tired, bruised and humiliated body down. It is usually at this point that even the most stubborn of us surrender to the will of God – well, at least for a while.

To be perfectly honest, learning to listen and obey the will of God was not an easy thing for me to do. It took many lessons for me to finally stop and pay attention to what I was being directed to do. My life had been like a roller coaster with no one at the wheel. It wasn't until I began to listen that things started to change. It didn't happen at once, but over years of trial and error. I suppose I was pretty stubborn, but eventually I figured it out.

It was only recently that I had an experience that, for me, fully validated the importance of listening to my inner voice. It started about four months earlier after I'd had a flat tire and began driving my car on the spare. Now you have to understand, my spare tire is full-sized and not one of those mini-tires, but the rim that I used for my spare was out of round, so it made the front end of my car wobble a little.

As you have probably already surmised, I didn't fix the punctured tire right away. I knew I would have to get to it eventually but it wasn't a priority. One thing I did notice was that every time I drove the car, my inner voice would say to me, "You need to change the tire." Needless to say I didn't listen.

Four months went by and I still had done nothing. Until one bright Saturday morning, I was driving to a breakfast meeting when my inner voice, instead of reminding me gently as it had been, demanded, "*You need to get a new tire, NOW!*" The voice was so loud, so adamant, that I said to myself with conviction, "You know what, I think I'm going to get a new tire today!"

You would think the story would end here, but it doesn't. The meeting ended and I got in my car and headed home. Naturally, I drove slowly – I needed a new tire and didn't really want fate to take its toll just then. As I pulled down the street I lived on and got closer to my driveway I noticed the left rear of my husband's car was up on a jack. He had a flat tire.

I thought that perhaps the message I received that morning wasn't really for me. I rationalized that I must have been picking on up the fact that he had gotten a flat tire. (Isn't denial grand?) Since my husband's spare was also flat, we had no choice but to go purchase at least one new tire, so I figured I might as well get a replacement tire as well.

Ah, but the story continues. The next day, I went to visit a friend who lived about seventy miles away. Taking a shortcut in hopes that I would get there more quickly, I ended up overshooting her house by about thirty miles. As I headed back down the freeway I came upon four 18-wheeler trucks that rode behind each other as if in a procession. In a hurry and unsure of where I was, I decided to pass the row of trucks. Moving into the fast lane and working my way down the line of vehicles, I felt as if there were something wrong with the steering of my car. It felt very stiff. I decided that once I passed the trucks, I would pull over and see what was going on.

Exiting the freeway, I pulled into a gas station that was just off the road. I stepped out of my car and immediately looked at my new tire. It was fine. Walking around the car, I quickly found out what the problem was. My other front tire was flat.

To this day, I am so grateful that I had listened. Within minutes, a man stopped and volunteered to change my tire. The part of this story that enamors me the most is the fact that, had I not listened, had I not paid attention and fixed my one tire, I would have been stuck out in the middle of nowhere, 100 miles away from home without a spare. As I drove away, I could only imagine the trouble and inconvenience I would have experienced had that been the case.

As well as being the bringer of Justice, Geburah is also the bringer of Truth. When we reflect upon our lives, the information provided through the action of Geburah will always be an honest assessment of where we are and where we need to go. It can be used to help rid us of our failings, identify thoughts and beliefs that are no longer working for us and help us to identify a new plan of attack. It is only when we can accept the good and the bad parts of ourselves that we can begin to experience balance. We do this by getting rid of useless mental and spiritual programming, which then allows us to become our authentic selves.

As we work to become our authentic selves, situations are presented to us that test our ability to listen to the guidance being provided. It is like taking a final exam of lessons learned. If we pass the test, we can move on. If we fail the test, we get to experience the pain and frustration over and over until the lesson is finally learned.

These tests are given to see if we truly understand. These tests can be seen as carrots that are dangled out in front of us to see if we will bite. The carrots represent those things that can cause us to deviate from the will of God. The carrots can appear to be so wonderful, so enticing, so tempting that many times it is hard to say no. The lure can be money, power or prestige. These things are often the hardest for us to pass up. But be wary: if your inner voice is directing you to follow a specific path and you choose not to follow, take heed or pay the price.

One last topic to be addressed when talking about the fifth chakra is the concept of telepathy. Telepathy is our ability to communicate with each other on nonverbal levels. As we discussed earlier, our chakras transmit, receive and assimilate information from the world around us. The fifth chakra is no different. The concept of telepathy suggests that we radiate what we think and feel as well as have the capability to sense the thoughts and feelings of others.

We most often recognize our ability to receive information on telepathic levels in situations of crisis where we may know something is wrong. This is especially true among family members. The reality is that we all receive information this way. This is seen when we are thinking about our friend Mary and shortly after Mary calls us on the phone. We use this ability when we finish each other's sentences or know what someone is going to say before they utter a word.

My husband and I often have moments such as this. There have been countless occasions when I have tried to call him on the telephone and I would get a busy signal, to subsequently discover that he had been on the phone trying to call me. We often laugh as we try to figure out who had the idea first.

When the fifth chakra is balanced, we can experience divine energy and insights because we listen and surrender to the will of God. These insights may provide us with the opportunity to change the course of our actions or help us to better know others. We are able to express ourselves and may be good speakers or musically or artistically inclined. If there is an imbalance in this chakra, we may be timid or shy or have difficulty expressing our thoughts and ideas. By contrast, an imbalance in the fifth chakra may cause us to be arrogant, self-righteous or opinionated, whereby we let our mind overrule the promptings God or our soul is providing for us.

The Sixth Chakra

We go where our vision is.

— Joseph Murphy

The primary mode of the sixth chakra is that of sight and insight. Physiologically, the sixth chakra is associated with the pineal gland and the hypothalamus/pituitary nerve plexus. Associated with the color indigo, the sixth chakra is located in the center of the forehead and is often referred to as "the third eye." Called Ajna in Sanskrit, the sixth chakra is the last of the major chakras that are represented by two distinct energy centers on the Tree of Life. Called Chokmah and Binah, which correspond to the second and third sephiroth respectively, these sephiroth represent the movement of energy as it begins to crystallize and take form.

Chokmah is unbridled energy and unlimited potential. It has no form. It is energy that has just entered into the realm of manifestation. It is where we first recognize our energy as being different and separate from God's. It is often thought of as the origin of consciousness or as self-consciousness itself.

Binah, on the other hand, binds the free flowing energy of Chokmah and limits it. Limitation helps us to differentiate ourselves from the collective energy of which we are a part. It is critical for the creation of discrete entities. We experience limitations on spiritual, mental, emotional and even on physical levels. They make us unique and distinctive, with our own thoughts, wants, needs, desires, opinions, strengths and weaknesses. These limitations control the direction and focus of our lives and form the basis and foundation of our life path and life experiences.

It is through limitation that form is created. Limitation gives shape to energy in order for us to see it and comprehend it. In fact, the sixth chakra provides us with the ability to access perceptual information directly. It allows us to see visual images in our mind's eye. These include images brought up from our memories, our imagination and our ability to visualize.

From here, we can see things as they really are, that is, if we choose. We are beyond the judgment, prejudice and programming found in the fifth chakra. From here we can view things neutrally and objectively. Visual information is nonlinear in nature. It just is. In order for it to be expressed, it has to be translated or interpreted so that we can communicate or express it to others. This is the function of the fifth chakra.

Our ability to receive and process information on sixth chakra levels is called *clairvoyance*. Clairvoyance means "clear seeing" or "clear vision." Clairvoyance suggests that we are receiving mental images in the same way we receive information from the other chakras. The only difference is that this information comes to us in visual terms.

When I was twelve years old, there was a television program called *The Sixth Sense*. This was not the recent movie that starred Bruce Willis about a child who saw dead people. *The Sixth Sense* was a weekly whodunit that starred Gary Collins as Dr. Michael Rhodes. Dr. Rhodes was a college professor who was interested in paranormal phenomena and investigated mysteries involving extrasensory perception, spirits, possessions and other paranormal topics. The show was like *Murder, She Wrote* with a psychic twist. The best part of the show was that, in addition to studying this phenomenon, Rhodes had extrasensory perception (ESP) and, with this ability, worked as a psychic detective solving crimes.

During a typical episode, someone would die of mysterious causes and Dr. Rhodes would be called in to help solve the mystery. As Dr. Rhodes worked to resolve the predicament of that particular episode, many times he would walk into a room and have a clairvoyant experience where he would see the ethereal image of Mr. Green, the recently deceased, float across the room. Mr. Green would then provide the good doctor with a clue or the location of an additional piece of evidence.

Other times he would pick up an item like a piece of paper or a drinking glass, and have a precognitive flash where he'd see the image of one of the episode's main characters drive a car off a cliff. Running out in just the nick of time, he would use this information and stop the impending catastrophe before it happened. Invariably, the character would be prevented from driving off, discovering that the brake lines had been cut.

From that point forward in my life, I wanted to be clairvoyant. I wanted to have visions just like he had. I read books and studied trying to get to the point in which I too could do what he did. I anxiously waited for years to see something float across the room as it provided me with a deep insight or an answer to my question. Well, that never happened.

It wasn't until years later that I discovered the truth regarding our ability to see things on clairvoyant levels. Limited by the constraints of filmmaking at that time, the show's producer portrayed Dr. Rhodes' intuitive insights as appearing in this world as if they were visible to the naked eye. Now, while the show did wonders to promote the idea of clairvoyance and ESP, it also presented its viewers with an inaccurate expectation of what a clairvoyant experience is.

It is a common misconception that clairvoyant experiences occur with the physical eyes. The reality is that when we see things on clairvoyant levels, we see things on our internal movie screen in our mind's eye. For example, as you read these words, can you bring into your visual awareness an image of your home or apartment? Can you visualize your mother or father? What about the first person you kissed or had a romantic relationship with? This is the type of inner seeing we do on sixth chakra levels. Most people are able to conjure up these images easily and effortlessly and many times with surprising detail.

Many people don't trust the information they receive on this level and often dismiss clairvoyant insights as being the work of their imagination. As we learned in the fourth and fifth chakras, if you ask a question, you will always be provided with an answer. Here too, the question is the key. If you don't ask, you can find yourself waiting for hours for something to happen. So again, instead of words that we may receive on fifth chakra levels or the warm and fuzzy feeling we get in the fourth, the answers provided by the sixth chakra are always in the form of pictures or visual images. The visual images obtained on sixth chakra levels are always there for you and it is important to learn to trust the information you receive.

The questions we ask to access our intuitive information play a pivotal role in the answer we receive. While we don't need to ask a yes or no question, our questions must be clear and concise. Even a small change in the intention of our question can leave us with very different answers. Let me share a story to further clarify this.

A few years ago I was teaching a class on intuition development. During the class we explored the use of gauges.

Gauges are an easy way to access information on clairvoyant levels. If you ask a question, you always get an answer, so when you work with gauges, questions need to be phrased in terms that will provide a numeric response.

Individualized questions were given to the group regarding different members of the class. The class members were given the opportunity to utilize their intuitive gauges to provide their fellow classmates with their insights.

The question asked on behalf of one of my students was, "Expressed in a percentage, how open is she to a new relationship?" Going around the room, all but one of my students identified that she was about 10 to 20% open to a new relationship. The remaining student stated that the answer she received was 70%. I found it interesting that out of the entire class there was only one person that received a different number, so I decided to find out why.

As we began to discuss this response, it became clear that the question she internalized was not "What percentage is she open to a new relationship?" but instead, "How much does she want a new relationship?" This small change in her question provided her with a completely different response.

When the revised question was posed to the class, the entire class validated that she "wanted" a new relationship. The subject of the question also verified this fact she wanted a relationship. When asked if she was "open" to having the relationship, she quickly stated that relationships were a pain and while she wanted one, she was really enjoying the freedom and independence that being single offered her.

At times we can put in a lot of effort in trying to get

an answer. This can occur on any chakra level, not only the sixth. Many times these attempts meet with failure. It can be likened to when we are trying to think of someone's name – it may be on the tip of our tongue but we just can't recall it. Often it is not until a few hours later, when we are no longer making an effort, that we are able to remember.

When we go into effort, we are slowing down our life force energy. We are creating an imbalance within ourselves. To be specific, we are creating a third chakra imbalance because we are putting our willpower into trying to *make* something happen. The harder we try, the less it works; the less it works, the more effort we put into it and so on. In the end, instead of receiving insights, we get frustrated. This never-ending do-loop will continue until we step away from the situation, quiet our minds and regain balance.

Many times it is difficult for us to quiet the incessant chatter of our conscious mind so that we can think and see clearly. We've all had the experience of lying in bed trying to sleep, but instead of sleeping, our minds are racing instead. Perhaps we're trying to resolve a problem at work where we keep reviewing what needs to be done and trying to come up with a solution. Perhaps we've had a disagreement with a friend or loved one and we find ourselves reviewing over and over what happened in a futile effort to relieve the hurt, pain or humiliation. As we work to create and establish balance, wholeness and harmony within ourselves, it is helpful to quiet the ongoing conversations of the conscious mind so we can allow the subtle promptings of spirit to emerge. This can be achieved through meditation.

When some people think of meditation, they envision an image of a guru sitting with his legs crossed, palms up, chanting. Others conjure up images of transcendental meditation where participants work to clear their minds of all thought. While there is truth to both of these images, neither reflects the true intent of meditation. The purpose of meditation is to focus the mind on a singular thought or action. This helps to get our energy moving and flowing through our bodies. It allows us, devoid of ego, expectation and desire, simply to be, to exist.

Take a moment to think about what you have going on in your life right now that requires your energy and attention at least on some level. How many projects do you have going on at work or at home? Even if you are not working on the project currently, do you think about it, dream about it? This also requires your energy. What about children, friends and family that require your time and attention? If you made a pie chart of all of the things you are concentrating on, how many pieces would be in the pie? For many of us, ten, twelve or twenty would not be out of line.

On a sixth chakra level, we create little energy bubbles to hold onto or encapsulate the energy or image of each of these projects. We carry them in our aura, especially around our heads so that we can look at them and check in on them. Depending on what is going on, we may check in on them daily or weekly, but if one is really important we may check in on it constantly.

As we move our energy from project to project, it gets

spread out thinner and thinner, leaving very little of it for us. Meditation helps us to bring our energy back into focus. Meditation will not cause us to drop the projects we are working on. Rather, it will help us to utilize our energy better so that we are able to focus on each project more directly.

Meditation can take two major forms, active and passive. Most people are familiar with passive meditation, in which practitioners work to clear their minds of all unnecessary thought. Some use the repetition of a tone such as OM or a mantra to assist them. A mantra may include prayers used in the Christian faith, especially the saying of the rosary.

Active meditation takes on a whole different flavor. Many of us actively meditate but don't realize it. Gardening, sweeping and other rote tasks can all work to help us focus our mind, energy and intention on one thing, one goal. The same holds true for dancing, exercising, yoga and Tai Chi. The important concept here is the focusing of intention. In that aspect, creating artwork, doing healing or energy work or designing a new widget will all help you to find and be in "the groove."

Here is an exercise you can use to eliminate the endless chatter that is goes on in your head. The easiest way I have found to soothe your mind is to create what I call a Sacred Space. This exercise is from my book entitled *The Power Within*. Your Sacred Space is where you can be at peace and neutrality within yourself. It can be visualized as a mountain retreat, a bungalow out in the woods, or even as a glass or crystal cathedral. Allow your imagination to take you to the place that is yours alone and no one else's.

- *Close your eyes.*
- *To begin, let go of your old grounding cord and allow it to fall to the center of the planet. (We discussed how to make a grounding cord when we explored the first chakra.)*
- *Now, let's create a brand new one right here, right now, in present time.*
- *Beginning at the base of your spine, at your first chakra, release a new grounding cord that goes all the way down to the center of the planet and anchor it there.*
- *There are many different types of grounding cords that will work for you.*
- *Check and see what you are using for a grounding cord this time.*
- *Are you still using a Redwood tree or are you using a chain and anchor? Maybe it's time to try a new one.*
- *Maybe a waterfall or clear glass tube or even a feather boa.*
- *It may also be time to make your grounding cord bigger.*
- *Take a deep breath.*
- *Go ahead and let your grounding cord do its job. You don't have to do anything. No effort. It just drains the energy you don't want out of you.*
- *Take this time to allow your body to release any unwanted energy.*

- You don't have to worry about what you have to get done right now.
- Let go of those problems you are trying to solve.
- Notice if there is some pain or discomfort in your body. Are you carrying it around with you every day?
- Right now, at this moment, let it go.
- That's right; drop it down your grounding cord. You don't need it.
- In this moment, you don't have any problems; you're giving to yourself.
- This is your time for you.
- Bring your energy and attention to a point behind the third eye or sixth chakra.
- This is where we are going to create your Sacred Space. Be in the center of your head right now.
- If you have trouble finding that spot, put the index finger of one hand on your forehead and the other index finger at the back of your skull. Draw an imaginary line between your two fingers. Then move those fingers to the sides of your temples and draw an imaginary line there also. Where the two lines intersect is the center of your head.
- This is where you want to be. Bring your energy and attention to this spot.
- Go ahead and be there. This is your place of peace and neutrality.
- To create your Sacred Space, first visualize an indoor location.

- Say hello to this space.
- Is there a sofa, chair or ottoman in your space or is it filled with pillows and cushions?
- Look around and see what is in your Sacred Space.
- Is your space decorated?
- What color are the walls?
- Are there knick-knacks on the furniture?
- Does your space have windows and a door?
- Is there a fireplace with a roaring fire or is the sun shining in, filling your space with warmth and a golden light?
- Say hello to your sacred space.
- Now, on the floor, in the far left-hand corner of your Sacred Space, notice the trap door.
- Open the trap door.
- Create a grounding cord that goes from the trap door opening all the way down to the center of the planet.
- You've just created a grounding cord for your Sacred Space.
- Pretend you are reaching into your back pocket and pulling out a large plastic trash bag.
- Slowly and carefully look in each direction of your Sacred Space.
- Do you see any papers, empty soda cans, junk food or candy wrappers lying around?
- Place these items into the plastic trash bag.
- Is your bag getting full?
- When the trash bag is filled up, close it and toss it into

- the trap door and allow it to go down your grounding cord.
- Reach into your back pocket and pull out a new trash bag.
- Go around your Sacred Space and pick up Christmas wrapping paper, old toys or clothes that don't fit anymore and throw them into the bag.
- You may also notice items given to you by other people. If you don't want them in your space, throw them into the bag. It's up to you.
- Again, check your bag to see if it's getting full.
- Use as many bags as is required for you to pick up all the garbage, tossing the full bags into the trap door and down the grounding cord.
- Notice how it feels to have all of the garbage picked up from your sacred space.
- Take a deep breath.
- Once the garbage is all picked up, reach into your back pocket and pull out a feather duster.
- Go around the room and dust your space. Dust the walls, lamps, knick-knacks, and any furniture that is in your space.
- If you would like, wash out your space with soap and water.
- Polish the furniture and clean the windows, if you think they need it.
- It's your space and you have the right and ability to clean it in any way you want.

- *Create any tool that will assist you with this process.*
- *Now that the walls and furniture in your space are sparkling clean, pull out a broom, and sweep the floor of your space, or use a vacuum cleaner. If your sacred space is outdoors, you might want to use a rake or even a backhoe.*
- *Sweep the dust into the trap door and down the grounding cord.*
- *How does your space feel now?*
- *Does it feel cleaner, more refreshing?*
- *Is it easier being in this space than it was before?*
- *Go ahead and take another deep breath.*
- *Take another moment to look around your Sacred Space.*
- *Do you have any company?*
- *If so, say, "Hello, I see you," and then move them out of your head.*
- *Show them the way to the trap door.*
- *Ask them to leave or gently push them through and down your grounding cord.*
- *Just do it.*
- *No problems, no effort – this is your head.*
- *Is your mother or father there?*
- *What about sisters or brothers or close personal friends or business associates?*
- *How about your dog, cat or other pet?*
- *Carefully look around your room, behind the furniture, under knick-knacks and even in the closet.*

The Sixth Chakra / 205

- *That's right. Whoever you find, show them the way to the trap door.*
- *Assure them that they will be okay and no harm will come to them, but tell them this is your space and you are not interested in sharing it with them.*
- *Close the trap door and hang a "Do not enter" sign on any other doors in your space.*
- *Take a deep breath and exhale.*
- *Find a comfortable place to sit in your Sacred Space.*
- *Look around.*
- *You have created this space for yourself.*
- *Notice how your body feels now that you've cleaned out this space.*
- *Does it feel as if there is more room for you to be in?*
- *Enjoy being in this safe, Sacred Space for five minutes.*
- *This is your Sacred Space.*
- *Before ending this exercise, let's take a moment to call back some more energy.*
- *Visualize a ball of golden white light over your head.*
- *Summon your energy back from where you have left it in your past, from the things or individuals you found in your Sacred Space.*
- *Watch as your energy comes back to you, causing the ball of golden white light to get bigger.*
- *Reach up and poke a hole in the sphere, allowing your energy to cascade down and around your body.*
- *Pretend that you can breathe your energy in through your sixth chakra.*

- *Notice how good if feels to have your own energy recharging your Sacred Space.*
- *When your body feels full, vital and refreshed, bend over and stretch out your body, opening your eyes when you feel comfortable.*

Before you move on, take a moment and ask yourself the following questions:

- *What did your Sacred Space look like?*
- *What kind of things did you find in your Sacred Space?*
- *Were there many people in your Sacred Space?*
- *How did your body feel as you cleaned out your Sacred Space?*

Imbalances in the sixth chakra can leave us feeling uncertain, or lacking clarity in what we want to do in our lives. They can leave us judgmental, proud, arrogant or egotistical. When the sixth chakra is balanced, we are open to receiving guidance and vision for our place and role in society. We are able to come from a place of balance, harmony and neutrality because we are no longer attached to material things or outcomes. In this space we are able to see things for how they truly are versus how we think they should be.

The Seventh Chakra

> *Inspiration may be a form of superconsciousness, or perhaps of subconsciousness – I wouldn't know. But I am sure it is the antithesis of self-consciousness.*
> — AARON COPLAND

Ending our journey through the chakras, we come the last of the major chakras, the seventh or crown chakra. Located on the top of the head, this chakra is often associated with the soft spot found on the heads of newborns. Occupying the first sephirah on the Tree of Life, this energy center is called Kether in Qabalistic literature and Suhasrar in Sanskrit. The seventh chakra is the seat of wisdom and enlightenment and is associated with the color purple, the fastest vibrating color of the visible light spectrum. Physiologically it is linked to the pineal gland, the cerebral cortex and the central nervous system.

The seventh chakra is the point where all life wells up from the energy of pure existence. It is the gate between all that is yet to manifest and the physical world. Energy that exists prior to its formation at the seventh chakra is described in Qabalistic literature as existing beyond the "veil of negative existence." It is important to recognize the preceding energy because all things come from the energy of infinite potential, or God. This energy is not limited by time or space. It is believed that the energy that exists beyond the veil is so vast it cannot be described because it is beyond the reaches of the rational mind.

The veil of negative existence condenses at Kether, the seventh chakra. The energy that flows through the seventh chakra can be thought of as the seed from which all life sprang into existence. The outflowing and indrawn breath represents this initiating force as do the concepts of birth and death. It is believed that this is the point from which all things begin and to which, in the end, all things return.

This boundless, limitless energy flows in through the seventh chakra and through the body via the Sushumna to the first chakra where it is output or grounded. The connection to our power source is critical because without it, we would be nothing. It can be thought of as the battery that provides the body with electricity, which in turn causes our energetic current to flow. It is the flow of this energy that animates us and energizes the chakras, filling us with a never-ending supply of life force energy.

In the first chakra we discussed the importance of having a grounding cord. It was through our grounding that we manifest onto the physical plane and into the physical world. Likewise, at the seventh chakra, there is a nadi that extends outward up and over our head that connects us to this unlimited power source. The nadi works to channel energy and information into the subtle body.

Through the seventh chakra we tune in to our divine consciousness, our higher self, the cosmic conscious or God. When we connect with the flow of this energy, we feel inspired. Information provided on seventh chakra levels is always abstract and without form. If you think about it, it is only one step away from nonexistence. It takes the unfettered energy of potential and transforms and consolidates it into a new vibration, the vibration of "I am."

It is difficult to describe the energy and function of the seventh chakra. Descriptions are often based upon its relation to the sixth chakra or the sephiroth Binah and Chokmah. This is because it is beyond all of our physical senses as well as our thoughts, beliefs and ideas. By the time we are able to form a mental image of the inspiration provided by the seventh chakra, the energy has already moved into the sixth chakra where an image of it can be formed.

Information that we recieve on seventh chakra levels is called *knowingness*. Knowingness is often thought of as an intuitive ability. It implies that we just know something, even though we don't know how we know. Inventors, scientists and engineers often have a strong sense of knowingness. In fact, this ability is often very strong in men. This is not to say that women are deficient in this area, but rather that men tend to ignore or invalidate the energy and information that flows through their other chakras. In general, women are more open to their feelings, they tend to trust their intuition and listen to their inner voice. Men are often less aware of these other energetic vibrations. To compensate for this imbalance, men tend to utilize their sense of knowingness to make up for the discrepancy.

When we experience knowingness, it is as if we know something right off the top of our heads. We don't know how we know, but we do. We experience it when we wake up in the middle of the night with the answer to a problem or when we know how to do something or achieve a goal even though we don't have any experience in that area.

I have come to recognize that the energy that flows through the seventh chakra is pure energy, unrestricted and unfiltered. Based on my experiences, I have found that my knowingness is directly connected to my fifth chakra because what comes in through the seventh inevitably exits my mouth.

I first noticed the flow of this energy many years ago when I was working at an electronics company as a drafter. In the office next door was a technician who was about my age and his boss, who was "older." He must have been all of forty-five years old. I didn't interact with my friend's manager very much. We would say hi and exchange pleasantries but that was the extent of our relationship.

One day, the manager didn't come in to work, which was very unusual for him. The following day, when I stopped by to say good morning to my friend, I saw that his manager was back at work. Walking over to him, I noticed that he had one of those small round band-aids on the top of his balding head. My rational mind thought, "Oh, he must have that band-aid on to cover a nasty pimple." I cannot say for sure, but I am assuming that this is when the flow of energy through my seventh chakra flooded my body and exited my mouth because instead of saying good morning, I looked at him, my hands on my hips, and said, "Where were you yesterday, having them check for a brain tumor?"

His face turned white as he quickly made his way out the office door. With my heart pounding and in a state of shock, I went back to my desk, confounded by what had just happened. Within seconds, my friend made his way to my desk. Clearly flustered, he stammered, "He thinks I told. He thinks I told you." "Told me what?" I exclaimed back. "That's where he was yesterday, having them check for a brain tumor."

Needless to say, my cognitive mind was certainly surprised.

Similar to knowingness is the concept of channeling. Channeling is a way in which we are able to access information that is "channeled" through the seventh chakra. Channeling dictates that the mind, the ego and the personality are set aside, in what would be considered a disassociated state, so that energy is allowed to flow in freely. Channeling was used in ancient times in Egypt and Asia as well as in Assyria and Greece and by the Celts. Performed by the priestly class, who developed the skills necessary to channel, it was used to communicate with the Gods and provide divine guidance to those who sought it.

A few years ago, I was working at a health and wellness expo. On the table in front of my booth I had a sign that read "Enter to Win a FREE Psychic Reading." It was late in the afternoon when a young couple in their early twenties walked up to the booth. The young man looked at me and announced that he wanted his free reading. Jokingly, I held up the 8 ½" × 11" sign, informing him that he could *enter* to win a free reading, but I wasn't doing free sessions.

His girlfriend, almost begging, said, "Oh, tell me something about us, tell me something about us." I found the two of them to be quite humorous, so I told the girl that if she got rid of her boyfriend and came back, I would tell her something. The couple left and in fewer than ten minutes, she was back, anxiously awaiting my insightful words. Walking over to her and looking her straight in the face, I blurted out, "He's an ---hole."

Shocked at my own words, I looked up over my left side trying to figure out where those words had come from. I know they didn't come from me. It wasn't that I didn't think her friend was a jerk, but it wasn't what I had planned on saying. I could feel my face turn red from embarrassment. As I looked back at the girl, somewhat bewildered, she threw her arms up in the air and exclaimed, "I know!" With that we both laughed.

What I have come to acknowledge is that information that flows in through the seventh chakra, and in my case, out my fifth, always carries truth. It is transmitted unedited, unrestricted and unfiltered. The energy of the seventh chakra vibrates at a level that is beyond our beliefs and opinions. It bypasses the sixth chakra where our consciousness is applied, for it is in the sixth chakra that we become aware of the thought or idea and work to describe it based on our life experiences. When someone channels, this filtering processes is suspended.

Like the other chakras, the flow of energy through the seventh chakra can become inhibited. This can occur because the seventh chakra has shut down, but more often than not, the nadi that connects us to the source of our universal energy is disconnected or pulled down into the body. This leaves us cut off from the flow of energy from the source and stops the flow of energy through our bodies. When this occurs, we end up feeling stuck, isolated or as if we are in a shell. It can also leave us feeling as if we lack purpose or direction in our lives.

An extreme imbalance of the seventh chakra manifests itself in bi-polar disorder. Individuals who are bi-polar (manic-depressive) have issues on seventh chakra levels. Granted, each of us has our ups and downs, but not on the same scale as those who suffer from this disorder. When a bi-polar person is in the manic state, the flow of energy in through their seventh chakra is intensified because their seventh chakra is fully open. In this state, they are able to access information and insights that are beyond those of most people. They feel confident, empowered and enthusiastic or as if there are no limits to what they can accomplish. They experience a sense of unfettered freedom, where responsibility and guilt are no longer a consequence. That is, until the energy shifts.

With each up or manic state experienced by someone with bi-polar disorder, there is an equal and opposite reaction. Where once the flow of energy through their seventh chakra was free-flowing and unlimited, when these individuals enter the depressive stage of this disorder everything changes. Their seventh chakra all but shuts down. The flow of energy in through their body is greatly diminished. This can leave them feeling fatigued, unfocused, restless, irritable and withdrawn.

When energy is flowing through the seventh chakra, we are open to and connected to the divine. We are able to access information that is clear, pure and unfiltered. When it is imbalanced, we may feel stuck, frustrated or out of touch with ourselves and the world around us.

Section 4

Avoiding the Cosmic 2 × 4

Finding Wholeness

> *Pain (any pain – emotional, physical, mental) has a message. The information it has about our life can be remarkably specific ... Once we get the pain's message, and follow its advice, the pain goes away.*
>
> — PETER MCWILLIAMS

Many people think disease is cruel. Pain, discomfort, illness and disease, however, when looked at from a place of wholeness, can be beneficial, if we choose to listen to the messages they contain. When we experience physical, emotional and even mental discomfort, our body is saying to us, "Excuse me, there is something wrong, I'm imbalanced and I want to move back into wholeness." When we experience pain, illness and disease, on the other hand, it is the body's way of saying to us, *"HEY!* I have something you must pay attention to. I've been trying to get you to notice me for months. Now you *have* to acknowledge me."

From this perspective, every issue that manifests in the physical body represents an aspect of ourselves that needs healing. It can be thought of as the final stage of a much deeper issue or complaint. It is an indication that there is resistance somewhere within our energetic system. It is a sign that something is out of balance and the body is seeking a way to bring itself back into wholeness. Elida Evens, in her 1926 book entitled *A Psychological Study of Cancer*, said, "Cancer is a symbol, as most illness is, of something going wrong in the patient's life, a warning to him to take another road." Canker sores, for example are the body's way of warning us that we are withholding communication, which is now festering inside. A bladder infection may literally let us know just how pissed off we really are.

Our bodies are always sending us signals, but, more often than not, we ignore them. Instead of paying attention to the aches, pains, frustrations, anxieties and stresses we experience, we allow our conscious mind to overrule them. Instead of following the guidance they offer us, we push them to the side and tell ourselves that what we are experiencing is wrong or unimportant. We allow our ambitions, our fears, our jealousies or our greed to rule, yet each of our should-a, would-a, could-a's are aspects of our personality that are in need of healing and have nothing to do with our true self.

Unfortunately, we are taught to focus our attention on the expression of the personality and the external world.

We are taught to ignore our deepest wants, needs and desires. In the end, we are left with little understanding of our true inner nature and how to recognize the messages from our soul. Inadvertently we become disconnected from our bodies and end up dulling our minds and our emotions. We numb ourselves with drugs and alcohol. We watch television, play video games or peruse other external distractions that overload our senses. We spend our days lying around, overeating or keeping ourselves constantly busy all in an attempt to avoid conflicts between our inner and outer worlds.

Diversions such as these allow us to avoid dealing with any discrepancies that may exist between our personality and our inner world. As you may recall, the goal of the personality is to maintain the image it created of itself. This is why many people avoid going inside. When we go inside, we are faced with the truth of who we really are. The personality is afraid we will find out that *who* we are is not who we *think* we are. It persuades us to ignore the promptings from our inner world all in an effort to avoid change.

All of our pain, suffering, illnesses and diseases endeavor to guide us towards perfection. So while it may seem bad or negative on the outside, the potential for transformation and change it offers is immense. Those who accept the challenge change presents often find that it can actually be a blessing in disguise. Most of us, however, change only when we have to. In fact, the majority of us spend a lot of time and energy running away from ourselves rather than changing.

When we resist changing, our problems don't go away. Resistance is the personality's way of holding on to an old self-image instead of letting it go. It is only when we let go and stop resisting that we can change and grow. We can try to fight change, suppress change, ignore it or deny it, but in the end the underlying issue will rear its ugly head again in another way or form. These problems are lessons provided for us by the soul to help us heal an aspect of our personality. Ultimately the choice is this: we can make the changes required of us, or we can choose to learn the same lesson over again, reexperiencing the same hurts, pain or confusion as before.

Many of us will only change when we feel as if we have no other choice. This occurs when we have reached a point in our lives where our problems have bothered us for so long or created so much pain and discomfort that we just can't stand it any longer. It is through personal and professional crises, extraordinary circumstances, profound suffering, broken promises, missed opportunities, life-altering events and even the diagnosis of a terminal illness that we can become clear about who we are.

It is at these times that we can typically experience the most profound, life-altering changes. Each of these life crises has the ability to rock our world and shake us to our very foundation. The self-image created by our personality begins to break down and we can begin to see that our view of ourselves is no longer working.

To bring changes into your life, the trick is to start paying attention to the signals your body is receiving and honestly interpret them. It is only when we have succeeded in observing our thoughts, emotions and physical sensations that we can begin to know ourselves. By paying attention to all aspects of ourselves we will begin to see the lessons our illness holds. It will also give us the opportunity to discover how our illness came into being in the first place and why.

Change isn't hard but it does take time, commitment and courage. It can be scary and can create confusion, but if you think about it, most of our pain comes from our digging our heels in the sand as we fight it. Change doesn't happen all at once, but in small, almost undetectable ways. As we work to change, we will stumble and fall, and experience setbacks and failures. Each of these experiences will help us as we move forward because they cause us to grow. They help us become conscious of what is and isn't working for us, giving us the opportunity to practice and integrate new ways of being.

On physical levels, we achieve awareness by listening to our body and paying attention to its needs. This includes a proper diet, regular exercise and relaxation. On emotional levels, it includes paying attention to how we feel and expressing our emotions as necessary. It is important to express our feelings and let them out. The larger the range of emotions that we experience, the happier and healthier we are. When we express our emotions we are allowing energy to move through us as opposed to suppressing it within us, even if the emotion we are experiencing is anger, pain, frustration and even rage.

On mental levels, awareness is achieved by paying attention to our actions. We act based upon our beliefs and intentions. If you are uncertain what beliefs are getting in your way, look at the source of your confusion, frustration, resistance, anxiety or stress. Follow these feelings back to their core beliefs. It is by acknowledging our underlying beliefs that we can change them and move on. Letting go of an old belief can be daunting, but you will never know what or who you will become unless you do.

How to Avoid the Cosmic 2 × 4

> *There is no need to go to India or anywhere else to find peace. You will find that deep place of silence right in your room, your garden or even your bathtub.*
>
> — Elisabeth Kubler-Ross

Simple as this may sound, the first step down the road to wholeness is to just be silent. Turn off the TV and the computer, put down the book, take a break from your project and just be still. Many of us never take the time to just be silent: silent with our thoughts, silent with our feelings and silent with ourselves. It is through silence that we can begin to become aware of the communications that each of our parts provides.

One way to become more aware of our inner world is to "check in." Checking in is easy and can be done in a few moments. In order to check into your inner environment the first thing you need to do is simply stop what you are doing and become silent. Close your eyes and take a deep breath. As you exhale, allow yourself to let go of any stress or anxiety you may be experiencing – just let it go. From this relaxed, receptive place, ask yourself, "What am I thinking?" "How am I feeling?"

Notice how your body feels, where your emotions are or what you have been focusing your attention on. Positive, joyful emotions tell us that we are moving in the right direction, following our passions and the promptings of the soul. Negative feelings and painful emotions indicate that something is out of balance and is in need of healing. Often it is an indication that we have ignored our feelings or that a change is required.

When we feel anxious, uncomfortable or frustrated, it is an indication our body is trying to tell us something important. Treat the discomfort as if it contains a form of intelligence and is trying to communicate with you. Let yourself stay with the feeling instead of ignoring it or trying to escape from it. Say to yourself, "I know you are trying to tell me something. What am I supposed to acknowledge?" Allow yourself to be open to receiving its message, even if it is something you don't want to hear.

We all receive answers to our questions in different ways. In the same way that we are all unique and diverse beings with distinct backgrounds, the way in which we receive and process information varies. For some, the answers to their questions may come to them via one of their chakras. Are you experiencing a vague impression or noticing a gut feeling as you open yourself up to receiving information on a second chakra level? Perhaps your inner voice is whispering your next step to you, so be sure to listen to this fifth chakra communication. Maybe an image immediately appeared in your mind's eye. This not your imagination but your sixth chakra at work. But then again, you may just have a knowingness about what you should do or what your next step should be. If this is the case, acknowledge and validate the flow of information through your seventh chakra.

Others may receive answers to their questions when they talk to a friend or read a book. Sometimes a song playing on the radio or a strange or unexpected event may provide them with guidance they seek. Regardless of the way or medium in which our questions are answered, it is important to corroborate the message by asking ourselves, "How does this feel to me?" As you may recall, it is through the fourth chakra that we can access all of our parts. By verifying how it feels to all our parts, we can be assured that we are coming from a place of wholeness.

When we check in, we are in point of fact seeking guidance from our inner self, our soul. It is our soul that provides us with the answers to the questions we ask. But nine times out of ten, we only seek the guidance it provides when everything else has failed.

Through the causal body and the soul we connect with the impulses of the universe, or God. The function of the soul is to guide us to perfection. When we listen to the dictates of the soul, we move closer to God or in a more synchronous vibration with the universe. When we ignore the dictates of the soul, we move further away from God or out of sync with the universe. The further we move away or resist, the more "static," pain and suffering we will experience in our lives as the universe tries to reestablish harmony.

The soul prompts us to seek wholeness and will remind us each and every day of its mission until we finally acknowledge it. The guiding presence of our soul is always there, ready, willing and able to help us, but we often choose not to pay attention to its requests. Over time, it can recede into the background and leave us to our own devices, the calling of the material world, and the lure of the illusions of our personality. Then, in order to access the information provided by our soul, we must search diligently within ourselves to find it.

When we don't pay attention to the messages provided to us by our soul, it will get our attention in symptoms such as obsessions, worry, mental anguish, fears, addictions, violence, heart disease, high blood pressure, diabetes or cancer. If its message is received, acknowledged and acted upon, health and harmony will ensue. If it is ignored, the problems being experienced will intensify until we finally get the message. It is only then that balance can be restored.

It must be remembered that the messages we receive from our soul are always the truth, so it doesn't make sense to avoid it, disregard it, go into denial about it or try to change the meaning of the communication you get. As palatable or unpalatable as it may be, truth is always truth, even if it sometimes stings. Also, it is best to catch these imbalances when they are in a beginning stage of dysfunction as opposed to waiting until they have manifested into something larger. When doctors take an in-depth history of someone diagnosed with a chronic or terminal illness, in almost every case earlier symptoms were ignored or treated superficially. The sooner we "get" the message and address the issues or concerns it contains, the sooner we can move back into health and wholeness.

Following the soul involves allowing ourselves to yield to its dictates and control. Once this occurs, our subtle bodies will act in unison and follow the directive of this higher energetic vibration. When we choose to follow and act on the information provided we surrender to it, opening ourselves up to an increased flow of our life force energy.

Surrendering implies that we are willing to let go of the limitations, illusions and false beliefs created by the personality and consciously choose to follow the dictates of the soul. Surrendering is not submission, nor does it render you pathetic or spineless. Actually surrendering to the "will of God" can require the greatest act of courage we have ever mustered, because the advice provided could at times be in direct conflict with some of our deeply ingrained beliefs. This can make the thought of following its directives downright terrifying.

Think about the countless number of people who stay in unhealthy relationships even though they are unhappy, or those that stay in jobs that they hate, forcing themselves to get out of bed every morning and go to work. If asked, the majority of them know deep within themselves that their situation is untenable. They are caught up in a web of dysfunctional beliefs that perpetuate behaviors and emotional responses that are all driven by the fear of change. They are trapped in the world they've created, acting as both jailer and prisoner alike until they hit rock bottom.

It is usually in a defining moment when we finally surrender and let go of our inner resistance and limiting beliefs. Surrendering frees us of the chains that bind. In the immortal words of Janis Joplin, "Freedom's just another word for nothing left to lose." It is only when we have nothing else to lose that we let go. We are free to leave "good" jobs or walk out on harmful relationships, with only the clothes on our backs, and feel right and whole about it.

If you wonder what it feels like to surrender, think of when you've had "one of those days," and just when you think nothing else could possibly happen, you find out you've locked your keys in your car. In and of itself, locking our keys in our cars is annoying, but at certain times, it can be the straw that breaks the proverbial camel's back. It is in these moments that we let go and surrender. Then for a period of time after that moment almost anything could happen to or around us and we would remain unaffected; it would just roll off our backs.

Now, it doesn't mean that we have to like what is going on, but in these moments, if we search hard enough, we somehow find a level of unconditional acceptance within ourselves. It is at these times that we are willing to risk it all because we are doing what feels right to us, not from a place of ego, power or greed, but from a place of wholeness that comes from deep within us. It is from this place that we are empowered.

As we learn to surrender, by acknowledging and acting on soul information, it is important to keep focused on only one thing: how we feel inside. It is easy to get lost in other people's problems, issues, goals and desires, but if our soul tells us to leap, we have to be willing to leap without question. If it tells us to wait, then we should use the time to relax and regroup until we are directed to move forward again. It may tell us to do something unexpected or different from what we had originally planned, but we must trust this inner knowing. Sometimes the requests of our souls may seem strange or illogical, but over time, we can see the perfection of these choices and decisions.

When we have faith and trust the direction our soul provides, we can let go of fear. This means we can stop trying to control our lives by planning out every detail or forcing things to happen. It means that we can now allow ourselves to be guided toward perfection and trust that whatever happens to us was meant to be and will ultimately serve our highest purpose, which is bringing us back into wholeness. This includes every obstacle or stumbling block we may encounter. Instead of getting upset every time we experience a setback, we can be thankful for receiving another opportunity to learn, grow and transform our inner being even more.

As we learn to align ourselves with the promptings of the soul, we are sent little tests that try to lure us with power, money, or perhaps a position of authority or gifts.

They can reveal inner strength, conviction and our ability to trust our inner knowing. These tests are sent to see how well we are listening, following and submitting. It is like taking the final exam for a specific lesson we are learning. Once we pass the test, we don't have to learn that lesson again. It doesn't mean that we won't have other lessons that we will have to learn, but we will not have to experience that one again.

Sometimes it's difficult to honor the guiding principles of the soul. When we listen to and heed the guidance our soul provides we can become masters of our reality. We have the opportunity to become our authentic selves, unhindered by self-imposed limitations and fearful fantasies. We are free from the opinions, rules and constructs of man because we live by the dictates of our inner guidance. We are free to act spontaneously as opposed to inhibiting our self-expression in order to gain love and approval. We are willing to stand alone and do what feels right to us even if nobody else understands our motives.

In the end, wholeness implies becoming an autonomous, self-determining being, true to ourselves in thought, word and deed. We are willing to follow where our inner guidance leads us instead of ignoring or avoiding it or feeling pressured to act in a certain way. In the end we will have to face our fears, for it is only when we overcome our fears, ignorance and self-deception that we will be liberated from self-imposed limitations and health, harmony and balance can be restored.

Experiencing Wholeness

> *The journey to wholeness requires that you look honestly, openly and with courage into yourself, into the dynamics that lie behind what you feel, what you perceive, what you value, and how you act. It is a journey through your defenses and beyond so that you can experience consciously the nature of your personality, face what it has produced in your life, and choose to change that.*
>
> — GARY ZUKAV

Most people don't recognize the source of their problems. Typically when we think about creating and maintaining health, we only think about the physical part of our makeup. Little attention is paid to our thoughts, feelings and emotions, even though they are intimately connected to the state of our health and well-being. So while modern medicine routinely utilizes biochemical solutions to heal the body, these remedies can only superficially repair damage, ease symptoms or provide temporary relief.

It seems obvious, then, that any hope for a cure will be ineffective until the underlying cause is also removed. Efforts directed at the physical body do little to address the fundamental or causal source of disease for this simple reason: disease is not material in origin. If the underlying cause of disease is not addressed, it is only a matter of time before the same issue presents itself in another form. The secret to treating disease and its underlying causes lies in finding or reexperiencing wholeness.

While wholeness on physical levels implies freedom from bodily pain, wholeness on emotional levels implies freedom from emotional pain. It entails the recognition of both our positive and negative feelings. It means taking the time to identify what we are feeling and expressing these feelings appropriately. It means we are willing to face our fears and confront the truth about ourselves.

Emotional wholeness is characterized by our ability to give and receive love, and our ability to forgive as well as our ability to trust. It is also seen in our ability to maintain both intimacy and independence in our relationships. To have any of these things in our lives, the awareness and communication of our feelings is essential.

On mental levels, wholeness implies that we take responsibility for our thoughts as well as our behavior. Our world is a reflection of our state of mind. This includes our beliefs, expectations and assumptions.

On soul levels, wholeness means creating skills of self-awareness and conscious decision-making. Through self-examination, we can often uncover patterns of thought or behavior that create or contribute to mental and emotional stress as well as to the physical tensions we experience in our bodies. These might take the form of a rigid attitude, a particular habit or an expectation or pretense that acts as a barrier or obstruction to our true self. By identifying these barriers we can begin to let them go. We must be willing to endure temporary pain, discomfort or hardship to and recognize that this is simply a necessary part of the process of making us whole.

As we begin to become more aware of our bodies and our thoughts, beliefs, feelings and emotions, we can start to see patterns of actions and reactions that have become our habitual responses to life's challenges. Granted, sometimes recognizing these patterns in ourselves isn't easy, but it is an important step in our ability to transform our lives and ourselves. Without this awareness we will never be able to understand the impact our thoughts, feelings and emotions have on our health. It has been found that those who benefited the most and were able to bring health and wholeness back into their lives were those who were willing to examine all areas of their being.

Disease provides us with an opportunity to work through trapped energy or resistance in our bodies. As we learn more about ourselves and become increasingly aware of our different parts, we can begin to recognize the parts of us that are seeking expression. If we allow this inner knowledge to tell us the reason for our illness or disease and what we need to do to recreate health in our lives, we can act on it, bringing the needed changes into our lives. Sometimes this may mean that we have to confront our worst enemy, ourselves.

For true healing to occur, our life force energy must flow unhindered through our subtle bodies and through every aspect of our nature. Healing occurs when we let go of constricting thoughts and personal attachments and work to become our authentic selves. It is only when we have released the pent up vital energy that formed the foundation for the disease in the first place that can we begin to experience health.

There is no longer a need for disease when we allow the energy and guidance of our soul to direct us through the right use of mind and will. It energizes our subtle bodies. This energy filters down and energizes our physical body including its organs, glands and tissues. These higher vibrational impulses create a healing resonance that is transmitted and manifested in the lower bodies. Our soul, now liberated to the flow of our life force energy, leaves us feeling less fragmented, less scattered. In essence we feel united, centered and whole. As the body begins to respond to the flow of our life force energy through it, health returns.

Healing and wholeness represent an integration of body, mind, spirit and emotions. They result from the acceptance and balance of the positive and negative, desirable and undesirable and inner and outer aspects of the self. These parts of ourselves need to be integrated and balanced in the same way that we need to eat a balanced diet. Healing necessitates an integration and synthesis of the whole. Wholeness can be found when we look deep inside ourselves for those parts of us which are out of harmony with the dictates of our soul. At that point, the illness may no longer be necessary and it will leave of its own volition.

> *A person becomes whole physically, emotionally, mentally and at deeper levels, resulting ideally in an integration with the underlying inward powers of the universe.*
>
> — RENÉ WEBER

Appendix

Guidance on Your Path to Wholeness

Guidance on Your Path to Wholeness

As you move forward and work to bring wholeness back into your life, you may require some assistance. Below is a list of alternative health care techniques and modalities that can help you restore health, harmony and wholeness in your life. If you are unsure about what would be the best direction to take or need guidance as to the method that would be best suited for you, take a moment to check in and ask your inner guide. It is there, waiting to help.

ACUPRESSURE

Oriental healing system using the application of fingertip pressure on specific tension spots on the body to reduce stress and pain and to treat specific symptoms or disorders.

Jin Shin Do Foundation for BodyMind Acupressure
P.O. Box 416, Idyllwild, CA 92549
Phone: 909-659-5707 Fax: 909-659-5707
http://www.jinshindo.org/

ACUPUNCTURE

Ancient Oriental healing therapy which stimulates or disperses the flow of subtle energy or chi' within the body by inserting fine needles into specific points on the skin, by massage, by thermal therapy or by a combination of all three. Each point is located along a meridian and is associated with specific organs. Every acupuncture point is considered to have a particular therapeutic effect.

Acupuncture and Oriental Medicine Alliance
6405 43rd Avenue CT NW Suite B
Gig Harbor, WA 98335
Phone: 253-851-6896 Fax: 253-851-6883
Website: www.aomalliance.org

American Academy of Medical Acupuncture
4929 Wilshire Boulevard #428
Los Angeles, CA 90010
Phone: 323-937-5514 Fax: 323-937-0959
Website: www.medicalacupuncture.org

American Association of Oriental Medicine
5530 Wisconsin Avenue Suite 1210
Chevy Chase, MD 20815
Phone: 888-500-7999 Fax: 301-986-9313
Website: www.aaom.org

ALEXANDER TECHNIQUE

F. Matthias Alexander created the method after concluding that bad posture was responsible for his own chronic voice loss. Practitioners use gentle hands-on guidance, verbal instruction, teach simple, efficient ways of moving as a means of improving balance, posture, coordination and to relieve tension and pain.

> American Society for the Alexander Technique
> PO Box 60008
> Florence, MA 01062
> Phone: 800-473-0620 Fax: 413-584-3097
> Website: www.alexandertech.com

APPLIED KINESIOLOGY

Knowledge of techniques for obtaining and using information from the position, movement, and tension of parts of the body, especially from the nerves, muscles, tendons and joints. For example, diagnosis of physical ailments may be obtained from the subconscious level by naming the ailment, asking the subject to tense an arm and noting whether the tension is maintained or released when the arm is depressed.

> International College of Applied Kinesiology – U.S.A.
> 6405 Metcalf Avenue Suite 503
> Shawnee Mission, KS 66202
> Phone: 913-384-5336 Fax: 913-384-5112
> Website: www.icak.com

AROMATHERAPY

The use of various aromatic herbs, volatile oils and similar preparations from plants, flowers, trees and herbs to achieve health, vitality and rejuvenation of the body, mind and spirit.

> The National Association for Holistic Aromatherapy
> 4509 Interlake Avenue North #233
> Seattle, WA 98103
> Phone: 888-ASK-NAHA Fax: 206-547-2680
> Website: www.naha.org

AYURVEDIC MEDICINE
Ancient Indian medical-metaphysical healing life science based on the harmony of body, mind and universe. It emphasizes the capability of the individual for self-healing using natural remedies to restore balance. Therapy consists of maintaining a balance between diet, daily routine and activities.

Maharishi Ayurved Products Intl.
1068 Elkton Drive
Colorado Springs, CO 80907
Phone: 800-345-8332 Fax: 719-260-7400
Website: www.mapi.com

Maharishi College of Vedic Medicine
2721 Arizona Street NE
Albuquerque, NM 87110
Phone: 800-811-0550 Fax: 989-803-6000
Website: mcvmnm.org

BIOFEEDBACK
A scientific technique to tune into and consciously control bodily functions by hooking up to a monitoring device that reads certain physiological responses and feeds information back to the user.

Biofeedback Certification Institute of America
10200 West 44th Avenue Suite 310
Wheat Ridge, CO 80033
Phone: 303-420-2902 Fax: 303-422-8894
Website: www.bcia.org

BIOENERGETICS
A body-mind therapy created by Dr. Alexander Lowen that uses the body to heal the mind. The simultaneous duality and unity

of the human personality is its underlying principle. The technique includes direct bodywork to release unresolved emotional blocks stored in muscle groups.

American Association of Acupuncture and Bioenergetic Medicine
AAABEM
2512 Manoa Road
Honolulu, HI 96822
Phone: 808-946-2069 Fax: 808-946-0378

BREATHWORK

A general term for a variety of techniques that use patterned breathing to promote physical, mental and/or spiritual well-being. Some techniques use the breath in a calm, peaceful way to induce relaxation or manage pain, while others use stronger breathing to stimulate emotions and emotional release.

International Breathwork Foundation
Rue Driesbos 25 bte 1
B-1640 Rhode St Genése
Belgium
Website: www.ibfnetwork.org

Rebirthing Breathwork International
P.O. Box 1026
Staunton, VA 24402
Phone: 540-885-0551
Website: www.rebirthingbreathwork.com

CHIROPRACTIC

A system of therapies based upon the theory that disease is caused by abnormal function of the nervous system. It attempts to restore normal function by manipulation and treatment of the structures of the body, especially those of the spinal column.

American Chiropractic Association
1701 Clarendon Boulevard
Arlington, VA 22209
Phone: 703-276-8800 Fax: 703-243-2593
Website: www.acatoday.com

Federation of Straight Chiropractors and Organizations
2276 Wassergass Road
Hellertown, PA 18055
Phone: 800-521-9856 Fax: 610-858-3031
Website: www.straightchiropractic.com

International Chiropractors Association
1110 North Glebe Road Suite 1000
Arlington, VA 22201
Phone: 800-423-4690 Fax: 703-528-5023
Website: www.chiropractic.org

National Directory of Chiropractic Foundations
PO Box 10056
Olathe, KS 66051
Phone: 800-888-7914 Fax: 877-568-4694
Website: www.chirodirectory.com

COLONIC IRRIGATION THERAPY

The flushing of the intestines with a series of inflows and outflows of purified water into the colon for cleansing and corrective purposes.

International Association for Colon Hydrotherapy
P.O. Box 461285
San Antonio, TX 78246-1285
Phone: 210-366-2888 Fax: 210-366-2999
Website: i-act.org

COLOR (LIGHT) THERAPY

A natural healing technique using the scientific application of the correct color vibrations to the body, often as white light projected through films of various colors.

Dinshaw Health Society
100 Dinshaw Drive
Malaga, New Jersey 08328
Phone: (609) 692-4686

CRANIOSACRAL THERAPY

An offshoot of traditional osteopathic medicine. This work is a diagnostic and healing tool that deals with a very subtle rhythm in the body. Traditionally used for head and tailbone dysfunction, it works well for chronic headaches, whiplash injury, facial or cranial trauma and other sensory, motor and/or intellectual dysfunction.

CSTA/NA
12 Sato Street
Whitby, ON
Canada L1R 2E6
Phone: 905-666-6081
Website: www.craniosacraltherapy.org/

DENTAL, HOLISTIC

Holistic Dental Association
PO Box 5007
Durango, CO 81301
Website: www.holisticdental.org

The Holistic Dental Digest & Referral Service
263 W End Avenue #2A
New York, NY 10023
Phone: 212-874-4212 Fax: 212-874-4212

FELDENKRAIS METHOD

The Feldenkrais Method uses gentle movement and directed attention to improve movement, increase your ease and range of motion, improve your flexibility and coordination, and rediscover your innate capacity for graceful, efficient movement.

Feldenkrais Guild of North America
3611 SW Hood Avenue Suite 100
Portland, OR 97239
Phone: 800-775-2118 Fax: 503-221-6616
Website: www.feldenkrais.com

FLOWER ESSENCES

A modality that uses extracts from flowering plants in homeopathic proportions as catalysts for healing. They are intended to alleviate negative emotional states that may contribute to illness or hinder personal growth. Each liquid potentized preparation carries the imprint of a specific plant, which speaks a subtle language that works on the root causes of disease. The appropriate essences are chosen, focusing on the client's emotional state rather than on a particular physical condition. Originated by Dr. Edward Bach.

Flower Essence Society
PO Box 459
Nevada City, CA 95959
Phone: 800-736-9222 Fax: 530-265-0584
Website: www.flowersociety.org

The Bach Flower Essences International Education Program
100 Research Drive Wilmington, MA 01887
Phone: 800-334-0843 Fax: 978-988-0233
Website: www.nelsonbach.com

GUIDED IMAGERY

The use of mental energy to create positive thoughts to manifest life changes; a process by which a facilitator suggests the types of pictures to imagine in the mind as a technique to create thought forms for a desired end result which will later manifest in the physical world.

Academy for Guided Imagery
PO Box 2070
Mill Valley CA 94942
Phone: 800-726-2070 Fax: 415-389-9342
Website: www.interactiveimagery.com

ENERGY HEALING/BALANCING

Healing technique, which involves working in the body's subtle energy field to promote mental, emotional, physical or spiritual healing.

American Polarity Therapy Association
PO Box 19858
Boulder, CO 80308
Phone: 303-545-2080 Fax: 303-545-2161
Website: www.polaritytherapy.org

International Association of Reiki Professionals
PO Box 104
Harrisville, NH 03450
Phone: 603-881-8838 Fax: 603-882-9088
Website: www.iarp.org

International Foundation of Bio-Magnetics
5634 East Pima Street
Tucson, AZ 85712
Phone: 520-323-7951 Fax: 419-844-3110
Website: JustTouch.com

EXERCISE/FITNESS

American Council on Exercise (ACE)
4851 Paramount Drive
San Diego, CA 92123
Phone: 800-825-3636 Fax: 858-279- 8064
Website: www.acefitness.org

International Fitness Professionals Association
14509 University Point Place
Tampa, FL 33613
Phone: 800-785-1924 Fax: 813-979-1978
Website: www.ifpa-fitness.com

HELLERWORK

A system of somatic education and structural bodywork, which is based on the inseparability of body, mind and spirit, making the connection between movement, body alignment and personal awareness.

Hellerwork International
3435 M Street
Eureka, CA 95503
Phone: 800-392-3900
Website: www.hellerwork.com

HERBALISM

Uses natural plants or plant-based substances to treat a range of illnesses and to enhance the functioning of the body's systems.

American Herbalists Guild
1931 Gaddis Road
Canton, GA 30115
Phone: 770-751-6021 Fax: 770-751-7472
Website: www.americanherbalist.com

HOLISTIC MEDICINE

Therapies that treat the whole person, mind and body as opposed to just the part of the body where symptoms occur.

American Board of Holistic Medicine
1135 Makawao Avenue #230
Makawao, HI 96768
Phone: 808-572-4616 Fax: 808-572-6968
Website: www.amerboardholisticmed.org

American College for Advancement in Medicine
23121 Verdugo Drive Suite 204
Laguna Hills, CA 92653
Phone: 800-532-3688 Fax: 949-455-9679
Website: www.acam.org

American Holistic Medical Association
12101 Menaul Boulevard NE Suite C
Albuquerque, NM 87112
Phone: 505-292-7788 Fax: 505-293-7582
Website: holisticmedicine.org

HOMEOPATHY

A school of medicine based on the theory of "like cures like." Minute quantities of natural substances stimulate the body's own self-healing ability. If taken in larger doses, they would produce side effects similar to those of the disease being treated.

National Center for Homeopathy
801 North Fairfax Street Suite 306
Alexandria, VA 22314
Phone: 703-548-7790 Fax: 703-548-7792
Website: www.homeopathic.org

HYPNOTHERAPY

A state of mind in which one's focus of attention is narrow and a higher level of awareness of the focal point is attained than is normal when one is awake. The power of conscious criticism is suppressed and suggestions move directly into the unconscious mind. Suggestions are acted upon more powerfully than is possible in the normal waking state.

> **American Board of Hypnotherapy**
> 2002 E McFadden Avenue Suite 100
> Santa Ana, CA 92705-4706
> Phone: 800-872-9996 Fax: 714-245-981
> Website: www.hypnosis.com

> **The American Society of Clinical Hypnosis**
> 140 N Bloomingdale Road
> Bloomingdale, IL 60108
> Phone: 630-980-4740 Fax: 630-351-8490
> Website: www.asch.net

MAGNETIC FIELD THERAPY

Magnetic field therapy or biomagnetic therapy involves the use of magnets, magnetic devices or magnetic fields to treat a variety of physical and emotional conditions, including circulatory problems, certain forms of arthritis, chronic pain, sleep disorders and stress.

> **Biomagnetic Therapy Association**
> PO Box 394
> Lyons, CO 80540
> Phone: 303-823-0307
> Website: www.biomagnetic.org

MASSAGE THERAPY

This is a general term for a range of therapeutic approaches with roots in both Eastern and Western cultures. Involves the practice of kneading or otherwise manipulating a person's muscles and soft tissue.

> **American Massage Therapy Association**
> 820 Davis Street Suite 100
> Evanston, IL 60201
> Phone: 888-843-2682 Fax: 847-864-1178
> Website: www.amtamassage.org
>
> **Associated Bodywork and Massage Professionals**
> 271 Sugarbush Drive
> Evergreen, CO 80439
> Phone: 800-458-2267 Fax: 800-667-8260
> Website: www.abmp.com

MYOFASCIAL RELEASE

Trauma, posture, or inflammation can create a binding down of fascia resulting in excessive pressure on nerves, muscles, blood vessels, osseous structures and/or organs. This hands-on technique seeks to free the body from the grip of tight fascia, or connective tissue, thus restoring normal alignment and function and reducing pain. Therapists apply mild, sustained hand-pressure in order to gently stretch and soften fascia. Treatment is used to treat neck and back pain, headaches, recurring sports injuries, scoliosis and other conditions.

> **National Association of Myofascial Trigger Point Therapists**
> 325 East 52nd Street
> New York, NY 10022
> Phone: 800-845-3454 Fax: 212-826-1088
> Website: www.myofascialtherapy.org

NATUROPATHIC MEDICINE

A healing system acknowledging the body's natural healing power. Fosters health through education and the use of natural substances such as herbs, foods, air and sunshine. No drugs or surgery are used.

American Association of Naturopathic Physicians
3201 New Mexico Avenue NW Suite 350
Washington, DC 20016
Phone: 202-895-1392 Fax: 202-274-1992
Website: www.naturopathic.org

American Naturopathic Medical Association
PO Box 96273
Las Vegas, NV 89193
Phone: 702-897-7053 Fax: 702-897-7140
Website: www.anma.com

NEURO EMOTIONAL TECHNIQUE

A methodology used to normalize unresolved physical and/or behavioral patterns in the body. It is used to assist the body's healing process by identifying and balancing unresolved emotional influences.

Neuro Emotional Technique, Inc.
510 Second Street
Encinitas, CA 92024
Phone: 800-888-4638 Fax: 760-753-7191
Website: www.netmindbody.com

NUTRITIONAL COUNSELING

American Association of Nutritional Consultants
400 Oak Hill Drive
Winona Lake, IN 46590
Phone: 888-828-2262 Fax: 219-269-4060
Website: www.aanc.net

Price-Pottenger Nutrition Foundation
PO Box 2614
La Mesa, CA 91943
Phone: 619-462-7600 Fax: 619-433-3136
Website: www.price-pottenger.org

Society of Certified Nutritionists
10632 Primrose Arbor Avenue
Las Vegas, NV 89144
Phone: 800-342-8037
Website: www.certifiednutritionist.com

ORIENTAL MEDICINE

American Association of Oriental Medicine
5530 Wisconsin Avenue Suite 1210
Chevy Chase, MD 20815
Phone: 888-500-7999 Fax: 301-986-9313
Website: www.aaom.org

POLARITY THERAPY

Asserts that balancing the flow of energy in the body is the foundation of health. Specific points along the currents are said to hold positive or negative energies. Practitioners use gentle touch and guidance in diet, exercise and self-awareness to help clients balance their energy flow, thus supporting a return to health.

American Polarity Therapy Association
PO Box 19858
Boulder, CO 80308
Phone: 303-545-2080 Fax: 303-545-2161
Website: www.polaritytherapy.org

PSYCHOLOGY/MENTAL HEALTH

American Psychiatric Association
1000 Wilson Boulevard Suite 1825
Arlington, VA 22209
Phone: 888-35-PSYCH Fax: 703-907-7322
Website: www.psych.org

Association for Humanistic Psychology
1516 Oak Street #320A
Alameda, CA 94501
Phone: 510-769-6495 Fax: 510-769-6433
Website: ahpweb.org

International Association of Counselors and Therapists
10915 Bonita Beach Road SE #1101
Bonita Springs, FL 34135
Phone: 239-498-9710 Fax: 239-498-1215
Website: www.iact.org

REFERRALS, GENERAL

American Association for Health Freedom
PO Box 458
Great Falls, VA 22066
Phone: 800-230-2762 Fax: 703-759-6711
Web site: healthfreedom.net

American Association of Drugless Practitioners
708 Madelaine Drive
Gilmer, TX 75644-3140
Phone: 903-843-6401
Website: www.aadp.net

American Holistic Health Association
PO Box 17400
Anaheim, CA 92817-7400
Phone: 714-779-6152
Website: www.ahha.org/

American Organization for Bodywork Therapies of Asia
1010 Haddonfield-Berlin Road Suite 408
Voorhees, NJ 08043
Phone: 856-782-1616 Fax: 856-782-1653
Website: aobta.org

REFLEXOLOGY
Based on the concept that specific points on the feet and hands correspond with organs and tissues throughout the body. With fingers and thumbs, the practitioner applies pressure to these points to treat a wide range of stress-related illnesses and ailments.

Reflexology Association of America
4012 South Rainbow Suite K-PMB #585
Las Vegas, NV 89103-2059
Phone: 508-364-4234
Website: www.reflexology-usa.org

REIKI
Practitioners of this ancient Tibetan healing system use light hand placements to transmit healing energies to the recipient. While the practitioners may vary widely in technique and philosophy, Reiki is commonly used to treat emotional and mental distress as well as chronic and acute physical problems, as well as to assist the recipient in achieving spiritual focus and clarity.

International Association of Reiki Professionals
PO Box 104
Harrisville, NH 03450
Phone: 603-881-8838 Fax: 603-882-9088
Website: www.iarp.org

ROLFING
A technique that uses deep manipulation of the fascia to restore the body's natural alignment, which may have become rigid through injury, emotional trauma, and inefficient movement habits. The process, developed by biochemist Ida P. Rolf, involves ten sessions, each focusing on a different part of the body.

Rolf Institute of Structural Integration
205 Canyon Boulevard
Boulder, CO 80302
Phone: 800-530-8875 Fax: 303-449-5978
Website: www.rolf.org

TRAGER BODYWORK
Movement-education approach that gently rocks, cradles, and moves the client's body. Meant to promote relaxation, increase mobility and mental clarity. Used by athletes for performance enhancement and by people with musculoskeletal and back problems.

Trager International
24800 Chagrin Boulevard Suite 205
Beachwood, OH 44122
Phone: 216-896-9383 Fax: 216-896-9385
Website: www.trager.com

THERAPEUTIC (HEALING) TOUCH
Is used to accelerate wound healing, relieve pain, promote relaxation, prevent illness and ease the dying process. The practi-

tioner uses light touch or works with his or her hands near the client's body in an effort to restore balance to the client's energy system.

Nurse Healers-Professional Associates International
3760 S Highland Drive #429
Salt Lake City, UT 84106
Phone: 801-273-3399 Fax: 509-693-3537
Website: www.therapeutic-touch.org

YOGA

An Eastern philosophy involving spiritual discipline and using various techniques to experience union with a Supreme Being. Many Yogic paths exist and include work on the physical body as in Hatha yoga, which uses breathing exercises and sustained physical postures to gain physical and mental control over the body, and Bhakti, the yoga of devotion and love using the heart as a vehicle for transcendence.

International Association of Yoga Therapists
2400A Country Center Drive
Santa Rosa, CA 95403
Phone: 707-566-9000 Fax: 707-566-9185
Website: www.iayt.org

About the Author

At the age of twelve, Rita Louise, Ph.D., became fascinated with the concept of extrasensory perception (ESP), a passion which has lasted a lifetime. After years of intense study and in-depth research into the fields of health and wellness, psychology, philosophy and the esoteric arts and sciences, she has emerged as a leading voice in the fields of holistic health and mind/body healing. The author of the book "The Power Within," Dr. Louise is a naturopathic physician and a twenty-year veteran in the Human Potential Field. But perhaps most importantly, it is her unique gift as a medical intuitive and clairvoyant that illuminates and enlivens her work.

Dr. Louise is a foremost authority on health and healing, and she possesses the caliber of knowledge and experience that people demand. A regular contributor to many alternative health and wellness publications, her monthly columns can be found in magazines and newspapers around the world, while her groundbreaking work has been featured on radio and television all over the United States and abroad.

Dr. Louise is a regular speaker at conferences throughout the United States. She infuses every speaking engagement with both credibility and content, and has the unique ability to deliver a serious message through intriguing stories and her own brand of humor. "Fran Dresher's delivery without the whine," is how one audience member described Dr. Louise's frank, funny yet honest approach. Her high content presentations offer many down-to-earth strategies and empowering solutions that inspire, invigorate and empower participants by helping them to understand the messages their bodies and their lives are giving them and to energize them into taking action.

Her unique insights bridge the worlds of science, spirit and culture, and are changing the way the world views physical, mental and emotional well-being. Most importantly, she helps individuals reclaim their most valuable asset – their health.

Dr. Rita Louise can be reached by calling 972-475-3393 or you can visit her on the web at www.soulhealer.com.

Contents

Introduction   10

Story of Buddha   14
The Early Years, The Turning Point
The Search, The Enlightenment
After The Enlightenment
The Nirvana, The Philosophy

Buddhist Wisdom   30

Stories from Buddha's Life   36
The Sower, The Peacemaker
The Mustard Seed, Angulimala
Queen Kshema, Buddha's Advice to Rahula
The Goat That Laughed and Wept
The Sound the Hare Heard

Buddha Parikrama   50
Varanasi, Sarnath, Bodh Gaya, Rajgir,
Nalanda, Patna, Vaishali, Kushinagar,
Lumbini, Kapilavastu, Sravasti

76 Sacred Sites in India
*Nagarjunakonda-Amravati, Tawang
Dharamsala, Tabo, Leh, Sanchi
Ajanta-Ellora, Dhauli
Lalitagiri-Ratnagiri-Udaygiri
Rumtek-Pemagyantse*

94 The Buddhist World

113 Sacred Sites in the World
*Nepal, Sri Lanka, Thailand
Cambodia, Indonesia, Tibet
China, Japan*

123 Glossary

126 Directory

Let a person be
a light to himself and
learn wisdom...

When he is free from delusion, he will go beyond birth and death.

Introduction

"Do not believe in anything simply because you have heard it. Do not believe simply because it has been handed down for many generations. Do not believe in anything simply because it is spoken and rumoured by many. Do not believe in anything simply because it is written in the holy scriptures. Do not believe in anything merely on the authority of teachers, elders or wise men. Believe only after careful observation and analysis, when you find that it agrees with reason and is conducive to the good and benefit of one and all. Then accept it and live up to it."

- Gautama Buddha

I am not a Buddhist scholar. I am just a lay person who believes and lives by what Buddha has said above, without knowing that he had said it thousands of years ago.

My first brush with Buddha happened when I was just twelve years old, through a lesson in our Hindi textbook. I was not happy with the way he left his wife and newborn son and went to seek answers to his seemingly inane questions. Thus began my quest about Buddha. It has been more than three decades now and my fascination about this great philosopher has turned into deep respect. Some time back I met a few people who were also equally intensely charged about Buddha, one of them was a Korean. We decided to travel the Buddha *parikrama* (circuit), to see and feel all the places visited by Buddha from Lumbini, where he was born to Kushinagar, where he passed away, though not in the same order. We went on the footsteps of Buddha, and the seed of this book, lying within me for years, started to germinate.

Buddha was a great philosopher who came near to revolutionizing the religious thought and feeling of all Asia. The starting point of Gautama Buddha's philosophy was his own question as a fortunate young man, "Why am I not completely happy?" It was an introspective question. It was a question very different in quality from the Self-forgetful externalized curiosity with which the philosophers of that time were attacking the problems of the universe. Buddha concentrated upon Self and sought to destroy it. All suffering, he said, was due to the greedy desires of the individual. Until man has conquered his personal cravings, his life is troublesome and his end sorrowful. All the forms of desire had to be overcome to escape from the distresses and chagrins of life. When they were overcome, when Self had

vanished altogether, then serenity of soul, *nirvana* was attained. This was the gist of Buddha's philosophy, very subtle and metaphysical indeed, and not nearly so easy to understand.

It was a philosophy much beyond the understanding of even Buddha's immediate disciples, yet the world gained substantially from it. If *nirvana* was too high and subtle, people could at least grasp something of the intention of what Buddha called the Noble Eightfold Path in life. In this there was an insistence upon mental uprightness, right conduct and honest livelihood. There was an awakening of the conscience.

I went on the Buddhist pilgrimage as a believer, wanting to feel the land where Buddha lived, preached, walked…. I came back with a firmer resolve to try and make others feel what I felt. To feel the person who lends an elevating perspective to our routine confusing existence, who compels us to look inwards, who makes compassion the easiest emotion to practice… The next time I travel on the path he took so many years ago, that has since been revisited by so many questing pilgrims; I shall not walk on the footsteps but shall walk with Buddha.

This book is an attempt to initiate the readers to sensitise themselves to Buddha's way of thinking. If done with an open

Introduction

mind it would take root and grow within, changing one's perspective towards life, resulting in the spiritual growth in the direction of enlightenment. After all the footsteps of Buddha *did* reach their goal of enlightenment!

Story of Buddha

The Early Years

Gautama Buddha was born Siddhartha, in 623 BC, in the kingdom of Shakyas, located on the present day Indo-Nepalese border with its capital at Kapilavastu. He was born to the royal couple, Shuddhodana, and Mahamaya. It seems that before Siddhartha was born, his mother dreamt that a silver white elephant entered her womb from the side. Experts in the court predicted that the dream was an indication of a great man who would either become a universal monarch or the enlightened one, that is a *buddha*.

According to their customs the pregnant Queen left for her mother's place to deliver the baby. But on the way in

Lumbini, when queen Mahamaya rested in a garden, the baby was born. With great joy he was named Siddhartha, meaning 'wish fulfilled'. Seven days after he was born, queen Mahamaya died. Fearing that the prediction about the young prince becoming an ascetic might come true, the King surrounded Siddhartha with great luxury. Mahamaya's younger sister Prajapati looked after Siddhartha as her own son.

At the age of seven Siddhartha began his lessons in literature and the military arts, but his thoughts ran to other things as well.

A very remarkable incident took place in his childhood. To promote agriculture, the King arranged for a ploughing festival. It was indeed a festive occasion for all. Both nobles and commoners participated in the ceremony in their best attires. On the appointed day, the King, accompanied by his courtiers, went to the field, taking with him the young

prince Siddhartha and his nurses. Placing the child on a screened and canopied couch under the cool shade of a solitary rose-apple tree to be watched by the nurses, the King participated in the ploughing festival.

In striking contrast to the mirth and merriment of the festival, it was all calm and quiet beneath the rose-apple tree. Siddhartha, young in years but old in wisdom, noticed a bird flying down to the ground and carrying away a little worm which had been

Story of Buddha

thrown out of the ground by the farmer's plough. He was deeply affected by the sight and thought, "Do all living creatures kill each other?" While he was immersed in his thoughts, the day passed by as usual for everyone else. But, when the King returned to the young prince, he saw that the shadow of the tree had not moved at all. The tree continued to shade the prince while the sun had moved on.

The King was increasingly worried as he recalled the prophesy and tried in every possible way to cheer the prince and to turn his thoughts in other directions. At the age of sixteen, the King arranged the marriage of prince Siddhartha to princess Yashodhara, who was the daughter of Suprabuddha, brother of the late Queen Mahamaya.

For nearly thirteen years, Siddhartha led a luxurious married life, blissfully ignorant of the vicissitudes of life outside the palace gates. His father built three palaces for him, one for each season: summer, winter and monsoon. Within the narrow confines of the palace the prince saw only the rosy side of life, and the dark side, the common lot of mankind, was purposely veiled from him.

The Turning Point

When he was twenty nine years of age, there occurred a series of revelations that irreversibly changed the course of life for Siddhartha.

One glorious day as he went out of the palace to the pleasure park to see the world

outside, he came in direct contact with the stark realities of life. What was previously conceived only mentally, he now saw in vivid reality.

On his way to the park his observant eyes met the strange sights of a decrepit old man, a diseased person, a corpse and a hermit. When the truth about the certainty of old age, sickness and death, dawned on him, he was shocked. The fourth signified the means to overcome the ills of life and to attain peace. Realizing the worthlessness of sensual pleasures, so highly prized by the world, and appreciating the value of renunciation in which the wise seek delight, he decided to leave the world in search of Truth and Eternal Peace.

Such was Siddhartha's state of mind when returning to the palace after seeing the hermit that on being informed about the birth of his son, the royal prince named him Rahula, which meant fetters or bond.

That night, Siddhartha left the city of Kapilavastu, on his favourite horse Kanthaka accompanied by his trusted companion, Channa.

Great was his compassion for his dear ones at this parting, but greater was his compassion for suffering humanity. He was not worried about the future of worldly happiness and comfort of his wife and child as they had everything in abundance and were well protected. It was not that he loved them less, but that he loved humanity more. It was not the renunciation of an old man who had had his fill of worldly life. It was not the renunciation of a poor man who had nothing to leave behind. It was the renunciation of a prince in the full bloom of youth and in the plenitude of wealth and prosperity - a renunciation unparalleled in history.

After crossing the river at the border of his father's kingdom, Siddhartha rested on its banks. Here he shaved his hair and beard and handing over his garments and ornaments to Channa with instructions to return to the palace, assumed the simple yellow garb of an ascetic and led a life of voluntary poverty. He had no permanent abode. A shady tree or a lonely cave sheltered him by day or night. Bare-feet and bare-head, he walked in the scorching sun and in the piercing cold. With no possessions to call his own, but a bowl to collect his food and robes just sufficient to

cover his body, he concentrated all his energies on the quest of Truth.

The Search

Thus as a wanderer, searching for eternal peace, Siddhartha approached Alara Kalama, a distinguished ascetic. Alara Kalama introduced him to the 'realm of nothingness,' an advanced stage of concentration. Siddhartha was quick to learn the doctrine but it brought him no realization of the highest Truth. Alara Kalama was very happy with his pupil's rapid success in achieving what had taken him so long, and invited Siddhartha to join him as a teacher to teach others in need. Siddhartha was not satisfied with a discipline and a doctrine which only led to a high degree of mental concentration, but did not lead to 'detachment, cessation (of suffering), tranquillity, and enlightenment.' Nor was he anxious to lead a company of ascetics even with the co-operation of another generous teacher of equal spiritual attainment, without

first perfecting himself. It was, he felt, a case of the blind leading the blind. Dissatisfied, he politely took leave.

Then Uddaka Ramaputta, another great teacher, taught Siddhartha to attain the 'realm of neither-perception-nor-noperception', a higher mystical state than the previous one.

This was the highest stage in worldly concentration when consciousness becomes so subtle and refined that it cannot be said whether the consciousness exists or not. Ancient Indian sages could

not proceed further in spiritual development. However, Siddhartha was still not satisfied. He felt that his quest of the highest Truth was still not achieved.

He had gained complete mastery of his mind, but his ultimate goal was far ahead. He was seeking *nirvana*, the complete cessation of suffering, the total eradication of all forms of craving. Dissatisfied with this doctrine too, he left.

He realized that his spiritual aspirations were far higher than those under whom he chose to learn. He realized that there was none capable enough to teach him what he yearned for - the highest Truth. He also realized that the highest Truth is to be found within oneself and ceased to seek external aid.

Disappointed but not discouraged, Siddhartha wandered through the district of Magadha. He eventually arrived at Uruvela (modern Gaya), the market town of Senani. There he found a peaceful place in a charming forest grove near the flowing river Niranjana. The place was congenial for his meditation. Alone, he resolved to settle down there to achieve his desired object. Hearing of his renunciation, Kondanna, the youngest of the brahmins who predicted his future, and four sons of the other sages - Bhaddiya, Vappa, Mahanama, and Assaji - also renounced the world and joined him in his quest.

In ancient India, great importance was attached to rites, ceremonies, penances and sacrifices. It was popularly believed that no

Deliverance could be gained unless one leads a life of strict asceticism. Accordingly, for six long years Siddhartha made a super-human struggle to practice all forms of the severest austerity and self-mortification. But, his prolonged painful austerities proved utterly futile. They only resulted in the exhaustion of his valuable energy. His delicately nurtured body could not stand the great strain. His graceful form completely faded almost beyond recognition. His golden coloured skin turned pale, his blood dried up, his sinews and muscles shrivelled up, and his eyes were sunk and blurred. To all appearance he was a living skeleton. He was almost on the verge of death. The more he tormented his body the farther his goal receded from him.

Siddhartha was now fully convinced from personal experience of the utter futility of self-mortification which, though considered indispensable for Deliverance, actually weakened one's intellect, and resulted in lassitude of spirit.

He abandoned this painful extreme as he did the other extreme of self-indulgence which tends to retard moral progress. He conceived the idea of adopting the 'middle path'

which later became one of the salient features of his teaching.

He realized that denial of food took its toll on his body and distracted him from his goal. So he decided to nourish the body sparingly. He bathed in the river and accepted a bowl of food from the hand of Sujata, a young woman who lived in the neighbouring village. The five companions who had lived with Siddhartha for the six years of his ascetic practices looked on with amazement that he could receive food, and that too from the hands of a woman; and left him in disgust.

The Enlightenment

Finally, Siddhartha sat cross-legged at the base of a *peepal* tree, determined to attain enlightenment. He sat in deep meditation.

It was an intense struggle. His mind was desperate, filled with confusing thoughts; dark shadows overhung his spirit; he was beset with all the lures of evil. But carefully and patiently he examined them one by one and rejected them all. It, indeed, was a hard struggle, that made his blood run thin, his flesh creep, and his bones crack.

He soon gained insight into his past births.

He recalled his varied forms in former existence in details, the pleasures and pains he had undergone; then both the dissolution and evolution of many world cycles and his departure from there to come into existence here. Then he attained the power to see the passing away and rebirth of beings.

With clairvoyant vision, purified and supernormal, he perceived beings disappearing from one state of existence and reappearing in another; he beheld the base and the noble, the beautiful and the ugly, the happy and the miserable, all passing according to their deeds.

He knew that the individuals, by evil deeds, words, and thoughts, after the dissolution of their bodies and after death, had been born in sorrowful states. He knew that the individuals, by good deeds, words, and thoughts, after the dissolution of their bodies and after death, had been born in happy celestial worlds.

Dispelling thus the ignorance with regard to the future, he directed his purified mind to the comprehension of the 'cessation of sorrow.' He realized in accordance with the fact: "This is Sorrow (*dukkha*); this, the Arising of Sorrow; this, the Cessation Sorrow; this, the Path leading to the Cessation of Sorrow". Thus cognizing, thus perceiving, his mind was delivered from the Corruption of Sensual Craving; from the Corruption of Craving for Existence; from the Corruption of Ignorance. Being delivered, He knew, "I am Delivered" and He realized, "Rebirth is ended; fulfilled the Holy Life; done what was to be done; there is no more of this state again." Ignorance was dispelled, and wisdom arose; darkness vanished, and light arose. The struggle was over and Siddhartha's mind was as clear and bright as the daybreak. He had found the path to enlightenment at last.

Prince Siddhartha was thirty-five years of age when he became Buddha. The word Buddha was attached as a suffix to indicate that he was the Enlightened One.

After The Enlightenment

Buddha then preached his philosophy and trained his followers to do the same. He propagated *dharma* and advocated following the Middle Path between worldly attachments and extremes of self-denial. He went first to Varanasi where the five mendicants who had lived with him during the six years of his ascetic life were staying. At first they shunned him, but after he had talked with them, they believed in him and became his first followers. Then he went to Rajagriha and won over King Bimbisara. From there he went about the country living on alms and teaching people his philosophy and way of life. Buddha's father, King Shuddhodana, Prajapati, Buddha's foster-mother, and Princess Yashodhara, his wife, and all the members of the Shakya clan, believed in him and followed him. And multitudes of others became his devoted and faithful followers.

The Mahaparinirvana

For forty-five years Buddha went about the country preaching and persuading men to follow his way of life. At last, at Vaishali on the way from Rajagriha to Sravasti, he predicted that after three months he would enter *mahaparinirvana*. Still he journeyed on until he reached Pava where he fell critically ill by food offered by Chunda, a blacksmith. Then in spite of great pain and weakness, he reached the forest on the border of Kushinagar. Lying between

two large *sal* trees, he continued his teachings to his favourite disciples until the last moment. At the age of eighty, on a full moon day of the month of Vaishakha, Buddha attained *nirvana*. A week after he passed away, he was cremated. When there was a fight over the claims of his remains, it was divided into eight portions and placed at eight different places. Stupas were built at these eight places, in honour of the Enlightened One.

The Philosophy

After a stupendous struggle of six strenuous years, in his 35th year, Siddhartha, solely relying on his own efforts and wisdom, eradicated all defilements from within, realizing things as they truly are, by his own intuitive knowledge, and became a Buddha - the Enlightened or Awakened One. Siddhartha was not born a Buddha, but became a Buddha by his own efforts.

The Pali term Buddha is derived from 'budh' meaning, to understand, or to be awakened.

Gautama, the Buddha, essentially preached these truths: that life is fundamentally disappointment and suffering; that suffering is a result of one's desires for pleasure, power, and continued existence; that in order to stop disappointment and suffering one must stop desiring; and that the way to stop desiring and thus suffering is the Noble Eightfold Path, namely, 'right views, right intention, right speech, right action, right livelihood, right effort, right awareness, and right concentration'.

Buddha admitted his past wanderings in existence which entailed suffering, a fact that evidently proves his belief in rebirth. He was compelled to wander and consequently to suffer, as he could not discover the architect that built his body. In his final birth, while engaged in solitary meditation which had become highly developed in the course of his wanderings, he discovered through his own inner wisdom the elusive architect, residing not outside but within the recesses of his own being. It was craving or attachment, a self-creation, a mental element latent in all.

How and when this craving originated is incomprehensible, but what is created by oneself can also be destroyed by oneself. The rafters of this self-created house are the passions such as attachment, aversion, illusion, conceit, false views, doubt, sloth, restlessness, moral shamelessness, and moral fearlessness. The pole that supports the rafters is the ignorance.

The shattering of this pole of ignorance by wisdom results in the complete demolition of the house. The pole and rafters are the material with which the architect builds this undesirable house. With their destruction the architect is deprived of the material to rebuild; his role gets over. With the demolition of the house, the eradication of the architect, one is free. This is Enlightenment.

Buddha did not claim to be an incarnation (*avatara*) of any God, nor did he call himself a 'saviour' who saves others by his personal salvation. Buddha exhorted his followers to depend on themselves for their Deliverance, since both defilement and purity depend on oneself. One cannot directly purify or defile another. Dependence on others would also mean a surrender of one's effort. Buddha indicated the path and method whereby he delivered himself from suffering and death and achieved his ultimate goal. It is left for people who wish their release from the ills of life to walk on his footsteps.

"Be an island unto yourselves; be a refuge unto yourselves; seek no refuge in others." These significant words uttered by Buddha in his last days reveal how vital is self-exertion to accomplish one's ends, and how superficial and futile it is to seek redemption through saviours, and crave for illusory happiness in an afterlife through the propitiation of imaginary Gods by fruitless prayers and meaningless sacrifices.

Buddhist Wisdom

Buddha's teachings were always in the form of parables, as has been the age old Indian way of teaching. He was a good story-teller and encapsulated the most complex of life's philosophies in simplest of stories.

The oldest Buddhist canonical writings began as oral literature. It seems that in the First Buddhist Council in Rajagriha, Buddha's disciples Upali and Ananda recited their Master's teachings from memory. Upali recalled the *Vinaya Pitaka* and Ananda the *Sutra Pitaka*.

The earliest Buddhist literature to have survived is in Pali, as **Tripitaka**, an anthology of *Vinaya, Sutra* and *Abhidharma Pitakas*.

Vinaya Pitaka is the book of discipline, dealing with the rules of Monastic Order. It comprises three works: *Sutra-vibhanga*, an exposition of the monastic rules and the disciplinary actions prescribed for each offence; *Khandhaka*, a series of 22 pieces dealing with such matters as admission to the order, monastic ceremonies, rules governing food, clothing, lodging, and the like, and procedures for handling offences and disputes; *Parivara*, a classified digest of the rules in the other *Vinaya* texts.

Sutra Pitaka is the book of discourses, dealing with the ethical principles of Buddha's teachings. Consisting of five collections (*nikayas*), it makes rewarding reading because of the richness of the illustrative similes that it contains. The discourses are chiefly in prose, except for stanzas illustrating or summing up a particular point. The *Digha Nikaya* (Collection of Long Discourses) contains 34 *sutras*, some of considerable length, presenting a vivid picture of the different aspects of life and thought at Buddha's time. Divided into three books, it contrasts superstitious beliefs, various doctrinal and philosophical speculations, and ascetic practices with Buddhist ethical ideas, which are elucidated with the help of similes and examples taken from the everyday life of the people. The *Majjhima Nikaya* (Collection of the Middle Length Sayings) contains 152 *sutras*, presenting Buddhist ideas and ideals, illustrating them by similes of great literary beauty. The *Samyutta Nikaya* (Collection of Kindred Discourses) has altogether 2,941 *sutras*, classed in 59 divisions (called *samyutta*)

grouped in five parts (*vagga*). In a kind of questioning and answering style, the Collection deals with the important principle of dependent origination - the chain of cause and effect affecting all things; the rejection of ego and the transitoriness of the elements constituting reality.

The *Anguttara Nikaya* (Collection of the Gradual Sayings) contains 2,308 small *sutras* arranged according to the number of topics discussed, ranging from one to eleven. It states that there are three areas in which training is needed - in conduct, concentration, and insight - and that there are eight worldly concerns - gain, loss, fame, blame, rebuke, praise, pleasure, and pain. The *Khuddaka Nikaya* (Collection of Small Texts) comprises 15 separate titles:

1. *Khuddaka-patha* (Short Passages), a compilation of 9 items, including the Buddhist creed, 10 precepts for novices, a hymn of praise to Buddha, and verses accompanying oblations to departed spirits.

2. *Dhammapada*, an anthology of ethical teaching.

3. *Udana* (Inspired Utterances), 82 sayings of Buddha, mostly in verse, each accompanied by the story of what occasioned it.

4. *Itivuttaka* (from the words 'Thus it is said,' with which each verse begins), a collection, in 112 short *sutras*, of Buddha's ethical teachings in prose and verse.

5. *Suttanipata*, concerned with the faith of a hermit.

6. *Vimanavatthu* (Stories of Celestial Mansions), 85 poems on the happiness of persons reborn in heavenly realms and on the worthy deeds that led to this reward.

7. *Petavatthu* (Stories of Spirits of the Dead), 51 similar poems on those whose misdeeds have condemned them to a sorrowful fate after death. This and the preceding work are among the latest in the canon.

8. and 9. *Theragatha and Therigatha* (Hymns of the Elders/Senior Nuns), lyrics in which 264 monks speak of their inner experiences and of nature and 100 nuns tell of their daily lives. The latter verses are informative about the position of women in ancient India.

10. *Jatakas* (Births) are the extremely popular stories of former lives of Buddha. There are about 550 *Jataka* stories, some of which are quite brief while others are as long as novelettes. Each tale begins by noting the occasion that prompted its telling and ends with Buddha identifying the current people with those from the past. Buddha himself may appear in the stories as a king, an outcast, a god, an animal - but, in whatever form, he exhibits some virtue that the tale thereby inculcates. Many *Jatakas* have parallels in the Mahabharata, Panchatantra, Puranas and elsewhere in non-Buddhist Indian literature. The *Jataka* stories have also been illustrated

frequently in sculptures and paintings throughout the Buddhist world.

11. *Niddesa* (Exposition), a commentary within the canon itself, attributed to Sariputra.

12. *Patisambhida-magga* (Way of Analysis), a late work consisting of 30 chapters of *Abhidhamma,* or scholastic like analysis, of various doctrinal concepts.

13. *Apadana* (Stories), a collection of legends about Buddhist saints.

14. *Buddhavamsa* (History of the Buddhas), a narrative in verse in which Buddha tells of the lives of the preceding 24 buddhas. (Earlier works know of only the last six of these.) Buddha himself, in former lives, knew and worshiped each of them, and each foretold his future Buddhahood.

15. *Cariya Pitaka* (Book of Conduct), 35 *Jataka* stories told in verse and emphasizing the *paramita*s (perfections) requisite to Buddhahood that Buddha acquired in his former lives.

Abhidharma Pitaka is a collection of abstract philosophies elaborating the metaphysical principles underlying Buddha's doctrine. Unlike *Sutra* and *Vinaya*, the seven *Abhidharma* works are not generally claimed to represent the words of Buddha himself but of disciples and great scholars. These are not systematic philosophical treatises but a detailed scholastic reworking,

according to schematic classifications, of doctrinal material appearing in the *Sutras*. The *Abhidharma Pitaka* encompasses the following texts, or *pakaranas*: (1) *Dhammasangani* (Summary of Dharma), a psychologically oriented manual of ethics for advanced monks; (2) *Vibhanga* (Division, or Classification), a kind of supplement to the *Dhammasangani,* treating many of the same topics; (3) *Dhatukatha* (Discussion of Elements), another supplementary work; (4) *Puggalapaññatti* (Designation of Person), classifying human characteristics in relation to stages on the Buddhist path; (5) *Kathavatthu* (Points of Controversy), attributed to Moggaliputta, president of the Third Buddhist Council (3rd century BC), the only work in the Pali canon assigned to a particular author; is a series of questions with their implications refuted in the answers; (6) *Yamaka* (Pairs), a series of questions on psychological phenomena, each dealt with in two opposite ways; (7) *Patthana* (Activations, or Causes), a complex and voluminous treatment of causality and 23 other kinds of relationships between phenomena, mental or material.

Stories From Buddha's Life

The Sower

Bharadwaja, a wealthy brahmin farmer, was celebrating his harvest-thanksgiving when Buddha came with his alms-bowl, begging for food. Some of the people paid him reverence, but the brahmin was angry and said: "It would be more fitting for you to go to work than to beg. I plough and sow, and having ploughed and sown, I eat. If you did likewise, you, too, would have something to eat."

Buddha answered: "I too, plough and sow, and having ploughed and sown, I eat." The brahmin asked: "Where, then, are your bullocks? Where is the seed and the plough?" Buddha said: "Faith is the seed I sow; good work is the rain that fertilizes it; wisdom and modesty are the plough; my mind is the guiding-rein; I hold the handle of the law; earnestness is the goad I use, and exertion is my ox. This ploughing is ploughed to destroy the weeds of illusion. The harvest it yields is the immortal fruit of *nirvana*, and thus all sorrow ends." Then the brahmin poured rice-milk into a golden bowl and offered it to Buddha, saying: "Let the teacher of mankind partake of the rice-milk, for he ploughs a ploughing that bears the fruit of immortality."

The Peacemaker

Two kingdoms were on the verge of war for the possession of a certain embankment. And Buddha seeing the kings and their armies ready to fight requested them to tell him the cause of their quarrel. Having heard the complaints from both the sides, he said: "I understand that the embankment has value for some of your people; has it any intrinsic value aside from its service to your men?" "It has no intrinsic value whatsoever." was the reply. Buddha continued: "Now when you go to battle, is it not sure that many of your men will be slain and that you yourselves, kings, are liable to lose your lives?" And they said: "It is sure that many will be slain and our own lives will be jeopardized." "Does the blood of men," asked Buddha "have less intrinsic value than a mound of earth?" "No," the kings said, "The lives of men and above all the lives of kings, are priceless."

Then Buddha concluded: "Are you willing to stake that which is priceless against that which has no intrinsic value whatsoever?" The wrath of the two monarchs abated, and they came to a peaceful agreement.

The Mustard Seed

Kisa Gautami was a young woman from a well-to-do family and was married to a wealthy merchant. When her only son was about a year old, he fell ill and suddenly died. Overcome with grief, Kisa Gautami took the dead child in her arms and went from house to house asking people if they knew of a medicine that would restore her child to life. Of course, no one was able to help her. Finally, she met a monk, who advised her to meet Buddha.

When she carried the dead child to Buddha and told him her sad story, He listened with patience and compassion, and then said to her: "There is only one way to solve your problem. Go and get me four or five mustard seeds from any family in which there has never been any death."

Kisa Gautami set off to look for such a household, but without success. Every family she visited had experienced the death of some person or another.

At last, she understood what Buddha had wanted her to find out for herself - that death comes to all. Accepting the fact that death is inevitable, she no longer grieved. She returned to Buddha to become one of his followers.

Angulimala

In Sravasti there was a great scholar who had many disciples. One day the king summoned the scholar to the palace. In order to keep watch over his house and also over his wife, the scholar left behind one of his main disciples. The scholar's wife felt great desire for the disciple and when the scholar and his disciples left, she approached him in a very alluring way. However, the boy told her that she was like a mother to him and he would not have anything to do with her. And in order to avoid her, the boy ran away.

The woman became very distressed. She tore her clothes, scratched her body in many places and beat herself with a stick. When her husband returned home, she complained that his disciple had done all that to her when he was away. The scholar believed her and decided to destroy the boy. But he thought that since the boy was very clever he would need a very special method to destroy him. So he decided that he would tell the boy that it was through his actions that he had lost his caste of a Brahmin, and also that he would never be able to gain liberation or gain a state of rebirth in heaven unless he rectified it by killing 1,000 people. He called the boy back and told him about that.

At first the boy refused to do it as he felt that this could not be right. But the teacher convinced him that he must believe the teacher who was teaching him the ways of gaining proper understanding of things in this world.

Believing what his teacher had said, the boy went out and killed 1,000 people. He went back to tell his teacher what he had done. But the scholar told him that he had to show proof of what he had done by cutting off the finger of those whom he had killed and to string them into a garland and wear it around his neck. The boy again went out and killed another 999 people and became Angulimala or 'one who

wears the garland of fingers'. At that time when he had already killed 999 people, his mother, being worried about his absence for many days went searching for him. When the boy saw his mother coming towards him, he thought that it was time he should kill his mother and make her his 1,000th victim. He thought that he would then be able to gain the state of rebirth in heaven and would also be able to put his mother in heaven by killing her. So, he drew out his knife and approached his mother. Buddha, who was in the vicinity, had perceived what was happening through his omniscience. He saw that it was the right moment to place this boy on the *dharma* path and also to awaken his enlightenment thought. So he approached the boy and began to walk in front of him. The boy Angulimala found Buddha's appearance wonderful and told him to stop walking. He asked Buddha who he was, to have the audacity to wander in front of him. Buddha replied that he was the Fully-Awakened One. He continued walking in front of Angulimala who asked him to stop as he intended killing him. Buddha said to him that he was standing still and was not moving anywhere; that he had stopped but Angulimala had not (stopped killing, that is). Then Buddha told him that he should have realised that he had been tricked into following the wrong path which led to great suffering, that he was even about to kill his own mother. Speaking in this way Buddha was able to calm the mind of the boy and convince him that he was on the wrong path. Angulimala then took refuge in Buddha.

Queen Kshema

Kshema was the beautiful queen of King Bimbisara of Magadha. Although he had often urged her to meet Buddha, she had always refused. Knowing that she was attracted to beautiful things, the king arranged for poets to compose poems about the beauty of the Bamboo Grove where Buddha was staying. Fascinated by the poems, she decided to go to the Bamboo Grove and see its beauty for herself. While admiring the scenery there, she caught sight of an especially beautiful maiden, standing beside Buddha. As Queen Kshema went to look closer, she moved nearer and nearer to Buddha. Actually, the beautiful maiden was just a vision created by Buddha with his supernatural powers. While Queen Kshema was gazing at it, the maiden was transformed into an old woman with grey hair and wrinkled skin. She appeared to grow weaker and weaker and finally collapsed and died. The Queen was startled. Then, Buddha said, "Beauty is impermanent."

Then and there, Queen Kshema realised this vital fact of life. Buddha added, "Those who are slaves to desire are like spiders entangled in the webs they have made for themselves. Those who are free and have destroyed attachment to desire do not delight in the pleasures of the senses." On hearing these words, Queen Kshema became an Arhat and with King Bimbisara's consent, entered the Order of Nuns.

Buddha's Advice to Rahula

Being a young boy, Rahula often told lies for fun. Buddha decided to teach him the importance of truthfulness. On one occasion, Buddha showed Rahula a vessel with a small amount of water in it and said, "A person who is not ashamed of telling lies knowingly, has little virtue in him. He is just like this vessel which has but a small amount of water in it." Next, He threw away the water from the vessel and said, "A person who is not ashamed of telling lies knowingly, throws away his virtue just like this water being thrown away." Then, Buddha turned the vessel right way up and said, "A person who is not ashamed of continuously telling lies knowingly, is as hollow and empty as this vessel."

Buddha also used another example to show him how to cultivate good conduct. "What do you think of a mirror? What is its purpose?" Buddha asked Rahula. "It is meant to reflect one's appearance," he answered. "In the same way, one's actions, words and thoughts must be reflected upon as if one were looking at them in a mirror. Before actions are done, consider whether they are harmful to yourself, to others or to both yourself and others. Only when they are beneficial to all should they be done. In the same way, before you speak, consider whether your

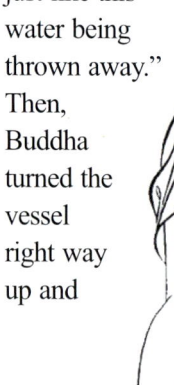

words are harmful to yourself, to others or to both yourself and others. Only if they are beneficial to all should they be spoken. When thoughts arise, consider whether they are harmful to yourself or to others or to both yourself and others. If they are not beneficial to all, they should be discarded. This is the way you must train yourself to consider your actions, words and thoughts. This is the way to purify yourself." Rahula was delighted by the words of Buddha and decided to discipline himself to become a good monk.

Jatakas

The Goat That Laughed and Wept

One day, while Buddha was staying in Jetavana, some *bhikkhus* (monks) asked him if there was any benefit in sacrificing goats, sheep, and other animals as offerings for departed relatives. "No, *bhikkhus*," replied Buddha. "No good ever comes from taking life, not even when it is for the purpose of providing a feast for the dead." Then he told this story of his past:

Long, long ago, when Brahmadatta was reigning in Varanasi, a brahmin decided to offer a feast for the dead and bought a goat to sacrifice. "My boys," he said to his students, "take this goat down to the river, bathe it, brush it, hang a garland around its neck, give it some grain to eat, and bring it back." "Yes, sir," they replied and led the goat to the river. While they were grooming it, the goat

started to laugh. Then, just as strangely, it started to weep loudly. The young students were amazed at this behaviour. "Why did you suddenly laugh?" they asked the goat, "and why do you now cry so loudly?" "Repeat your question when we get back to your master," the goat answered.

The students hurriedly took the goat back to their master and told him what had happened at the river. Hearing the story, the master himself asked the goat why it had laughed and why it had wept.

"In times past, brahmin," the goat began, "I was a brahmin who taught the Vedas like you. I, too, sacrificed a goat as an offering for a feast for the dead. Because of killing that single goat, I have had my head cut off 499 times. I laughed aloud when I realized that this is my last birth as an animal to be sacrificed. Today I will be freed from my misery. On the other hand, I cried when I realized that, because of killing me, you, too, would be doomed to lose your head five hundred times. It was out of pity for you that I cried."

"Well, goat," said the brahmin, "in that case, I am not going to kill you." "Brahmin!" exclaimed the goat, "whether or not you kill me, I cannot escape death today." "Don't worry," the brahmin assured the goat, "I will guard you." "You don't understand," the goat told him, "your protection is weak; the force of my evil deed is very strong."

The brahmin untied the goat and said to his students,

"Don't allow anyone to harm this goat." They obediently followed the animal to protect it. After the goat was freed, it began to graze. It stretched out its neck to reach the leaves on a bush growing near the top of a large rock. At that very instant a lightning bolt hit the rock, breaking off a sharp piece of stone which flew through the air and neatly cut off the goat's head. A crowd of people gathered around the dead goat and began to talk excitedly about the amazing accident.

A tree *deva* had observed everything from the goat's purchase to its dramatic death, and drawing a lesson from the incident, admonished the crowd: "If people only knew that the penalty would be rebirth into sorrow, they would cease from taking life. A horrible doom awaits one who slays." With this explanation of the law of *karma* the *deva* instilled in his listeners the fear of hell. The people were so frightened that they completely gave up the practice of animal sacrifices. Buddha ended his lesson and identified the Birth by saying, "In those days I was that *deva*."

The Sound the Hare Heard

One morning while some *bhikkhus* were on their alms round in Sravasti, they passed some ascetics of different sects practicing austerities. Some of them were naked and lying on thorns. Others sat around a blazing fire under the burning sun. Later, while the monks were discussing the ascetics, they asked Buddha, "Lord, is there any virtue in the harsh ascetic practices?"

Buddha answered, "No, monks, there is neither virtue nor any special merit in them. When they are examined and tested, they are like a path over a dunghill, or like the noise the hare heard."

Puzzled, the monks said, "Lord, we do not know about that noise. Please tell us what it was." At their request Buddha told them this story of the distant past:

Long, long ago, when Brahmadatta was reigning in Varanasi, the *bodhisattva* was born as a lion in a forest near the Western Ocean. In one part of that forest there was a grove of palms mixed with *bel* (woodapple) trees. A hare lived in that grove beneath a palm sapling at the foot of a *bel* tree.

One day the hare lay under the young palm tree, idly thinking, "If this earth were destroyed, what would become of me?" At that very instant a ripe *bel* fruit happened to fall and hit a palm leaf making a loud 'THUD!' Startled by this sound, the hare leapt to his feet and cried, "The earth is collapsing!" and immediately fled, without even glancing back.

Another hare, seeing him race past as if for his very life, asked, "What's wrong?" and started running, too. "Don't ask!" panted the first. This frightened the second hare even more, and he sprinted to keep up. "What's wrong?" he shouted again. Pausing for just a moment, the first hare cried, "The earth is breaking up!" At this, the two of them bolted off together.

Their fear was infectious, and other hares joined them until all the hares in that forest were fleeing together. When other animals saw the commotion and asked what was wrong, they were breathlessly told, "The earth is breaking up!" and they too began running for their lives. In this way, the hares were soon joined by herds of deer, boars, buffaloes, wild oxen, and rhinoceroses, a family of tigers, and some elephants.

When the lion saw this headlong stampede of animals

Stories From Buddha's Life

and heard the cause of their flight, he thought, "The earth is certainly not coming to an end. There must have been some sound which they misunderstood. If I don't act quickly they will be killed. I must save them!"

Then, as fast as only he could run, he got in front of them, and roared three times. At the sound of his mighty voice, all the animals stopped in their tracks. Panting, they huddled together in fear. The lion approached and asked why they were running away. "The earth is collapsing," they all answered. "Who saw it collapsing?" he asked. "The elephants know all about it," some animals replied. When he asked the elephants, they said, "We don't know, the tigers know." The tigers said, "The rhinoceroses know." The rhinoceroses said, "The wild oxen know." The wild oxen said, "The buffaloes know." The buffaloes said, "The boars know." The boars said, "The deer know." The deer said, "We don't know, the hares know." When he asked the hares, they pointed to one particular hare and said, "This one told us."

The lion asked him, "Is it true sir, that the earth is breaking up?" "Yes, sir, I saw it," said the hare. "Where were you when you saw it?"

"In the forest in a palm grove mixed with *bel* trees. I was lying there under a palm at the foot of a *bel* tree, thinking, 'If this earth were destroyed, what would become of me?' At that very moment I heard the sound of the earth breaking up and I fled."

From this explanation, the lion realized exactly what had really happened, but he wanted to verify his conclusions and demonstrate the truth to the other animals. He gently calmed the animals and said, "I will take the hare and go to find out whether or not the earth is coming to an end where he says it is. Until we return, stay here."

Placing the hare on his back, he raced with great speed back to that grove. Then he put the hare down and said, "Come, show me the place you meant." "I don't dare, my lord," said the hare. "Don't be afraid," said the lion. The hare, shivering in fear, would not risk going near the *bel* tree. He could only point and say, "Over there, sir, is the place of dreadful sound."

The lion went to the place the hare indicated. He could make out where the hare had been lying in the grass, and he saw the ripe *bel* fruit that had fallen on the palm leaf.

Having carefully ascertained that the earth was not breaking up, he placed the hare on his back again and returned to the waiting animals. He told them what he had found and said, "Don't be afraid." Reassured, all the animals returned to their usual places and resumed their routines.

Those animals had placed themselves in great danger because they listened to rumours and unfounded fears rather than trying to find out the truth themselves. Truly, if it had not been for the lion, those beasts would have rushed into the sea and perished. It was only because of the *bodhisattva's* wisdom and compassion that they escaped death. At the conclusion of the story, Buddha identified the Birth: "At that time, I myself was the lion."

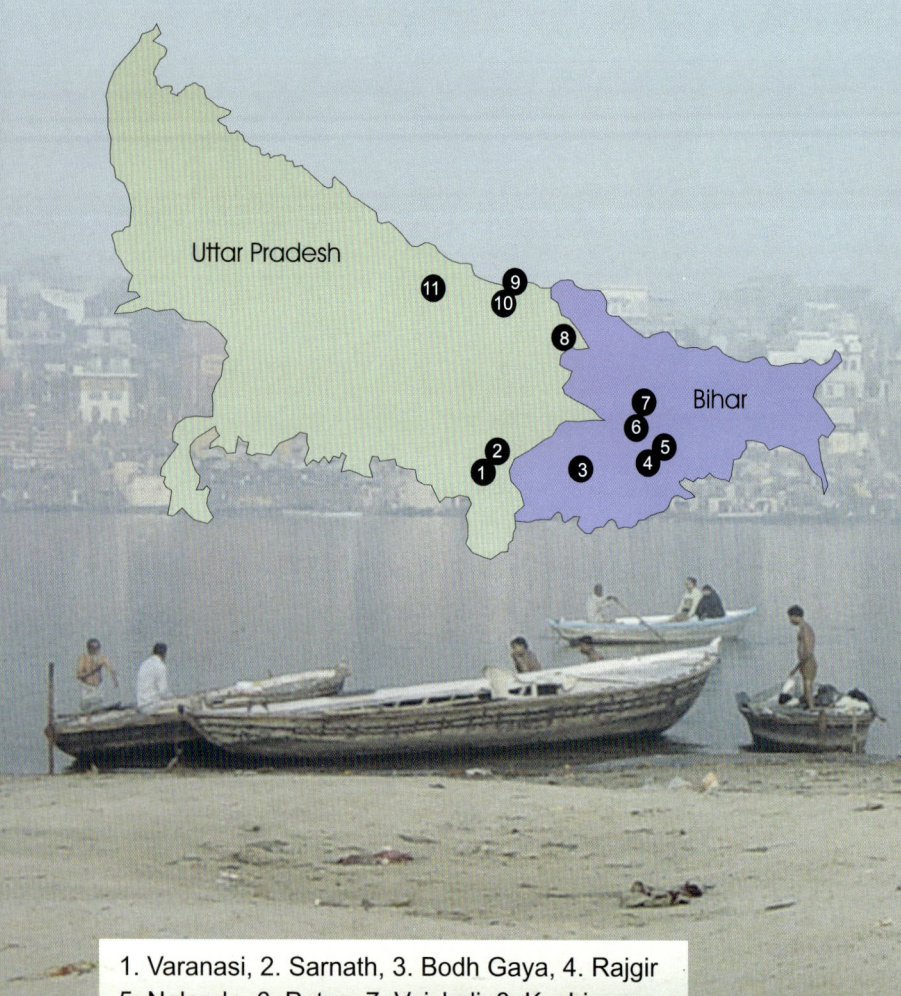

The journey begins from Delhi by train to Varanasi in Uttar Pradesh. Buddha came crossing the Ganga to the *ghats* (banks) of Varanasi (ancient Kashi), from Bodh Gaya, after attaining enlightenment, looking for his five companions who had abandoned him earlier. Early morning with the rising sun if you cross the river and go to the other side, from where you get a panoramic view of the ghats … it is not difficult to imagine Buddha walking alone on those sands…

Varanasi (Uttar Pradesh)

Varanasi is on the west bank of the river Ganga, in Uttar Pradesh, at a distance of 764 kms from Delhi. Varanasi is connected by good roads to Sarnath, Lumbini, Kapilavastu, Kushinagar and Sravasti.

On the Footsteps of Buddha

From Varanasi onwards, the journey is in a jeep, starting from the nearby city of **Sarnath**. Rishipattana, the Deer Park, in Sarnath, was where Buddha found his ex-companions. Chaukhandi Stupa marks the spot where he first met them. It is a derelict monument, but once you manage to climb up to the top, you are able to see the Dhamekh Stupa at a distance. A magnificent monument, the sheer size of which makes you feel very small literally and figuratively, Dhamekh Stupa was built by Ashoka to mark the spot where Buddha preached Dharmachakraparivartana for the first time to his five followers and started the *sangha*. In the same complex, Dharmarajika Stupa, now in ruins, marks the site where Buddha gave his first sermon. Remains

Dhamekh Stupa

of a massive monolithic Ashoka pillar mark the exact location. And Mulgandhakuti is the place where Buddha meditated during the monsoons. Anagarika Dharmapala built the temple Mulgandhakuti Vihara at the site in 1922, enshrining the relics of Buddha found in Taxila. Japanese frescoes adorn the temple walls depicting the life story of Buddha. A huge Bodhi tree outside in the courtyard completes the picture. Walking through the ruins, the realisation hits that one has entered the world of Buddha. The peace, the monks… there is a certain sanctity in the whole environment.

Sarnath (Uttar Pradesh)

Rishipattana or Mrigadaya, the Deer Park, in Sarnath, is only 10 kms away from Varanasi. The high mound with the remains of the Chaukhandi Stupa is topped by an octagonal tower commemorating the visit of the Mughal emperor Akbar to the city. Dhamekh Stupa, the most impressive sight in Sarnath, is a 33metres tall cylindrical stupa with its walls covered with delicately carved geometrical, floral patterns, birds and human figures. It was here that Yasha, son of a rich merchant of Kashi, renounced his worldly life to join the *sangha*. Sarnath museum is a treasure trove of Buddhist sculptures, pottery and inscriptions. It also houses the Ashoka pillar with the magnificent capital of four roaring lions, supporting the wheel or *dharmachakra*, facing the four cardinal directions. Over 15metres tall, the original pillar had a lotus, four small wheels, a lion, a bull, a horse and an elephant carved on its lower portion.

Mulgandhakuti Vihara

The next halt is at **Bodh Gaya**, situated on the banks of river Phalgu in Bihar. On the banks of the river, under the Bodhi tree, Buddha sat facing the east, till he attained enlightenment. Bodh Gaya jolts one back to the present, with its beggars accosting the tourists, pavements spilling over with vendors selling rosaries, incense, Buddha images et al. The roadside *dhabas* selling *chai-pakoras* are no different from any other tourist spot.

A little away from the main city, in the Pragbodhi caves, on the Brahmayoni hill, Buddha practiced severe austerities for 6 years. After which Sujata, daughter of the village chief of Senani, offered him a bowl of *kheer* (sweet made with rice and thickened milk). It is believed that the *kheer* was infused with *amrit* (ambrosia) by the gods. Sujata's village, her house, are not part of the regular tourist circuit, so not very many people get to see them; which is sad as this is the place where one can actually feel the presence of Buddha. After all it was here that he became Buddha!

The famous Mahabodhi temple in the city of Bodh Gaya has seven sacred spots within its precincts, including the Bodhi tree. The Bodhi tree

Mahabodhi Temple

here is said to have been planted from a sapling from the original tree under which Buddha attained enlightenment. The entire temple complex seems like a small monastery, with monks all over; praying, chanting, meditating… the vibrations make one sit, and if not pray, just watch the others praying and suddenly one realises that one has begun praying too.

Bodhi Tree

Bodh Gaya (Bihar)

As the place of Buddha's enlightenment, Bodh Gaya is the spiritual home of the Buddhists. Known as Uruvela earlier, Bodh Gaya is situated on the banks of river Phalgu (ancient Niranjana). It is in Bihar, 115 kms from Patna.

On the banks of the river Phalgu, under the Bodhi tree, prince Siddhartha sat crossed-legged, facing the east, determined in his quest. For forty-nine days, Mara (the tempter or devil) assaulted him with his weapons of water, fire, thunder and lightning and thereafter through his three beautiful daughters. But Siddhartha remained unfazed, entering deeper and deeper into meditation. His quest finally ended at the dawn of Vaishakha (April-May) *poornima* (full-moon). He attained *samma sambodhi* (enlightenment) and became the Buddha.

The main Buddhist attraction of Bodh Gaya, 52 metres tall Mahabodhi temple, is surrounded by beautifully carved votive stupas and chaityas. The Bodhi tree next to it is cordoned off, but its leaves that fall are picked up enthusiastically by the

Buddhapada

people who pray to it. Next to the tree is a shrine with a large circular stone with Buddha's footprints, known as Buddhapada.

The main temple shrine has a gilded statue of Buddha in the *bhumisparsha mudra*, with one finger touching the earth calling it to witness his awakening. A chamber at the top houses a figure of Mahamaya, Buddha's mother.

Seven spots within the precincts of the Mahabodhi temple are sacred because Buddha spent a week each here, soon after his enlightenment. Buddha spent the first week under the Bodhi tree. The tree was destroyed and replanted five times thereafter. The present tree has grown from the sapling brought from the tree planted by Ashoka's son Mahendra in Anuradhapura, Sri Lanka, in 3rd century BC. The Vajrasana or the diamond throne, a red sandstone slab, is kept at the spot where Buddha sat in meditation under the Bodhi tree.

Main Temple Shrine

Muchhalinda Pond

Buddha spent the second week at the Animeshlochana chaitya, from where he gazed at the Bodhi tree unblinking.

The Ratnachankrama or the jewelled walk is where Buddha spent the third week walking between the Bodhi tree and the Animeshlochana chaitya.

Buddha spent the fourth week in the Ratnaghar chaitya, where he reflected on the higher modes of exposition, *abhidharma nyaya*.

The fifth week was spent in the east, near the entrance, where in response to a brahmin's query, he expounded that good *karma* and not the birth makes a brahmin.

Buddha spent the sixth week at the Muchhalinda pond to the south of the temple.

The seventh week was spent in the southeast, where under the Rajyatna tree Buddha preached his doctrine.

The next destination is **Rajgir**, a city not as commercial as Bodh Gaya. Rajgir was the capital of Bimbisara. After renouncing his royal heritage, Siddhartha came to this city first, where Bimbisara impressed by him, offered half his kingdom to him if he stayed. Siddhartha declined promising to return after getting enlightened. And he kept his promise and visited the place many times. In the rock cut caves of the Griddhakuta hill (Vulture Peak), towards the south of the city, Buddha spent many rainy seasons meditating. Here he preached the Lotus Sutra and the Wisdom Sutra. Here Devadutta tried to kill him by hurling a boulder at him; and also by sending a mad elephant to him. Near the hill is Vishwa Shanti Stupa built by the Japanese. Close by are the ruins of Jivakamravana Vihara, a mango grove presented to the Buddha by Jivaka, the royal physician. The only place in Rajgir where one gets transported back to Buddha is Venuvana Vihara, a bamboo grove, where Buddha used to bathe in the Karanda tank.

Karanda Tank

Rajgir (Bihar)

Rajgir (ancient Rajagriha) is connected by road to Patna 100 kms away, Bodh Gaya 70 kms away and Nalanda 11 kms away. Entering the city from Bodh Gaya, one sees the remains of the thick city wall extending from east to west, from one hill to another. Once 40kms long, it encircled Bimbisara's kingdom. Down the Griddhakuta hill is the site of Mardakukshi Vihara, where Bimbisara's queen tried unsuccessfully to get rid of her unborn baby on the prophesy that he would kill his father. Along the road is the Jivakamravana Vihara, the mango grove presented to Buddha by Jivaka, who looked after him when he was injured. Only ruins of stone foundations remain, indicating the existence of a large monastery once. Across the road are the remains of the jail where Bimbisara was imprisoned and killed by his son Ajatshatru. Filled with remorse, he later joined the *sangha*. A couple of kilometres away is Venuvana Vihara, Bimbisara's first gift to Buddha. Saptaparni Caves, on another hill, is the place where the First Buddhist Council was held to codify Buddha's teachings.

Vishwa Shanti Stupa

On the Footsteps of Buddha

Sariputra's Stupa

The next halt is **Nalanda**, the most renowned university of ancient India. Buddha came here often and stayed at Setthi Pavarika's mango grove. Sariputra and Maudgalyayana, two chief disciples of Buddha, belonged to this region. Sariputra attained *nirvana* here and emperor Ashoka built a stupa at his shrine. To call the ruins of Nalanda impressive would be grossly understating the fact. It seems that besides what can be seen today, there is a lot more still unexcavated at Nalanda. Standing atop the ruins of one of the hostels in the Nalanda campus, hearing that in its heydays a hundred subjects were taught here to students from all over the world is a proud moment, worth experiencing indeed. It is not possible to capture in the photographs, the magnitude of the fact that once hundreds of students were living and studying here, in a well-planned, well designed university campus.

Nalanda (Bihar)

Nalanda, or Baragaon village, is 90kms from Patna, 11kms from Rajgir and 80kms from Bodh Gaya. Nalanda Mahavihara, the most renowned university in ancient India, derived its name from *na alam da*, meaning insatiable in giving, also one of the names of Buddha. It was established in the 5th century AD in the reign of Kumaragupta. During the reign of Devapala, in the early 9th century, Nalanda reached its zenith of fame and glory. Chinese pilgrims Hiuen Tsang and Hwui Li studied in this university and have left detailed accounts of the same. More than a hundred subjects were taught here including the art of debate and public speaking. Among the Indian scholars trained in Nalanda were, Nagarjuna, Aryadeva, Asanga, and thereafter Santarakshita and Padmasambhava, who went to Tibet to spread Budha's teachings. Spread over an area of 14 hectares, the ruins of Nalanda indicate eleven monasteries and five temples, with Sariputra's Stupa being the most imposing.

Nalanda

Situated on the banks of Ganga, **Patna**, is the next destination. Ajatshatru built a fort here, which Buddha saw in his last days and prophesied that the city would always be threatened by fire, flood and feud. The ruins of the city can be seen in Kumrahar. The remains are housed in the Patna museum.

Kumrahar

Patna (Bihar)

Situated on the banks of Ganga, Pataliputra (now known as Patna, State capital of Bihar) became the capital of Magadha Empire under the reign of Ajatshatru. Pataliputra reached its zenith under the Mauryas and Guptas from 6th century BC onwards, especially during the reign of Ashoka (260-239BC). The Third Buddhist Council was held here under his royal patronage. The ruins of Pataliputra city are in Kumrahar. The valuable antiques are housed in the Patna museum, along with the holy casket of Buddha's ashes unearthed from Vaishali.

From Patna one heads towards Vaishali. The vast stretches of fields overflowing with vegetables all through the drive takes away the discomfort of the long journey to a great extent. Because of being a part of the Ganga basin, Bihar happens to be a very fertile State. Buddha taught Ratna Sutra in Vaishali and women were ordained in the *sangha* for the first time here, starting from Buddha's foster-mother Gautami. At Kutagarshala Vihara, Buddha gave his last discourse, and declared the imminent *mahaparinirvana*. Vaishali is also known for Amrapali, the famous courtesan, who invited Buddha to her house. Amvara, the neighbouring village, is the site of her mango grove dwelling. She gifted it to the *sangha* and joined the order herslf. A well is there where her house must have been once. As this spot is not a part of the regular tourist circuit, so very few people know of it.

Kutagarshala Vihara

Vaishali (Bihar)

Vaishali, 60 kms away from Patna, is situated on the northern banks of the river Ganga, bound by the hills of Nepal on the north the river Gandak on the west. When Buddha entered the plague-infested city of Vaishali, there was a heavy rain that washed the city clean, purging it from all infection. Buddha taught Ratna Sutra here and 84,000 thousand people embraced the faith. Kutagarshala Vihara, was built by the ruling Lichchavis, 3kms away from the main city. The site has revealed extensive remains of a huge monastery, chaitya, courtyards and water tanks. Here a monkey gathered honey for Buddha. And it is here that Buddha gave his last discourse, declaring his imminent *mahaparinirvana*. Ashoka built a stupa to mark the spot. The remains of the stupa along with a pillar are also part of the extensive ruins at the site.

A kilometre away from the main city is Abhishek Pushkarini, the coronation tank. The sacred water of the tank anointed the elected representatives of Vaishali. Near the tank stands the Relic Stupa, where the Lichchavis enshrined their share of Buddha's relics. Ananda, Buddha's favourite disciple, attained *nirvana* on the outskirts of Vaishali. A hundred years after Buddha's passing away, the Second Buddhist Council was held in Vaishali. After his last discourse, Buddha set out for Kushinagar. The Lichchavis continued to follow him, even though he told them not to, and even when he gave them his alms bowl. Then Buddha created an illusion of a river in spate that compelled them to return back. The site is Deora, in the Kesariya village, where Ashoka built a stupa to commemorate the event.

Leaving Bihar at Vaishali one enters Uttar Pradesh again in **Kushinagar**. It was the place selected by Buddha for his *mahaparinirvana*. After his last sermon at Vaishali, he came here. The Mahaparinirvana temple enshrines a statue in that posture. On the seventh day after the *mahaparinirvana*, Mahakashyap lighted the funeral pyre at Mukutabandha Vihara. Remains of the stupa can be seen. In fact more than the Mahaparinirvana temple, it is here at this stupa that one gets a sense of peace and a strong desire to meditate.

Mahaparinirvana Temple

Kushinagar (Uttar Pradesh)

Rambhar Stupa

Kushinagar is 176 kms away from Lumbini and 148kms away from Kapilavastu.

Kushinara, as it was known then, the capital of the Malla republic, was the place selected by Buddha for his *mahaparinirvana*. After his last sermon at Vaishali, he came here. On the way he stopped at Pava, where Chunda, a metalsmith, gave him his last meal.

On the banks of Hiranyavati River, on a bed, prepared by Ananda, under two *sal* trees, Buddha attained *mahaparinirvana*. For six days people from far and wide came to pay their obeisance to the mortal remains of Buddha. On the seventh day after the *mahaparinirvana*, the revered *bhikshu* Mahakashyapa lighted the funeral pyre at Mukutabandha Vihara. Today remains of the Rambhar Stupa can be seen there in a small park. The Mahaparinirvana temple in Kushinagar enshrines a six metres long statue of Buddha in the *mahaparinirvana* posture. Close to the temple is the Mathakuar shrine, where he spoke for the last time.

Buddha Parikrama

Kushinagar is close to the Indo-Nepal border and one can cross it to reach Lumbini in Nepal. There is a custom check at the border, so it is advised not to carry much luggage. Lumbini is the sacred site of Buddha's birth. A temple complex houses the tank where Mahamaya had her bath before delivery. The *sal* tree and the sacred stone slab are present at the exact location. Ashoka erected a pillar, to mark the place. Hardly any tourists are seen here. The locals come to the Bodhi tree here and seek its blessings and when their wishes are granted, they come back to tie a flag on it.

Mahamaya Devi Temple

Lumbini (Nepal)

Lumbini grove, the sacred site of Buddha's birth, is in a small village in Nepal, 27 kms from the Indian border at Sonauli. The entire area of the Lumbini village consists of many ruins of the structural remains testifying the birth of Buddha, making it a very important Buddhist site. The temple complex housing the tank where Mahamaya had her bath before delivery is surrounded by the ruins of a number of stupas. The *sal* tree and the sacred stone slab are present at the exact location near the tank. Beautiful stone panels in the Mahamaya Devi Temple depict the birth of baby Siddhartha. Ashoka erected a pillar, Rummendei (also known as Rupandhei) pillar, to mark the place, three hundred years after the *mahaparinirvana* of Buddha. The remains of the pillar are preserved in an enclosure. The Chinese traveller, Fa Hien also visited this site in the 5th century AD.

Sacred Tank and Tree

Back to Uttar Pradesh, this time to **Kapilavastu**. Buddha spent the first three decades of his life here. Ruins of the palace can still be seen. It is worth spending some time roaming about the ruins, imagining the grandeur that young Siddhartha must have left behind... so powerful must have been his urge to find the Truth...

Palace Ruins

Kapilavastu (Uttar Pradesh)

The village of Piprahwa in U.P., 93 kms from Lumbini via Sonauli, is identified as Kapilavastu. It was the capital of Shakya king Shuddhodana. His son Buddha, as prince Siddhartha, spent the first 29 years of his life here. Ruins of the royal palace can still be seen. One and a half kilometres away, excavations by the Archaeological Survey of India in 1971-77 have revealed ruins of the stupas of Devaputra Vihara of the Kapilavastu Bhikshu Sangha, dating back to the Kushan period.

The last destination is **Sravasti**, near Kushinagar. It was the annual monsoon retreat of Buddha. Jetavana Vihara built by Sudatta contains the ruins of Anandakuti and Gandhakuti, where Buddha stayed and expounded the Tripitakas. The vast lawns of the vihara and the ruins can transpose one yet again to Buddha's time. A few monks scattered here and there complete the picture. It was in Sravasti that Buddha performed the miracle of levitating on a thousand petalled lotus, causing fire and water to leap out of his body and multiplying in the air, in response to a challenge from some non-believers.

Sravasti (Uttar Pradesh)

Sravasti (ancient Savatthi), capital of the Kosala kingdom, was the annual monsoon retreat of Buddha for 25 years. It is 147 kms away from Kapilavastu. Sudatta, a rich and pious merchant, wanted to convert a beautiful park at the southern edge of the town into a vihara for Buddha. The land belonged to Jeta, son of the king Prasenjit of Sravasti. Jeta demanded that Sudatta cover the entire park with gold coins, which he did. Though the trees were left uncovered, Jeta agreed to part with the park, which was made into Jetavana Vihara by Sudatta. Once a seven-storied vihara, the site now contains the ruins of Anandakuti and Gandhakuti, where Buddha stayed and expounded the major part of the Tripitakas. Mahet, to the north of Jetavana, has the remains of two stupas, Kachchi Kuti said to be Sudatta's stupa and Pakki Kuti believed to be Angulimala's stupa. Angulimala was a dreaded dacoit who wore a necklace of fingers chopped off from his victims. Once in rage he decided to kill his mother, and met Buddha on the way. Buddha's words changed Angulimala's life.

Then back to Kushinagar to catch a train for Delhi, thus completing the full circuit.

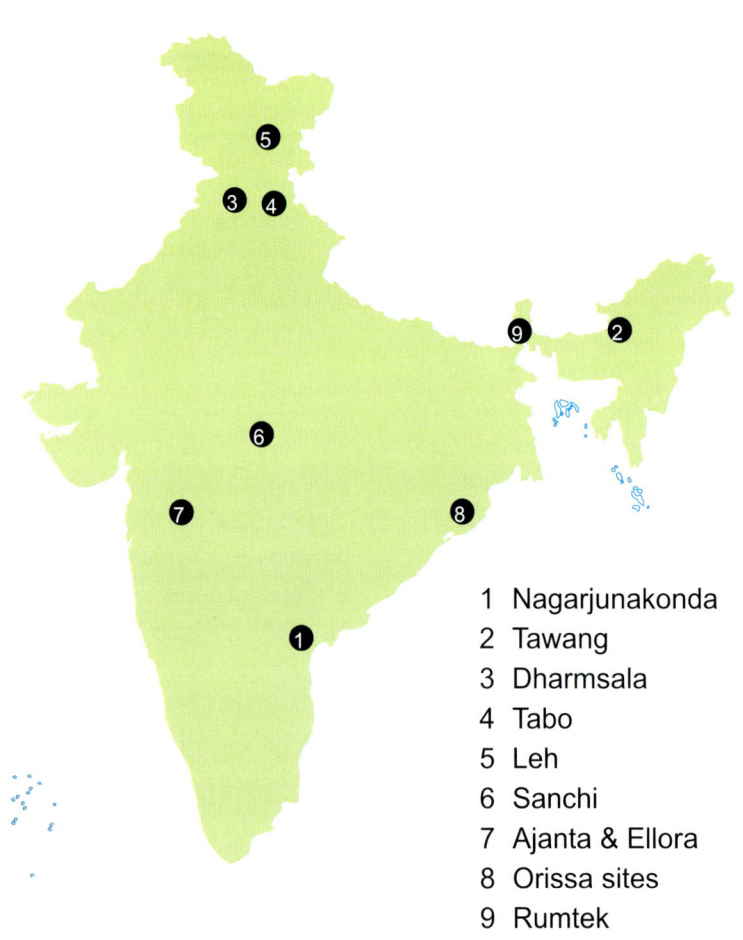

The Buddha *parikrama* covers all the important places associated with Buddha's life, including the four cardinal ones: Lumbini (birth), Bodh Gaya (enlightenment), Sarnath (first sermon) and Kushinagar (*mahaparinirvana*). Though Buddha himself did not go, but his teachings spread far and wide in India and beyond. The sacred Buddhist sites of India are described here.

Nagarjunakonda-Amravati (Andhra Pradesh)

Nagarjunakonda is about 150 kms southeast of Hyderabad, the State capital of Andhra Pradesh. Buddhist religion spread to Sri Lanka and Burma from the ports of the Andhra coast. One of India's richest Buddhist sites, Nagarjunakonda, now lies almost entirely under the Nagarjunasagar Dam. The monasteries and chaityas were reconstructed on top of a hill called Nagarjunakonda (*konda* is Telugu for hill), which rises from the middle of the lake. The main stupa of Nagarjunakonda called Mahachaitya is believed to contain the sacred relics of Buddha. The island takes its name from the Buddhist monk, Nagarjuna, who lived around the turn of the second century AD and was the exponent of the philosophy of *sunyata* (void). Statues, friezes, coins and jewellery found at the site are housed in a museum on the island and give a fascinating insight into the daily lives of this ancient Buddhist centre. Constructed In the shape of a

Buddhist vihara, the museum houses a stupendous collection of relics of Buddhist art and culture. Famous relics include a small tooth and an ear-ring believed to be of Buddha.

Amaravati lies on the right bank of River Krishna, 65 kms from Vijayawada in the State of Andhra Pradesh. It is famous for the ruins of a 2000-year-old Buddhist settlement and the great Buddhist stupa. The great stupa or Maha Stupa of Amravati is larger than the stupa at Sanchi, and it is also known as Deepaladinne or the Mound of Lamps. An envoy of Emperor Ashoka, who spread Buddhism in this region, laid the foundation of this stupa. It has a brick-built circular *vedica* (drum) and platforms projecting in the four cardinal directions.

Most of the archaeological findings from the site, the sculpted friezes, medallions and railings, are exhibited in the British Museum, London, and the National Museum, Delhi. Amravati is considered as one of the most sacred pilgrim centres for the Buddhists.

Tawang (Arunachal Pradesh)

Tawang monastery, situated at a height of 3400 metres, in the far west of the northeast Indian State of Arunachal Pradesh, is one of the largest monasteries in India. The present monastery was built at the site of an ancient monastery in the seventeenth century. Difficult to reach, Tawang stands isolated from the rest of the world with its community of 500 odd monks, attracting scholars and pilgrims from all over the world. The main attractions are a gigantic 10 metre tall gilded statue of the Buddha, a large collection of priceless manuscripts, books and *tangkhas*, depicting stories and important incidents from Buddha's life.

Tawang Monastery

Dharamsala (Himachal Pradesh)

Upper Dharamsala or McLeodganj, the seat of His Holiness, the XIVth Dalai Lama, is in the Kangra district of Himachal Pradesh. This hill station, with its magnificent view of the Dhauladhar range of the Himalayas, has a large Tibetan refugee settlement. The monks in maroon robes, street-side shops selling Tibetan exotica, old people in traditional Tibetan clothes walking past or sitting serenely, turning their prayer wheels, could well be in Buddha's time. The main road leads to Dalai Lama's temple, Namgyal Monastery, housing giant statues of Buddha, Avalokiteshwara and Padmasambhava.

Sacred Sites in India

Tabo (Himachal Pradesh)

Tabo is located at a height of 3050 metres in the Spiti valley of Himachal Pradesh. Founded in 996 AD by the great scholar, Rinchen Zangpo, as an institution for advanced learning, Tabo celebrated its 1000th anniversary in 1996. Unlike other monasteries, Tabo stands on barren, flat ground and is built with mud bricks. A small community of sixty odd monks resides here. The monastery has some rare *tangkhas*, clay statues of Buddha and breathtaking murals reminiscent of the Ajanta paintings.

Leh (Jammu & Kashmir)

Hemis Monastery

Surrounded by the snow-covered Himalayas, Leh the remote headquarters of Ladakh district, is situated at an altitude of 3500 metres. The Buddhist monasteries here are perched perilously on the precipices of the rocky mountains.

Not far from Leh, Shey is the oldest capital of Ladakh from where its earliest Tibetan kings ruled. Perched on top of a huge rock are the royal palace and temples adorned with brilliantly coloured murals and a 7.5 metre gold statue of Buddha. Basgo and Tingmosgang with their forts and palaces were also capitals of Ladakh. Stok Palace across the river from Leh is the home of the erstwhile royal family. The Palace Museum here has collections of beautiful royal costumes and jewellery, exquisite *tangkhas*, porcelain, jade, weapons and armours.

Within easy reach of Leh is the Spituk monastery with the view of the river Indus. It has fine *tangkhas* and a collection of ancient masks. Thiksey monastery, one of the most impressive in the area is spectacularly located and is noted for its beautiful murals. Hemis, founded in the seventeenth century, is the biggest monastery in Ladakh and best known for its magnificent summer festival that celebrates the birth anniversary of Guru

Padmasambhava. The largest *tangkha* in Ladakh is found here. It is unfolded only once every 12 years.

Other magnificent monasteries located in the vicinity include the splendid Lamayuru, Likir, Phyang, Rizdong, Stakna, Matho and Chemrey, all easily accessible from Leh.

Alchi, though no longer an active religious centre, is among Ladakh's most beautiful monasteries. Over a thousand years old, its wall paintings like those of Tabo in Spiti are comparable to the Ajanta style of painting.

The people of Ladakh are predominantly Buddhist and practise Mahayana Buddhism tempered with the old Bon animistic faith and Tantric Hinduism.

The living Buddhist heritage is manifest in the State where walls are engraved with the mantra *Om Mani Padme Hum* and stones are piled into commemorative mounds known as 'chortens'.

Thiksey Monastery

Sanchi (Madhya Pradesh)

Sanchi in Madhya Pradesh is 46kms away from the State capital of Bhopal. Perhaps the finest and most complete Buddhist monument in India is Sanchi's great stupa with its four magnificent free standing gates (*toranas*). The vast brick stupa dates from around the 3rd century BC. The Jataka stories, about Buddha's earlier incarnations, form the main subject of imagery in the carvings and sculptures of the stupa. The images at Sanchi also reflect the prosperity of the times (second century BC to seventh century AD) when

Sanchi Stupa

Sacred Sites in India

the city was at the height of its glory. Elephants and royal lions, Hindu-Buddhist deities and exquisite female nature spirits crowd most parts of the four *toranas*. The small archaeological museum nearby houses excavated sculptures; other important Sanchi pieces are in museums in Delhi, London and Los Angeles.

Ajanta-Ellora (Maharashtra)

Situated in Aurangabad district of Maharashtra, Ajanta caves are world famous for their wall paintings, done by Buddhist monks as well as highly trained artists under royal patronage.

Starting in the second century BC, twenty six caves were chipped out of a horseshoe shaped cliff, in a span of nearly a thousand years. The crescent-shaped ravine pierced with Buddhist cave temples makes this one of India's most spectacular sites.

Many genres of early medieval sacred art, from elaborately carved monastic halls, to sculptures and wall paintings, are represented here, and prominent among Ajanta's glories are murals painted in glowing reds, blues

Sacred Sites in India

and greens. The Jataka narratives form the main theme of the paintings, though scenes from the daily life in the royal courts are also depicted. The paintings flow into one another, in an interplay of human and divine forms, forming a colourful series.

The best paintings are in cave numbers 1, 2, 16, 17 and 19; and the best sculptures are in cave numbers 4, 17, 19 and 26.

Most sublime in grace, compassion and serenity is the incomparable figure of Padmapani, the lotus carrying aspect of the *bodhisattva* Avalokiteshvara in cave 1.

A visit to Ajanta is incomplete without visiting the nearby caves at Ellora. Since seventh century AD, Ellora carried on the great legacy of Ajanta. The sculptures of Ellora are massive but as graceful as those of Ajanta. There are twelve Buddhist caves in Ellora.

Ajanta Caves

Dhauli (Orissa)

The Buddhist heritage in Orissa is remarkable for its architectural wealth. The Kalinga war, which transformed Emperor Ashoka into a devout Buddhist, was fought on the banks of the river Daya near the temple city of Bhubaneshwar, the capital of Orissa. Ashoka's rock edicts, dating from 260 BC, at Dhauli, 8 kms from Bhubaneshwar, stand testimony to his conversion to the gentle faith of Buddha. These Kalinga Edicts differ from other Ashoka edicts which expound Buddhist principles. The Dhauli edicts give detailed instructions to Ashoka's administrators to rule his subjects with gentleness and fairness.

Lalitagiri - Ratnagiri - Udaygiri (Orissa)

Hundred and ten kms from Bhubaneshwar, these three hills represent the rich Buddhist heritage of Orissa. Once the seat of a flourishing Buddhist university called Tushpagiri Mahavihara, these hills still have extensive ruins of monasteries, sculpted stone portals and Buddhist images. Lalitagiri is situated on a small hill and has a large number of votive stupas and the remains of a chaitya hall. The earliest Buddhist complex of first century AD has a huge brick monastery and a renovated stone stupa at the apex of a small rugged sandstone hill, dominating the rural greenery around.

Ratnagiri excavations have revealed the establishment of a Buddhist centre from the time of Narasimha Gupta Baladitya (first half of the sixth century AD). Ratnagiri, the fertile Birupa river valley, 90 kms from Bhubaneshwar, was a great centre of Vajrayana Buddhism till the twelfth century and the Mahavihara of Ratnagiri played a great role in the development of the Kalachakratantra during the tenth century. Remains of this monastic university can be seen with the beautiful sculpted panels. In Udaigiri, 5 kms from Ratnagiri, the remains of a sprawling monastery can be reached through a long stairway. Rock-cut Buddhist sculptures adorn the hilltop.

Rumtek - Pemagyantse (Sikkim)

From its perch on a hilltop facing the city of Gangtok, the capital of Sikkim, the monastery of Rumtek is the seat of the Sixteenth Karmapa, Rangjung Rigpe Dorje. The monastery, largest in Sikkim, is home to the monks, the place where they perform the sacred rituals and practices of the Karma Kagyu lineage. Every year on the twenty-eighth and twenty-ninth day of the tenth lunar month (July) the *cham* dance is performed by monks

Rumtek Monastery

wearing masks and colourful dresses, culminating in a ritual dismembering of an effigy symbolising evil.

Many sacred objects are housed within the complex, and one of the most magnificent is the Golden Stupa, which contains the precious relics of His Holiness the Sixteenth Karmapa. In the precincts of the monastery is also Karma Shri Nalanda Institute for Higher Buddhist Studies. Members of the *sangha* practise in the community lhakhang just outside the walls of the monastery complex. Surrounding Rumtek Dharma Chakra Centre is the stupa walkway, where monks, pilgrims, and visitors alike perform *kora*.

A full day's trip by car, the monastery at Pemagyantse (the perfect sublime lotus) is 140 kms west of Gangtok. Situated at an altitude of 2085 metres, Pemagyantse presents a panoramic view of the high Himalayas. Legend has it that the great tantric saint, Padmasambhava or Guru Rinpoche, searching for a place to meditate, shot an arrow in the air. The place where the arrow landed is where Pemagyantse monastery stands. The monastery houses on its top floor a wooden, intricately crafted structure, depicting Guru Rinpoche's abode. The annual *cham* festival is held in February.

The Buddhist World

In the centuries following the Buddha's lifetime, his followers faithfully preserved his teachings and spread it not only throughout India, but also to many countries in Asia and lately even to Europe and America.

Three months after Buddha's *mahaparinirvana*, his immediate disciples convened a council at Rajagriha. Mahakashyapa presided over this First Council. He began by questioning Upali on the rules governing the life of the monastic community. Based on Upali's answers, the content of the Discipline (Vinaya) was agreed upon. Similarly, Mahakashyapa questioned Ananda on the sermons taught by Buddha. Based upon his answers, the Teaching (Dharma) was established. At the Council, Dharma was divided into various parts and each part was assigned to an Elder and his pupils to commit to memory. The Dharma was then passed on from teacher to pupil orally.

About a hundred years after Buddha's *mahaparinirvana*, a Second Council was held at Vaishali. The purpose of this Council was to settle a disagreement that had arisen between a group of monks and the Elders of the Order. This group of monks resented the exclusive authority of the Elders and wanted greater freedom in the application of the rules of the Discipline. At the Council, the practices of the dissenting monks were declared to be unacceptable. The dissenting monks, however, refused to accept the decision and proceeded to hold their own council elsewhere. They called themselves the 'Great Community' because they were sympathetic to the concerns of the majority of the ordinary monks. This division led to the appearance of two major Buddhist traditions: Theravada (Way of the Elders also known as Hinayana) and Mahayana (the Great Way). Although both traditions acknowledge Buddha as their teacher, they differ in some of the rules of monastic discipline. The Theravada tradition generally teaches that the highest goal, which most people can aspire to, is becoming an Arhat. The Mahayana tradition, however, teaches that the only worthy goal for all is the attainment of Buddhahood.

During the reign of Emperor Ashoka, the renowned Buddhist monarch of the third century BC, the Third Council was held in Pataliputra, to discuss the differences of opinion among the monks of different sects. At this Council differences of opinion were not confined to the Vinaya, but also concerned the Dharma. The President of the Council, Moggaliputta Tissa, compiled a book called the Kathavatthu which refuted the heretical, false views and theories held by some sects occurring at the time. The Council also compiled the Buddhist teachings, which by now included not only the Teaching and the Discipline, but also Buddhist Philosophy and Psychology (Abhidharma). After the Third Council, Ashoka sent missionaries to all over the Indian sub-continent, from the Himalayan regions up north and north-east upto Burma, to Madhya Pradesh in the centre to Maharashtra in the west, to Orissa and Andhra Pradesh along the eastern coast upto Sri Lanka in the south.

The Fourth Council was held in the first century CE under the patronage of Kanishka, a powerful king who ruled in the north-western part of India. For more than a thousand years after the Fourth Council, Buddhism flourished and enjoyed the patronage of many kings throughout India. Great monastic universities like that of Nalanda were built and generations of scholars from India as well as the rest of Asia were taught there. During this period also, Buddhist scholars composed outstanding works in the fields of Ethics, Philosophy and Logic. Eminent scholars like Nagarjuna, Asanga and Vasubandhu, made important contributions to the philosophy of Mahayana Buddhism. As a result, Mahayana Buddhism gained greater popularity throughout India. As Mahayana Buddhism became more popular, many Buddhists in India began to look to the great Bodhisattvas like Amitabha, Avalokiteshvara and Manjushri, for encouragement and inspiration. Vajrayana Buddhism (the Diamond Way) also appeared during this period. Like Mahayana, Vajrayana Buddhism teaches that Buddhahood is attainable by all. It differs from Mahayana, however, in some of the methods that it uses for achieving this goal. These methods, which include meditation upon special forms of the Buddha and the recitation of mantras, can help one attain Buddhahood more quickly.

After the thirteenth century, Buddhism largely disappeared from India, leaving only a few Buddhist communities in the Himalayan belt. In recent years, however, Buddhism has again won new followers and fresh recognition in India.

The Buddhist World

The Fifth Council was held from 1868 to 1871 in Mandalay, Burma where the Pali Canon was inscribed on 729 marble slabs. The Sixth Council was held at Rangoon, Burma in 1954-1956

Sri Lanka

Ashoka's son, Mahendra, headed the mission to Sri Lanka. There, he converted the king to Buddhism.

Later, Ashoka's daughter, Sanghamitra, brought a shoot of the Bodhi tree from Bodh Gaya to Sri Lanka. She also established an Order of Nuns in Sri Lanka. With the help of royal patronage, Buddhism became the dominant religion of Sri Lanka by the second century BC. The fifth century saw the arrival of the famous scholar, Buddhaghosha, from South India. He made an outstanding contribution to the literature of the Theravada tradition.

Burma

During the time of King Ashoka, monks were sent to Thaton to spread Buddha's teachings. Thaton soon became an important centre for Theravada Buddhism.

In later centuries, Vajrayana Buddhism was introduced to the people in northern Burma. They practised it together with Hinduism and local folk beliefs. In the mid-eleventh century, king Anawratha made Theravada Buddhism the national religion. He had Buddhist texts and relics brought from Sri Lanka and built monasteries and stupas in the capital city of Pagan.

Thailand

By the thirteenth century, Buddhist influence had already been felt in this region as a result of contact with neighbouring countries. At the end of the thirteenth century, Theravada Buddhism gained the support of the Thai king, Ramkham-haeng. He invited Buddhist monks to teach in his capital city of Sukothai. Under his patronage, all the people in his kingdom became Buddhists.

About half a century later, king Luthai joined the Order for a period of time and initiated the Thai tradition of Buddhists becoming monks for a limited period of time, usually for three months.

Cambodia

By the end of the fourth century, Indian influence had spread throughout Cambodia. The Buddhist monks of the region were invited to China in the fifth century to translate Buddhist texts from Indian languages to Chinese. In the seventh century, Cambodia had a succession of rulers who patronised Hinduism and suppressed Buddhism. But in the ninth century Buddhism began to receive royal patronage again. King Jayavarman VII, who ruled from the end of the twelfth century to the early years of the thirteenth century, was a devout Buddhist. Under him Mahayana Buddhism became the dominant religion of the kingdom. He built the city of Angkor (Angkor Thom). It was also during his reign that Burmese monks began to teach Theravada Buddhism among the common people.

Laos

In mid-fourteenth century, Fa Ngoun, a descendant of a royal family of Laos, spent his earlier years in exile in Cambodia. He was looked after by a Cambodian monk who later took him to the court of the Cambodian king. There he married a princess who was a devout Buddhist. With the help of the king of Cambodia, he later returned to Laos to rule.

At his wife's request, Fa Ngoun invited Buddhist monks from Cambodia to teach in his kingdom. Thus Buddhism was brought to the people in Laos.

Vietnam

The earliest monks were said to have come to Vietnam from China at the end of the second century. Later, monks from India and Central Asia also arrived by land and sea. But the Chan (Chinese) school of Buddhism flourished in the monasteries and among Buddhist scholars.

Indonesia and Malay Peninsula

Late in the fifth century, an Indian Buddhist monk reached central Java and converted its queen to Buddhism. She in turn converted her son and made Mahayana Buddhism the official religion of the kingdom. In the eighth century, central Java was under the rule of the Sailendra kings who were Buddhists. They built various Buddhist monuments in Java, the most famous of which is the Borobudur. In the ninth century, a Sailendra prince became king of Srivijaya. Under the Sailendra kings, Srivijaya grew in wealth and power. By that time, the kingdom already included Sumatra, Java and the Malay Peninsula. During this period of prosperity, Vajrayana Buddhism also gained wide acceptance throughout the empire.

China

The Chinese people had their first contact with Buddhism through the Central Asians who were already Buddhists. When the Han Dynasty of China extended its power to Central Asia in the first century BC, cultural ties between China and Central Asia also increased. As interest in Buddhism grew, there was a great demand for Buddhist texts to be translated from Indian languages into Chinese. This led to the arrival of translators from Central Asia and India. The first notable one was Anshigao from Central Asia. With a growing collection of Chinese translations of Buddhist texts, Buddhism became more widely known and a Chinese monastic order was also formed. The first known Chinese monk was said to be Anshigao's disciple. The earliest translators had

some difficulty in finding the exact words to explain Buddhist concepts in Chinese, so they made use of Taoist terms in their translations. As a result, people began to relate Buddhism with the existing Taoist tradition. Among the Chinese monks, Dao-an who lived in the fourth century was the most outstanding. He collected copies of the translated scriptures and prepared the first catalogue of them and invited the famous translator, Kumarajiva, from Kucha. With the help of Dao-an's disciples, Kumarajiva translated a large number of important texts and revised the earlier Chinese translations. With the rise of the Tang Dynasty at the beginning of the seventh century, Buddhism reached out to more and more people. It soon became an important part of Chinese culture and had great influence on Chinese Art, Literature, Sculpture, Architecture and Philosophy of that time. By then, the number of Chinese translations of Buddhist texts had increased tremendously. The Buddhists were now faced with the problem of how to study this large number of Buddhist texts and how to put their teachings in to practice. As a result, a number of schools of Buddhism arose, with each school concentrating on certain texts for their study and practice, the two most prominent schools being the Chan and the Pure Land schools.

Korea

Buddhism came into Korea from Central Asia and China, sometime in the fourth century and flourished from the seventh century onwards under the royal patronage of the Silla rulers. Great works of art were created and magnificent monasteries built. Buddhism exerted great influence on the life of the Korean people. In the tenth century, Silla rule ended with the founding of the Koryo Dynasty. Under this new rule, Buddhism reached the height of its importance. With royal support, more monasteries were built and more works of art produced.

The whole of the Tripitaka in Chinese translation was also carved on to wooden printing blocks. Thousands of these blocks were made in the thirteenth century and have been carefully preserved to the present day as part of Korea's national treasures.

Japan

In the sixth century, the king of Packche (southwest Korea), anxious to establish peaceful relations with Japan, sent gifts of images of Buddha and copies of Buddhist texts to the Japanese imperial court. The Japanese people soon accommodated Buddhism along with their indigenous Shinto beliefs. During the early part of the seventh century, prince Shotoku wrote the first 'constitution' of Japan, which promoted moral and social values as taught in Buddhism. His devotion and royal patronage of Buddhism helped to make it widely known. Many Buddhist temples were built and works of art created.

Besides encouraging Japanese monks to read the Buddhist scriptures (from China), Prince Shotoku lectured and later wrote commentaries on some of these scriptures. His commentaries are said to be the first ever written in Japan and are now kept as national treasures. Towards the end of the eighth century, a Japanese monk Kukai introduced Vajrayana Buddhism (learnt in China) into Japan. At the end of the twelfth century, political power shifted to a group of warriors (Samurai). During this period, a number of distinctly Japanese Buddhist sects arose, and became popular because of their simplicity and directness of approach. Among these sects were the Jodo Shinshu, Nichiren and Zen.

Tibet

In the seventh century, the Tibetans, who had long been divided among many warring clans, were united under the rule of a great king, Srong-tsan-gam-po. His Chinese and Nepalese queens were both Buddhists and before long he, too, became interested in Buddhism.

Srong-tsan-gam-po sent representatives to India and China to study the Teaching of Buddha and to bring back Buddhist texts. He had many Buddhist texts translated into Tibetan and encouraged the people to practise the Buddhist teachings. He also constructed many temples throughout Tibet. In the eighth century, one of the later rulers invited Shantarakshita, a famous Buddhist scholar from Nalanda, to teach Dharma in Tibet. But he had to leave because of the opposition of the people. Then Padmasambhava, a famous master of meditation, was invited from India, who was able to remove all opposition to Buddhism in Tibet. Soon, Shantarakshita also returned. Padmasambhava and Shantarakshita together helped to establish the teachings of the Mahayana and Vajrayana firmly in Tibet. During the time of these two

great masters, great monasteries were built and the first Tibetans were ordained. The eleventh century saw a great increase in contacts between Tibet and India and a corresponding growth in Buddhist activity in Tibet. Of the many outstanding contributors are the famous Indian scholar, Atisha, and the great Tibetan meditator and poet, Milarepa. Over the course of several centuries, not only did many outstanding Indian masters visit Tibet, but also many Tibetans made the difficult journey over the Himalayas to study the Dharma in India. They brought back with them the Buddhist philosophy of India and also the knowledge of Music, Medicine, Logic and Art. Virtually the entire collection of Buddhist literature from India was translated into Tibetan.

Hundreds of monasteries were established and numerous Tibetan works on Buddhism were written.

By the thirteenth century, when Buddhism in India began to decline, Tibet was ready not only to preserve Buddhism, but also to transmit it to other lands. In the fourteenth century, yet another teacher influenced the development of Buddhism in Tibet. He was Tson-kha-pa, noted for his careful adherence to the code of monastic discipline and for the quality of his numerous writings. He soon attracted many followers and in the years after his death, his sect gradually gained a very large following in Tibet. Buddhism continued to flourish in Tibet from the fourteenth century right through to the present century. In the middle of the twentieth century, when Tibet came under the rule of the People's Republic of China, Buddhism was repressed. Many Tibetans fled to India and to the West to preserve their religion. In this way, through the Tibetan refugees, many people throughout the world came into contact with Tibetan Buddhist traditions.

Today, there are Tibetan Buddhist centres teaching the Dharma in many lands. Recently, a liberalisation in the policy of the government towards religion in China has permitted a revival of Buddhism within Tibet also.

The Buddhist World

Mongolia

The thirteenth century saw the rise of Mongolian power in Central Asia. By the middle of the century, links had been established between the Mongol court and Tibetan Buddhist masters. At that time, an army under a Mongol prince threatened Tibet. Sakya Pandita, the most outstanding Tibetan religious teacher of the time, was asked to negotiate with the Mongols. Sakya Pandita succeeded in converting the Mongol prince and his court to Buddhism. He began the work of translating the Buddhist scriptures into Mongolian and taught the Dharma to the Mongols until his death.

Later Sakya Pandita's nephew, Cho-gyal-phag-pa, became the personal religious teacher of Kublai Khan. He also continued the work of translating the Buddhist scriptures which had been started by Sakya Pandita.

The Institution of the Dalai Lama

By the sixteenth century, the number of Tson-kha-pa's followers in Tibet had grown dramatically and the Mongols came under the influence of the new sect. It was then that one of the Mongol rulers invited a chief monk from Tson-kha-pa's sect to Mongolia and gave him the title of Dalai Lama (master whose wisdom is vast like the ocean).

The Dalai Lamas are believed to be embodiments of the Bodhisattva Avalokiteshvara who, out of compassion for sentient beings, assumes human form. Upon the death of a Dalai Lama, a search is made for his successor, who is then recognised as the next embodiment of the Bodhisattva. Today as in the past, the Dalai Lama is held in high esteem by Tibetan and Mongolian Buddhists everywhere. In the eighteenth century, the Manchus intervened to end a long period of political strife in Tibet. They appointed the then Dalai Lama as the ruler of Tibet. In this way, the Dalai Lamas became political as well as religious leaders. This situation lasted until the People's Republic of China assumed control of Tibet in the middle of the twentieth century.

Sacred Sites in the World

Svayambhunath - Bodhnath (Nepal)

Other than Lumbini, the birthplace of Buddha, Nepal has some very important stupas in its capital city of Kathmandu, built by Ashoka to commemorate his missionary visit to the country. Two surviving examples are the Svayambhunath and Bodhnath stupas in Kathmandu. Both stupas share unique Nepalese architectural features. Surmounting the conventional dome is a steeple raised on thirteen diminishing tiers to symbolize the thirteen Buddhist heavens. The square base (*harmika*) is gilded, and a face gazes with immense eyes of inlaid metal and ivory from each side. The eyes are supposedly of the 'all-seeing' Buddha. One is followed by these eyes while circumambulating the stupa.

Bodhnath

Anuradhapura - Polonnaruwa (Sri Lanka)

Anuradhapura is a huge park containing the ruins of the great monastery (Mahavihara) established in 250 BC on the outskirts of the ancient Singhalese capital. It is connected by a 13 km pilgrim's path to Mihintale where Mahendra first preached. A stupa marks the spot.

Anuradhapura's stupas, monastic ruins, sculptures, reservoirs, and a descendant

of the original Bodhi tree, provide an intense experience of ancient Buddhism.

Dominating the site are two huge stupas with characteristic Singhalese 'bubble domes,' the Thuparama, probably the oldest monument in either India or Sri Lanka and the Ruwanweli Dagoba. Polonnaruwa, situated on Lake Topawewa, offers an unparalleled view of medieval Buddhist sculpture and architecture. There the visitors may see the immense recumbent *mahaparinirvana* Buddha and the 7.5m rock-cut figure of Ananda standing by the head of the Master. One can also see the colossal meditating Buddha, and the famous sculptured portrait of the sage-king Parakramabahu overlooking the lake and in contemplation of a manuscript. Then there are the early thirteenth century monuments situated on the Great Quadrangle. These include the classically proportioned pyramidal brick stupa (Sat Mahal Pasada), the carved stonework of the 'temple of the tooth relic' and the waving lotus-stem-shaped columns of the Nissanka Lata Mandapaya. The art of Polonnaruwa represents the final flowering of Singhalese Buddhist art.

Polonnaruwa

Wat Phra Kaeo - Ayutthaya (Thailand)

Much early and medieval Thai architecture was ruined in southeast Asian wars, but nineteenth and twentieth century Buddhist temples abound in Thailand. In Bangkok, the Wat Phra Kaeo temple, built by King Rama I (1782-1809) in the precincts of his Grand Palace is a spectacular monument to the Theravada Buddhism. This temple is a centre of Thailand's religious life, symbolizing the close bond between the *sangha* (religious community) and the State, and houses the Emerald Buddha, a figure of national importance to modern Thai people. Perhaps the most beautifully preserved of Thailand's medieval monuments are at the Ayutthaya historical park, north of Bangkok. Of special interest are stupas with characteristic Thai 'lotus bud' domes, and temple towers showing the influence both of medieval Khmer design and of 'honeycombed' south Indian *shikhara* towers.

Ayutthaya

Sacred Sites in the World

Angkor Thom

Angkor Thom (Cambodia)

Angkor Thom was the creation of the Khmer 'god-king' Jayavarman VII (1181-1219), who converted to Mahayana Buddhism following the destruction of Angkor by the Vietnamese during his father's reign.

Jayavarman's Buddhism seems to be a revised version of the Brahmanical religion which previous Khmer kings had exploited to deify themselves. The central deity in Jayavarman's religion was Lokeshvara (Lord of the Worlds), assumed to be an aspect of his own divine self. Rebuilding Angkor Thom on a stupendously grand scale, the king created a Buddhist city as a monument to Lokeshvara. This convergence of king and deity is still visible in the portrait masks of Jayavarman carved on the faces of the Bayon temple towers at the centre of an immense complex of shrines in Angkor Thom.

Borobudur (Indonesia)

The Borobudur Temple complex is one of the greatest Buddhist monuments in the world. It is of uncertain age, but thought to have been built between the end of the seventh and beginning of the eighth century AD. For about a century and a half it was the spiritual centre of Buddhism in Java, and then it was lost until its rediscovery in the eighteenth century.

The structure, composed of 55,000 square metres of lava-rock is erected on a hill in the form of a stepped-pyramid of six rectangular storeys, three circular terraces and a central stupa forming the summit. The whole structure is in the form of a lotus, the sacred flower of Buddha. Besides being the highest symbol of Buddhism, the Borobudur stupa is also a replica of the universe. It symbolises the micro-cosmos, which is divided into three levels, first in which man's world of desire is influenced by negative impulses; the middle level, the world in which man has control of his negative impulses and uses his positive impulses; the highest level, in which the world of man is no longer bounded by physical and worldly desires. In total, Borobudur represents the ten levels of a Bodhisattva's life which a person must develop to become a Buddha or an awakened one.

Borobudur Stupa

Sacred Sites in the World

Potala Palace

Lhasa (Tibet)

In the holy city of Lhasa, the Dalai Lama's Potala Palace, like many Tibetan monasteries, is now a State museum. Unlike countless shrines and monasteries destroyed during the Cultural Revolution, both the structure and contents of the Potala are preserved. Symbol of the protection of Avalokiteshvara and the Tibetan Buddhist community, Potala towers imposingly over Lhasa, and contains countless treasures from the seventeenth century, including murals, *tangkhas*, *mandalas*, altars, and the famous statue in sandalwood of Padmapani.

The Jokhang monastery, southeast of the Potala, is the most sacred of all Tibetan pilgrimage sites. Somehow surviving the Cultural Revolution, the Jokhang retains its famous gilded roof, and the 'Four Deities Radiating Light'.

On the Footsteps of Buddha

Yung-kang - Lung-men caves (China)

Yung-kang is one of the most remarkable Buddhist sites known for its massive rock-carved Buddhas and the delicate ornamentation of its narrative reliefs. Work on the cave shrines was started by the emperor of the first Wei dynasty in AD 460, in response to persecution of Buddhists over the previous twenty years. In the next decades, in the limestone river cliffs at Lung-men (fifth-sixth centuries), Wei dynasty's monumental carvings achieved a spiritual and aesthetic perfection. The giant Buddhas at Yung-kang recall Indian prototypes; at Lung-men early Buddhist and Mahayana motifs converge in a graceful Chinese style.

Southeast of Dunhuang City, along the eastern cliffs of Mingsha Mountain, are the

Mogao Caves

Sacred Sites in the World

Mogao stone caves decorated with dignified, mysterious Buddhist works of art in the form of murals and painted statues. Apart from these, about 50,000 hand-written documents and relics, including paintings on silk, engraved plates, embroideries, and a large amount of calligraphic works, are found in the Buddhist Sutra Cave. A treasure house of art, the Mogao Caves contain art styles of different historical periods, including the most brilliant period of China's Buddhist art, which occurred during the Tang Dynasty. The imposing statue of Buddha several dozen meters high; the exquisitely carved *bodhisattvas*, each only a little more than ten centimeters high; huge paintings depicting Buddhist scriptures, each showing a grand scene with many people, and paintings depicting religious activities are most impressive.

Nara - Kyoto (Japan)

Todai-ji

Nara, the Japanese imperial capital in the 8th century, remains one of the great centres of East Asian Buddhist history. In and around Nara's historical park are pagodas, early Buddhist and Shinto shrines, gardens, the Nara National Museum, and the Todai-ji temple with its immense bronze Buddha statue. The beauty of old Kyoto lies in its numerous Zen temples dating from the Hieian period, and the famous gardens ('hill gardens' featuring water and 'dry gardens' featuring rock and sand) of temples such as Tenryu-ji & Ryoan-ji.

Nara

Glossary

Anagarika — Homeless. Name adopted by David Hewavitarane, a Sri Lankan Buddhist who dedicated his life to the revival of Buddhism.

Amitabha — Japanese Amida. The primary Bodhisattva in the northern Mahayana pantheon.

Arhat — An enlightened person. One who has extinguished craving and achieved Nirvana, the ideal of the Theravada school of Buddhism.

Atman — The Self or individual soul in the Hindu tradition.

Avalokiteshwara — The Mahayana Bodhisattva of compassion. Known as Chenrezi in Tibetan and regarded as the protector of Tibet. His reincarnations are the successive Dalai Lamas.

Bhikshu — Bhikku. One who begs for alms. Also Buddhist monk.

Bodhi — Enlightenment, Self-realisation, samma sambodhi. The peepal tree (ficus religiosia) came to be known as the Bodhi (or Bo) tree after Buddha attained Enlightenment under this tree at Bodh Gaya.

Bodhisattva — The ideal of the Mahayana tradition, an individual who delays his own Enlightenment in order to lead other sentient beings to deliverance.

Brahmin — The highest (priestly) caste in the Hindu caste hierarchy.

Chaitya — A sacred place, commonly used as halls of worship.

Chakra — Wheel. A recurring motif in Buddhist art,

	symbol of the Buddha's teaching.
Deva	God in Hindu mythology.
Dharma	The Truth, teaching of Enlightened ones, religion, social order, morality, righteousness.
Gompa	Tibetan for monastery.
Guru	A teacher, one who shows the way.
Karma	Action. The consequences resulting from previous action is the doctrine of karma. According to it, all action involves a build-up in the soul of spiritual merit or demerit. Good action leads to favourable rebirth, while bad action, whether or not intentional, leads to unfavourable rebirth.
Kshatriya	The warrior caste and the second in the Hindu caste hierarchy.
Lama	A teacher or guru in the Tibetan Buddhist tradition.
Mahavihara	Monastic university.
Mandala	Ritual drawings representing the cosmos.
Manjusri	A Bodhisattva who dispels ignorance.
Mantra	Sacred syllables or words.
Mara	Personification of evil. The temptor in Buddhist mythology, who tried unsuccessfully to distract Buddha in his meditation.
Mudra	Gestures of the hand with a meaning, a symbolic language.
Nirvana	Enlightenment. It is also peace, the death of craving, detachment.
Om Mani Padme Hum	The powerful mantra of Avalokiteshwara.
Pali	The Indo-Aryan language in which the Buddha spoke and in which the Buddhist canon was originally composed.
Parinirvana	The final extinction from samsara, the cycle of birth, life and death.

Poomima	Full moon.
Sakyamuni	Another name of Buddha. Sakyamuni means the saint of the Sakyas, the clan to which Buddha was born.
Samsara	The endless cycle of birth and rebirth.
Sangha	The Buddhist community of monks and nuns, founded by Buddha in Sarnath.
Siddha	Yogic master or spiritual adept in Tantra.
Stupa	A dome-shaped Buddhist reliquary. Known as chorten in Tibetan.
Sutta	Aphoristic scripture, said to be the original teachings of Buddha.
Tangkha	Tibetan Buddhist religious painting on fabric.
Tantra	A ritual path to salvation, derived from the tantras, a class of esoteric religious texts in both Hindu and Buddhist traditions.
Tara	Female saviour in Mahayana tradition.
Tathagata	An epithet used for Buddha, meaning 'the thus gone'.
Vajra	Tibetan dorje. Thunderbolt or diamond. A Mahayana symbol of the Absolute.
Vajrayana	The vehicle of the vajra. The great movement in Mahayana Buddhism in Tibet. The four main sects of Vajrayana in Tibet are Nyingmapa, Sakyapa, Kagyupa, and Gelugpa, in the chronological order of development.
Varna	Colour, also caste in the Hindu social order. The four castes are: brahmin, kshatriya, vaishya and shudra.
Yantra	Sacred diagram used for ritual purposes.

Directory of Buddhist Organisations in India

Akhil Bhartiya Boudha Maha Sangha
Sanghmitra Buddha Vihar
Y.B.Cavhan Road
Maharastra Nagar No.1
Mankhurd Mumbai-88
Maharashtra

All Assam Buddhist Association
Namphake Buddhist Temple
P.O. Naharkatia
Dibrugarh 786610, Assam

All India Bhikkhu Maha Sangha
Sangharam Buddha Vihara
Dr.Ambedkar Marg, Shahdara
New Delhi 110091

All Buddhist Congress
Sakthi Nagar
Kavundampalayam

Coimbatore 641033
Tamil Nadu

Bhikkhu Sangha's United Buddhist Mission
Sarvodaya Buddha Vihar
Tilak Nagar, Chembur
Mumbai 400089
Maharashtra

Buddha Dharmamankur Sabha
1 Buddhist Temple Street
Kolkata 700012
West Bengal

Buddhist Society of India
216, Siddhartha Nagar
Juni Indore 452001
Madhya Pradesh

Buddhist Society of India
21, Mangal Vihar Extension,

Gopalpura Bypass
Jaipur 302015
Rajasthan

Bodhi Meditation Centre and Library
12-27-124
Seelamvari Street Kothapet
Guntur 522001
Andhra Pradesh

Boudha Dhamma Sanskar Sangha
Shravasti Vihar, Sanjay Nagar
Sangali 416416
Maharashtra

Dhamma Kranti Mahasangh
110/111, Shantinagar
Yerwada, Pune 411006
Maharashtra

Dzogchen Monastery
Dhondenling
P.O. Tibetan Settlement
Kollegal Taluk
Chamrajnagar Dist.
Karnataka

Gaden Shartse Monastic University
Lama Camp No 1, Tibetan
Settlement Tattihalli
Mundgod, Karwar 581411
Karnataka

Karmapa International Buddhist Institute
B 19-20
Mehrauli Institutional Area
New Delhi -110016

Mahabodhi International Meditation Centre (MIMC)
Devachan, PO Box 22
Leh, Ladakh 194101
Jammu & Kashmir

Office of His Holiness the Dalai Lama
Thekchen Choeling
P.O. McLeod Ganj
Dharamsala 176219
Himachal Pradesh

Sakya Centre
187 Rajpur Road
Dehradun 248009
Uttararanchal

Tushita Mahayana Meditation Centre
9 Padmini Enclave
Hauz Khas
New Delhi 110016

Vipassana International Academy
(Dhamma Giri & Dhamma Tapovana)
P.O. Box 6; Igatpuri 422 403
Dist. Nashik, Maharashtra

Zurmang Kagyud Buddhist Foundation
Lingdum, Gangtok
East Sikkim

Mahabodhi Societies of India

* Maha Bodhi Society (Bangalore)
14, Kalidasa Road, Gandhinagar, Bangalore 560009, Karnataka
* Maha Bodhi Society School (Arunachal)
Mahabodhi School, Diyun 792103, Arunachal Pradesh
* Mahabodhi Society (Kolkata)
4A Bankim Chatterjee Street, College Square, Kolkata 700073
West Bengal
* Mahabodhi Society (New Delhi)
Mandir Marg, New Delhi
* Mahabodhi Society (Mumbai)
Anand Vihara, Dr Anandrao Nair Road, Mumbai 8
* Mahabodhi Society (Mumbai)
Bahujana Vihara, Buddhist Temple Street, Parel, Bombay 12
* Mahabodhi Society (Bhopal)
Chetiyagiri Vihara, Sanchi, Bhopal, Madhya Pradesh
* Mahabodhi Society (Sarnath)
Dharmapala Road, Sarnath, Uttar Pradesh
* Mahabodhi International Meditation Centre
PO Box 22, Devachan, Leh, Ladakh 194101, Jammu & Kashmir
* Mahabodhi Society (Lucknow)
Buddha Vihara, Risaldar Park, Lucknow, Uttar Pradesh
* Mahabodhi Society (Chennai)
17 Kennet Lane, Egmore, Chennai 600008, Tamil Nadu
* Mahabodhi Maitri Mandala (Mysore)
Swimming Pool Road, Saraswathipuram, Mysore 570009
Karnataka